Constructive Work with Offenders

Constructive Work with Offenders

Edited by Kevin Gorman, Marilyn Gregory,
Michelle Hayles and Nigel Parton

Jessica Kingsley Publishers
London and Philadelphia

First published in 2006
by Jessica Kingsley Publishers
116 Pentonville Road
London N1 9JB, UK
and
400 Market Street, Suite 400
Philadelphia, PA 19106, USA

www.jkp.com

Copyright © Jessica Kingsley Publishers 2006

Reprinted twice in 2006

Library of Congress Cataloging in Publication Data

Constructive work with offenders / edited by Kevin Gorman ... [et al.].
    p. cm.
Includes bibliographical references and index.
ISBN-13: 978-1-84310-345-5 (pbk. : alk. paper)
ISBN-10: 1-84310-345-1 (pbk. : alk. paper) 1. Probation--Great Britain. 2. Social work with criminals--Great Britain. 3. Constructivism (Psychology) I. Gorman, Kevin, 1951-
    HV9345.A5C66 2006
    364.40941--dc22
                            2005034296

British Library Cataloguing in Publication Data
A CIP catalogue record for this book is available from the British Library

ISBN-13: 978 1 84310 345 5
ISBN-10: 1 84310 345 1

Printed and bound in Great Britain by
Athenaeum Press, Gateshead, Tyne and Wear

Contents

Acknowledgements

The editors very much appreciate the support, encouragement and advice received from a range of friends and colleagues at the Universities of Huddersfield and Sheffield during the compilation of this book.

Special thanks are due to Sue Hanson for her heroic contribution to the formatting, proof-reading and referencing of manuscripts; Professor Eric Blyth for his invaluable facilitation of a workshop for contributors; Jeremy Cameron for keeping the story alive by supporting and encouraging this book from the outset, for editorial advice, and for the contribution of his unique humour; Anthony McCann for very generously sharing his inspirational ideas with us; and all of the contributors for delivering so conscientiously and thought provokingly to the agreed deadline and specifications.

We are also particularly indebted to the offender inside each of us for reminding us that working constructively with those convicted of routine or very serious offences is only really possible if we approach the task in a spirit of shared humanity, critical friendship and humility.

Prologue

Jeremy Cameron

'Good morning, Mr Smith.'
'Good morning, Mr Jones.'
'You are late.'
'How much late?'
'Nine and a half minutes.'
'That's all right then, eh? Ten minutes and it's band-up, right?'
'You would be returned to court due to your fecklessness.'
'Bus was late, Mr Jones.'
'And irresponsibility. Now there are only five and a half minutes left.'
'That's a shame.'
'There is no time for isometric testing.'
'And I do love that isometric testing.'
'I want to talk about' [consults checklist] 'gaols.'
'Gaols?'
'Oh no, it was goals.'
'You see that one last night?'
'Targets. Mr Smith, you are not hitting society's bullseyes.'
'True, Mr Jones. Very true.'
'You are very low on the shafting scale.'
'Mr Jones, you hit the hamster on the head there. Very low mate.'
'You show predication to offend.'
'But I ain't committed no crimes.'
'You are offensive.'
'Got to agree with you there, mate. What my missus says all the time.'
'You must attend the offending behaviour course.'
'But I don't need it, right, since I ain't committing no crimes.'
'I believe you are too comfortable.'

'Not really, Mr Jones. Tell the truth, I'm a bit uncomfortable here and now. Them shackles in your office…'

'Your comfort zone leaves no space for responsible thinking skills. You must move your problem outside your living area. Remove yourself from the battleground.'

'Mr Jones, you reckon I could get a cup of tea here?'

'Any society simultaneously demands more retribution.'

'That Sandra, she always got me a cup of tea when she was my PO.'

'If you do not address your problem I shall breach.'

'Breach, Mr Jones?'

'I have been conducting a conceptual risk assessment while you have wriggled there. In accordance with the Data Protection Act I shall inform you of your score. It is 100 per cent.'

'That good?'

'You are a walking virus of public danger. You have expressed no remorse. You are your own trigger zone.'

'Wasn't he a horse?'

'Tell me, Mr Smith, where do you believe is your dominator?'

'I dunno, Mr Jones. I don't know if I can see it from here.'

'We must find your compulsory. What do you believe you want from life?'

'Money, Mr Jones. That's what I want.'

'Nonsense. You do not need money. You have not achieved citizenship.'

'We got the removals in. What you were saying about living area, well, I did what you said and we moved.'

'You will attend thinking group.'

'No, I won't. I thought about it and I won't.'

'And on your community punishment you will gain credits towards a masters in communication and empathy. Now your time is up. Make sure when I see you next, you have struck every one of your targets.'

'About that punishment Mr Jones.'

'Yes?'

'The court never gave me that punishment.'

'What? Everyone gets it.'

'Not me, Mr Jones. They reckoned I needed advice. And assistance. And they reckoned I needed a friend.'

'A friend!'

'They said I needed help.'

'Help!'

'Help!'

[Mr Jones has pressed the button for the breaching chute and Mr Smith disappears backwards through the wall.

Two minutes later the next client arrives.]

'Good morning, Mr Brown.'

'Good morning, Mr Jones.'

'You are nine and three quarter minutes late.'

'Kept on the right side then, eh?'

Chapter 1

Constructive Work with Offenders

Setting the Scene

Kevin Gorman, Patrick O'Byrne and Nigel Parton

This book is a collection of stories about inclusive and collaborative ways of working with those who are sometimes referred to as 'offenders'. None of these stories is true in any absolute sense, but each story describes and constructs a particular reality as perceived by the storyteller. We hope that the stories will achieve a measure of negotiated meaning through the process of being read. However, it is a healthy probability that not all of the stories will resonate with readers' own narratives. Indeed, as we explain a little later, there is no consensus even among the various contributors about the convenient, but reductionist and contradictory, use of the term 'offenders' in the title of this volume and within some of its chapters.

The stories themselves have been written against the backdrop of significant and continuing developments in criminal justice. For more than a decade, the pace of change has been relentless and has found expression in the apparent determination of each successive Home Secretary, whether Conservative or New Labour, to outdo the last in terms of being seen to be tough on crime, sensitive to the needs of victims and witnesses, and (cost) effective. The political rhetoric has been accompanied by:

- a raft of legislation, including the Criminal Justice Acts 1991 and 1993, Criminal Justice and Public Order Act 1994, Crime and Disorder Act 1998, Criminal Justice and Court Services Act 2000, Sexual Offences (Amendment) Act 2000, Criminal Justice and Police Act 2001, Criminal Justice Act 2003 and Sexual Offences Act 2003

- a series of Home Office publications and practice requirements, including *Three Year Plan for the Probation Service* (Home Office 1992a and 1996a), *National Standards for the Supervision of Offenders in the Community* (Home Office 1992b, 1995 and 2000), *The Victim's Charter* (Home Office 1990 and 1996c), *Protecting the Public* (Home Office 1996b), *Inter-Agency Work with Potentially Dangerous Offenders and Risks/Needs Tools* (Home Office 1998a), *Managing Offenders, Reducing Crime* (Carter 2003) and *Reducing Crime, Changing Lives* (Home Office 2004a).

For criminal justice agencies and those employed within them, the implications of these and other government initiatives have been enormous. Organizationally, there have been attendant increases in visibility, accountability and managerialism; a greater preoccupation with public protection, inter-agency partnerships and evidence-based practice; and, in agencies such as the Probation Service, an important shift of emphasis from the treatment of individual *offenders* to the classification and management of *offending* (Kemshall 1998; Kemshall *et al.* 1997; Worrall 1997). In addition, there have been major structural innovations, perhaps most notably the creation of Youth Offending Teams (Crime and Disorder Act 1998) and, from 1 June 2004, barely three years after the introduction of a National Probation Service, the establishment of the National Offender Management Service as recommended by Patrick Carter (2003) following a review of correctional services. Inevitably these continuing organizational and ideological changes have impacted on the everyday activities of individual practitioners, especially probation and prison staff, but also others working with young and adult offenders. Implicit in the changes is a 'decline in trust' in the expertise and decision-making of frontline practitioners (Parton 1996), whose role has gradually been redefined in terms of technical competence rather than professional autonomy (Pitts 1992) through the proliferation of standardized, heavily prescribed and closely audited assessment tools and programmes of intervention.

The extent to which these developments are understood as threats or opportunities can, of course, vary at both practitioner and organizational levels. Much will depend upon whether practitioners, managers and policy-makers anticipate a happy or disastrous ending to a story wherein the present situation might be seen as but the latest chapter, and/or how far they experience feelings of relief or regret about moving on from the past. At one extreme, for example, might be those whose attachment to the 'What Works' movement in general, and cognitive-behavioural programmes in particular, has been depicted as verging on the evangelical (Gorman 2001;

Mair 2004): they may be glad to be free from the wilderness of the 'Nothing Works' era (Martinson 1974) and to be heading for a Promised Land in which interventions with offenders are not left to the whims or variable expertise of particular practitioners but are based on hard evidence and scientifically proven effectiveness (Chapman and Hough 1998; McGuire and Priestley 1995). At the other extreme might be staff deeply demoralized by the absence of evaluation or affirmation of their own creative practice, living in fear that the Prison Service and/or the Probation Service are about to founder on the rocks of 'contestability' (Carter 2003), and/or resentfully enduring their perceived reduction to the role of 'minions who merely follow procedures from this or that manual...who are technically informed but insufficiently thoughtful' (Nellis and Chui 2003, p.274).

It is likely that between these extremes there lies a broad range of support, unease and mixed feelings about the direction in which the criminal justice system is currently moving. However, polarization of a different kind has characterized the response of the Probation Service to its centrally determined twin-remit of public protection and evidence-based practice through the provision of programmes of intervention which enable the safe and effective supervision of offenders in the community (Home Office 1996a). The caution which has arguably typified that organization's retreat into a procedural and pragmatic defensiveness when assessing and managing risks (Alaszewski, Harrison and Manthorpe 1998; Parton 1996) contrasts sharply with the unbridled and uncritical enthusiasm with which it has embraced the circumspect and questionable findings of meta-analytic reviews on recidivism. The Probation Service and the Home Office have unhesitatingly introduced a succession of pathfinder and accredited programmes across England and Wales, ignoring the cautionary counsel of meta-analysts themselves (Lipsey 1995; Losel 1995) and, whenever it has been expedient to do so, sidestepping supposedly key principles of effective practice (McGuire and Priestley 1995), such as matching the style of programme delivery to the learning style of participants and reserving the most intensive interventions for offenders posing the greatest risks so as to avoid contamination (McIvor 1992). These are mainly cognitive-behavioural groupwork programmes, some of which have been piloted in the very different context of custodial environments prior to being 'rolled out' in the community. They include generic offending behaviour programmes such as Reasoning and Rehabilitation (Ross, Fabiano and Ross 1986), and Enhanced Thinking Skills (developed by the England and Wales Prison Service), as well as a number of offence-specific programmes for addressing domestic violence, sex offending, aggression, racially motivated offending, drink-impaired driving and substance-related offending (crimereduction. gov.uk 2003).

There remains a notable absence of hard evidence as to the success of these community-based programmes in terms of discouraging participants from offending. Baroness Scotland of Asthal informed the House of Lords in March 2004 that independent research into the effectiveness of accredited programmes run by the National Probation Service would be published later in the year (Lords Hansard 2004). However, given the regularity with which promised research findings appear to fall victim to so-called 'slippage', it may well be that George Mair (2004) is correct in assuming that it is likely to be some time yet before reconviction data associated with these programmes are forthcoming, notwithstanding the notorious unreliability of such data as an outcome measure. Indeed, he argues that even then it would be wise to treat any early apparent successes with caution, given the incrementally disappointing reconviction indicators which emerged over time from the evaluation of the mid-Glamorgan 'STOP' initiative (Raynor and Vanstone 1997). Certainly this would be consistent with lessons from the recent evaluation of prison-based programmes. The initial promise of research into a pre-accredited cognitive skills programme, which revealed two-year reconviction rates for treatment groups that were 14 per cent lower than for matched comparison groups (Friendship *et al.* 2002), has not been echoed by subsequent research findings. An evaluation of accredited cognitive skills programmes for adult prisoners found no differences in the two-year reconviction rates for those who had participated during 1996–8 and a matched comparison group (Falshaw *et al.* 2003). Similarly, a later study found that there were no differences in the one- and two-year reconviction rates between adult men or young offenders who started custodially based cognitive skills programmes and their matched comparison groups (Cann *et al.* 2003).

Equally intriguing are statistics concerning programme throughputs rather than outcomes, which are published regularly by the National Probation Directorate and which provide national, regional and area breakdowns for England and Wales in relation to accredited programme completions against targets. The headline figure in the most recent of these Performance Reports (National Probation Directorate 2004) shows an overall programme completion rate of 78 per cent of target for the first quarter of the financial year 2004/5. Whilst this would suggest a relative decline in terms of the annual overall completion rate of 88 per cent for the financial year 2003/4, it is nonetheless a seemingly respectable figure when compared to the annual completion rates of 55 per cent and 64 per cent for 2001/2 and 2002/3 respectively. However, closer scrutiny of the data reveals that the overall completion figure of 78 per cent for April–June 2004 is heavily reliant upon slightly fewer than a quarter of the 45 probation areas involved exceeding their completion targets, with one area achieving a completion rate of 197 per cent against its target, and another 228 per cent. Leaving aside the perfectly valid question as to how these two areas managed to surpass their targets to such an extent without compromising any of the principles of 'What Works', the distorting effect of such overachievers disguises the fact that the majority of probation areas, no less than 34 of the 45, failed to meet their completion targets, and that ten of these areas achieved completion rates of less than 50 per cent. When considered carefully alongside an under-publicized halving of the annual national target for accredited programmes from 30,000 completions to 15,000 completions (National Probation Directorate 2004), these figures suggest that in most parts of England and Wales considerably fewer offenders are actually completing accredited programmes than was originally or even more recently projected.

There are several interconnected factors which might possibly account for the number of successful completions of community-based accredited programmes proving to be so much lower than was first expected and than is still being acknowledged. It may be, for example, that the programmes were significantly under-subscribed from the outset because of a combination of practitioner reluctance to make referrals and excessive 'cherry-picking' on the part of programme managers anxious to increase their prospects of meeting completion targets by excluding all but the seemingly most motivated, compliant and promising offenders. Certainly, explicit Home Office links between performance and funding, and the continuing threat of financial penalties if targets are not met (see, for example, Probation Circular 30/2004, Home Office 2004b), placed considerable pressure on probation officers to increase their referral rates and on Probation Service managers to widen the initially narrow window of programme eligibility as determined by recidivism predictors such as the Offender Group Reconviction Score (OGRS; Copas 1995). However, the resulting pendulum swing in programme referrals from a position of excessive selectivity to one of excessive abandon has had a twofold, if not entirely unpredictable, effect: first, to create a worrying, centrally recognized tendency for certain offenders to be allocated to inappropriate programmes (National Probation Service 2001); second, to produce programme attrition rates which are considerably higher than seem to have been anticipated at a management/policy level and which are reflected in a muted but steady adjustment downwards of completion targets quite at odds with governmental and organizational 'spin'.

The discovery that there are considerably fewer offenders in practice than there are in theory who are either suited to or able to cope with the characteristically intensive requirements of accredited programme groupwork has, of course, come as no surprise to experienced practitioners familiar with the high attrition rates typical of former probation centre programmes and other group interventions. More puzzling and counterproductive, however, is that a Probation Service ostensibly committed to the collaborative principles of motivational interviewing (Miller and Rollnick 1991) should routinely contradict many of those principles in its operationalization of the Effective Practice Initiative (Home Office 1998b). Small wonder in such an environment if significant numbers of those offenders with sufficient motivation to attend the early sessions of an accredited programme eventually decide to stay away. Indeed, this is arguably a perfectly rational decision in the context of their regular exposure to rigidly sequenced programme content and a didactic, often confrontational style of delivery, which clearly prize the expert knowledge of the worker and the programme designer(s) over the self-efficacy of the offender, and which are more likely to assume collective cognitive deficits than to recognize individual strengths or resources. Small wonder, too, if the success of efforts to improve attendance is limited by the widespread imposition of standardized agency objectives within an unhelpful discourse of 'resistance', 'lack of motivation' or 'pre-contemplation' (Prochaska and DiClemente 1994) rather than being enhanced through a process of building and nurturing therapeutic alliances (Cordess 2002) in which sometimes competing goals are carefully explored and negotiated (Miller and Rollnick 1991; Trotter 1999).

Seen from this perspective it could be argued that the hunger of the accredited programmes has not been satisfied because of a tendency on the part of the Home Office and the Probation Service to dine *à la carte* from the menus of meta-analysis, effective practice, motivational interviewing and pro-social modelling. If so, then the political and organizational appetite for case management might be said to be similarly picky and whimsical, despite much enthusiastic rhetoric. Heralded as a key component of the effective practice initiative (Chapman and Hough 1998), case management remains a largely ill-defined, undeveloped and uncoordinated activity (Holt 2002) which often demotivates and confuses practitioners (Kemshall *et al.* 2004) whilst being perceived by some managers as involving 'little…beyond assessment, assignment to the appropriate programme and enforcement of attendance' (Raynor 2003, p.84).

The fragmented evolution of different, poorly designed and ill-articulated models of case management in different probation areas inspires little confidence that what has essentially been reduced to a 'managerial device' (Spencer and Deakin 2004, p.214) for handling high workloads will meta-morphose into a highly professional role for coordinating services. On the contrary, it seems more probable that case management will continue to provide an organizationally expedient mechanism for eroding professional autonomy and the boundaries between qualified and unqualified staff. At the same time, whether intentionally or not, it has proven to be an effective means of systematically depersonalizing probation practice (McIvor 2004), so much so that offenders and their case managers are increasingly unlikely to be able even to recognize each other should they stumble across each other in the waiting room. This is all the more unfortunate and ironic given the rediscovery of constructive relationships between offenders and their supervisors as a potentially central component of successful intervention. The arguably pivotal importance of such relationships is recognized not only in literature directly related to case management and effective practice but also in the findings of desistance research, currently enjoying something of a renaissance.

Academic interest in why people stop offending is not new. For example, earlier studies suggesting correlations between decisions to desist from crime and employment (Farrington et al. 1986), significant partner-ships (Parker 1976), and parenthood (Sampson and Laub 1993), have some resonance with more recent research relating to young offenders in Scotland (McIvor, Jamieson and Murray 2000), which highlights increas-ing maturation and responsibilities as self-reported determinants of their desistance. However, new impetus has been given to the debate about desistance by the separate but complementary contributions of Stephen Farrall and Shadd Maruna.

From research interviews with 199 probationers and their supervising probation officers, Farrall (2002) discovered evidence of progress towards desistance from crime in more than half of the sample, but he concluded that this appeared to be largely due to changes in the behaviour or circumstances of the offender (e.g. employment, accommodation or personal relation-ships) which rarely had any direct linkage to professional interventions. Like Maruna, Immarigeon and LeBel (2004), Farrall is unsurprised by the seemingly limited extent to which desistance from crime is directly related to rehabilitative treatment given that the time spent in the company of their supervisors by even the most compliant probationers represents a relatively tiny proportion of offenders' waking lives, estimated to be 'about one third of one percent of this time' (Farrall 2002, p.175). Somewhat less discouragingly for practitioners, he suggests that their work may help improve offenders' motivation (Farrall 2002, 2004). Moreover, he argues that community-based supervision may have a significant indirect impact on offenders' lives by providing a context in which other, more important social interactions and changes can take place naturally and can even be enhanced by interventions that, instead of being exclusively cognitive in their orientation, also offer support in overcoming obstacles to desistance such as family problems, transition to parenthood or unemployment (Farrall 2002, 2004). Maruna (2000, 2001) similarly acknowledges the crucial, if relatively minor, role of intervention in the larger, complex process of desistance from crime and advocates a truce and marriage between unnecessarily polarized understandings of the phenomenon in terms of either spontaneous remission or professional cure.

It is still too early to tell how far key concepts and data from recent desistance literature will inform future criminal justice policy-making and everyday practice with offenders. However, Fergus McNeill (2003) offers some tentative suggestions as to what desistance-focused practice might actually look like. From his interpretation of the desistance research, he proposes that the most appropriate focus for professional assessment and intervention would be the interfaces between 'developing personal maturity, changing social bonds associated with certain life transitions, and the individual subjective narrative constructions which offenders build around these key events' (McNeill 2003, p.157).

Intriguingly, the third element of this triangle points towards diagnostic and therapeutic approaches more consistent with the social constructionist, narrative work of Michael White (1990) and Alan Jenkins (1990) than with currently fashionable cognitive-behavioural models based upon notions of deficient or distorted thinking. Furthermore, as McNeill rightly points out, desistance-focused practice would inevitably need to 'be thoroughly individualised' (McNeill 2003, p.156), implying a possible revival of interest in effective one-to-one working relationships with offenders quite at odds with the present appetite for groupwork interventions but entirely consistent with a central, if conveniently ignored, principle of Chris Trotter's otherwise enthusiastically received 'pro-social modelling' (Trotter 1999).

Signs of a cautious shift away from the hegemony of cognitive-behavioural groupwork programmes and towards customized, relationship-oriented practice are likely to be welcomed by seasoned, newly qualified and trainee staff in the field of criminal justice, whose voices have too often been muted and their practice wisdom, reservations and questions disqualified in the ideological pursuit of a universally applicable intervention. In this context, the present volume offers a timely, alternative vision of effective offender assessment, intervention and enforcement. Contributions from academic writers and from existing and former practitioners and managers in the Probation Service will seek to complement the embryonic critical analysis of current, standardized provision and the resurgent interest in desistance with a competing discourse about customized and productive ways of working with those convicted of criminal offences. Twin strands of this 're-storying' process will be:

1. an affirmation of the interpersonal skills and expertise of frontline practitioners, well accustomed to tailoring their interventions to the varied circumstances and the often messy reality of offenders' lives

2. an application to work with offenders of social constructionist ideas and narrative approaches (Parton and O'Byrne 2000).

Constructive work with offenders will be articulated as a complex and dynamic process of intervention which is more artistic than technicist, more creative than procedural, more collaborative than instrumental.

Social constructionism

In the context of the dramatic and rapid changes that have taken place in both policy and practice in relation to work with offenders, and its dominance by an evidence-based, managerialist and cognitivist set of approaches, we are attempting to articulate a rather different vision; something we call 'constructive work with offenders'. The general approach has been developed in relation to the human services more generally (Milner and O'Byrne 2002; Parton 2002, 2003; Parton and O'Byrne 2000). The term *constructive* has been chosen for two reasons. First, it reflects our wish to provide an approach which is explicitly positive, in its implications both for practitioners and for those with whom they work. For the core idea of *construction*, from the Latin to the present day, is that of *building* or of *putting together*. The *Oxford English Dictionary* defines *construction* as 'the action or manner of constructing', while *constructive* is defined as 'having a useful purpose; helpful'.

Second, however, the term *constructive* has been chosen to reflect more theoretical concerns. In trying to develop theoretical and conceptual ideas for practice an explicit attempt has been made to draw on perspectives which have been developed since the late 1960s, associated with social constructionist and narrative developments in social and psychological theory. In such perspectives an understanding of language, listening, talk and meaning are seen as central. The idea of understanding as a *collaborative* process is a core one in social constructionism. Here, meaning and understanding are matters of negotiation between the participants in conversation and thus the understanding of and use of language are seen as central to the process.

Constructionist perspectives have become increasingly widespread in various areas of Western intellectual life over a number of years (Hacking 1999; Velody and Williams 1998). They have become central to some of the most important changes and heated debates in literary studies, philosophy, history, socio-legal studies, anthropology, sociology and psychology. It would be incorrect, however, to assume that there is only one single stance or position that exemplifies the work of those it would be appropriate to associate with the term *constructionism* (Lynch 1998).

Perhaps the key event in introducing the notion of 'social constructionism' to a wide academic audience was the publication in 1967 of Berger and Luckman's *The Social Construction of Reality*. Drawing on the phenomenological philosophy of Edmund Husserl (1975) and Alfred Schutz (1962–6), they characterized everyday life as a *fluid, multiple, precariously negotiated interaction*. Their principal thesis was that individuals in interaction create social worlds through their linguistic, symbolic activity for the purpose of providing coherence to an essentially open-ended uniform human existence. Society is not a system, a mechanism nor an organization; it is a symbolic construct composed of ideas, meanings and language which is all the time changing through human action and imposing constraints and possibilities on human actors themselves. What such an approach did was to emphasize the *processes* through which people define themselves (their identities and their environments). People do so by participating in their social worlds, interacting with others and assigning meaning to aspects of their experience. *Constructing* social realities is seen as an ongoing aspect of people's everyday lives and relationships.

In more recent years, such approaches have recognized the *rhetorical* aspects of construction, in that it is partly a process of *persuading* oneself and others that one rendering of social reality is more legitimate or credible than any other. Michael Billig (1987) and John Shotter (1993) have, for example, analysed thinking as a rhetorical process, where conversation and language are key to understanding identity. Thinking is seen not as a private or personal activity, but as a micro-political and interactional process concerned with categorizing everyday life and developing arguments that justify preferred realities and courses of action. Similarly, Potter and Wetherell (1987) argue that language orders our perceptions and makes things happen. They suggest that what they call 'social texts' do not merely reflect or mirror social objects, events and categories existing in the social and natural world, they actively *construct* a version of those things. They do not just describe things, they *do* things and thus have social, practical and political implications. A part of what we must learn in growing up, if we want to be perceived as speaking (and writing) authoritatively about so-called factual matters, is how to respond to the others around us should they challenge our claims. This includes *conversations* with ourselves. We must *speak* with an awareness of the possibility of such challenges and be able to reply to them by justifying our claims. This is a *rhetorical* rather than a referential or representational form of language because, rather than merely claiming to depict or reflect a state of affairs or an external reality, talk and language have the effect of *moving* people to action in changing their views and perceptions. Language is thus seen as not just constituting reality but actively changing it.

While there is no one feature which could be said to identify a social constructionist position, there are a number of themes which can be seen to link them together (Burr 2003; Gergen 1999). First, it is argued that the terms by which we understand our world and ourselves are neither required nor demanded by 'what there is'. Constructionism insists that we develop a critical stance towards our taken-for-granted ways of understanding the world, including ourselves. It suggests we should be critical of the idea that our observations of the world unproblematically reveal its nature to us in any straightforward way. It *problematizes* the 'obvious', the 'real' and, crucially, the 'taken-for-granted'; it challenges the view that conventional knowledge is based upon unbiased observation and that we can therefore separate subject and object, the perceived and the real; and it cautions us to be ever-suspicious of our assumptions about how the world appears and the categories that we use to divide and interpret it.

Second, because the social world, including ourselves as people, is the product of *social processes*, it follows that there cannot be any given, determined nature of the world 'out there'. There are no essences inside things or people which are hidden and which make them what they are.

Third, social categories and concepts are seen as historically and culturally specific and therefore vary over time and place. Not only are particular forms of knowledge the products of their history and culture, and thus artefacts of it, but there are also numerous forms of knowledge available. We cannot assume that our ways of understanding are necessarily the same as others' and are any nearer 'the truth'. In the context of this book, the notion of 'offenders' is subject to continual problematization and questioning. It is a term which many contributors feel is very unhelpful. The manner in which the term marginalizes those to whom it is applied, and in the process assumes that they are qualitatively different from the vast majority of the population, is seen as ethically, politically and practically questionable.

Fourth, it is argued that knowledge of the world is developed between people in their *interactions*. These *negotiated* understandings can take a variety of forms which thereby invite different kinds of action. However, while constructions of the world sustain some patterns of actions, they exclude others. Thus rather than being able to separate knowledge and action it is important to recognize that they are intimately interrelated. Crucially, there needs to be a recognition that our modes of description, explanation and representation are derived from *relationships*. Such a view follows largely from the use-view of language. In this account language and all other forms of representation gain their meaning from the ways in which they are used within *relationships*. Meanings are born of coordinations with other persons – agreements, negotiations, affirmations. Nothing exists for us – as an intelligible world of objects and persons – until there are *relationships*. As we have noted earlier, one of the consequences of changes in criminal justice policy and practice in recent years is the downgrading of the importance of relationships in the work. In doing so, what is a key component, not just of professional practice but of social existence, is not recognized.

Fifth, as our practices of language are bound within relationships, so are relationships bound within broader patterns of practice, rituals, traditions and so on – for as we describe, explain or otherwise represent ourselves and the world, so do we fashion our future. If we wish to make changes, therefore, we must confront the challenges of generating new meaning and of becoming what Kenneth Gergen calls 'poetic activists' (1999, p.49). New patterns of social life are not secured by simply refusing or rejecting the meanings as given, but rather by the emergence of new forms of language and thus new ways of interpreting the world and patterns of representation. 'Generative discourses' provide ways of talking and writing (and any other way of representing) that simultaneously challenge existing traditions of understanding and at the same time offer new possibilities for action and change. This is a central theme throughout this book.

Sixth, constructionism has at its core the notion of *reflexivity* (Taylor and White 2000); that is, the continual attempt to place one's premises into question and to listen to alternative framings of reality in order to grapple with the potentially different outcomes arising out of different points of view. Reflexivity is not necessarily a prelude to rejecting the present or the past but underlines the importance of entering into *dialogue* in order to clarify what might lead to improvement and, in particular, to recognize that there are differing notions of what improvement might mean. In doing so, we are encouraged to recognize that in expanding on the range of valued considerations taken into account in any outcome, we need to set in motion dialogues in which these competing and potentially conflicting values or outcomes may be articulated and weighed. We are thus not attempting simply to reject the policy and practice changes we have described earlier but aim to enter into a *dialogue*, and in the process broaden and deepen what is understood as good practice.

While there is no singular set of practices that follow from a constructionist 'point of view', it is also clear the approach invites a reconsideration of what has become the dominant ethos. This is not a simple and straightforward change in style. It moves from a hierarchical to a collaborative approach and calls into question the top-down and increasingly centralized approaches which have been adopted in recent years. It is not simply a question of moving beyond the hierarchical and centralized approaches towards something more democratic, but of trying to develop a stance of being much more humble and thereby not being seen as the expert on a range of problems. There is a real attempt to move beyond problem-saturated discourses which lie at the heart of the notion of 'the offender' and which have recently become increasingly dominant. The approach emphasizes skills in *knowing how* as well as in *knowing what*, and thereby moving fluidly in relationships and of collaborating in a mutual generation of new futures which explicitly values the views, experiences and voices of all concerned, including those identified as 'the offender'. People are seen as inventing options and making them real, and in the process there is a recognition that in opening up individuals to the possibilities of choice and responsibility they are truly made up as moral (Bauman 1993, 1995).

The constructive approach we adopt here, therefore, emphasizes process, plurality of both knowledge and voice, possibility and the relational quality of knowledge. It is affirmative and reflexive and focuses on dialogue, listening to and talking with the other. It is concerned with the narratives of solutions to problems, and with change. Instead of providing the practitioner with information about the *causes* of problems, so that she or he can make an expert assessment and prescribe a 'scientific' solution, those with whom we work are encouraged to tell their *story* of the problem in a way that *externalizes* it, giving more control and agency and thereby creating new perspectives on how to manage or overcome it. Rather than thinking of *causative factors*, we prefer to think in terms of the *invitations* to crime to which people are subjected in society. 'Cause' is rather deterministic and it diminishes the role of decision-making and responsibility, whereas we can *decide* to accept an invitation or not and because we can do this we are accountable. While strong invitations can *restrain* responsible choices, they cannot totally remove the power to choose. Hence, talk of what invitations people experience and of how they resist these is a key component of constructive practice.

These *narratives* construct the future and anticipate change; questions encourage the identification of *exceptions* to the apparently overwhelming nature of the problems and occasions when resistance was successful. The constructive approach develops techniques and thinking associated with 'solution-focused' (De Shazer 1985, 1991, 1994; Miller 1997), 'narrative' therapy (White 1993; White and Epston 1990), 'possibility' (O'Hanlon 1993; O'Hanlon and Beadle 1994; O'Hanlon and Weiner-Davis 1989) and the 'strengths perspectives' (Saleebey 1997). Those with whom we work are encouraged to repeat successes, to identify solutions as theirs and as the steps to the achievement of their own goals.

Constructive work with offenders

It is these key themes associated with social constructionism which have informed our thinking about developing a specific focus on constructive work with offenders. However, as already intimated, this poses a number of quite specific challenges. First, the term 'offender' has become institutionalized in ways which particularly pathologize those who are so categorized; they are thereby seen as the most marginalized and potentially dangerous members of society. Since the late 1970s issues around law and order have escalated up the political agenda (Downes and Morgan 2002) such that all mainstream political parties wish to be seen as 'tough' on criminals. But, second, we should not underestimate the fact that those who are categorized as 'offenders' are themselves reluctant and captive participants in the criminal justice system. They are involuntary recipients of the 'services'. Both factors pose a particular challenge for those who wish to develop constructive approaches to work with offenders. Not only are such approaches likely to be perceived as being *soft* on crime and criminals, but they may also be seen as providing a weak basis for trying to engage people who do not wish to be engaged in the first place. With regard to being soft, we believe that, while the approach is supportive of those who want to resist temptations to offend, it is tough in its emphasis on responsibility/accountability for future actions. Moving from 'I can't help it – this is how I am made' to realizing that one can decide not to offend, and accepting responsibility, is tough work that needs a supportive relationship with a worker; though it is tough on the irresponsibility it does not need to be tough on the person.

Whilst such an approach may be seen as relevant for those who are willing to receive help and guidance, it can be seen as not being relevant for the involuntary 'client'. But our experience is that the so-called 'unwilling' are more likely to be engaged because of the different stance of the worker in constructive practice. The worker stands alongside the offender as they both confront crime. De Shazer (personal communication) found no significant difference between the motivation of Probation Service clients and that of the clients of other services, so long as they were listened to and 'what was different when they were not offending' was put to work. When the negative effects of crime on their lives and their relationships are talked about, the majority of those who have a close relationship with crime can engage in conversations about these effects and begin to be alienated from offending so that they start to stand up to the invitations, supported by the worker. The stance changes from:

Worker $\longrightarrow$ Offender

to:

Worker/Offender $\longrightarrow$ Crime

Recent experience of working with men who commit domestic violence is that this joint stance of worker and offender against violence makes motivation less an issue as the problem is externalized.

These issues about being 'soft' and the 'involuntary client' are two central themes throughout this book and are a focus in all of the chapters. In the process the authors challenge some of the currently taken-for-granted assumptions of policy and practice, and demonstrate how constructive approaches themselves can be developed and integrated into day-to-day work with offenders.

In recognizing that crime and the notion of offending themselves vary both historically and culturally, such that the language of offending does not merely describe reality but is constitutive of it, the possibility is opened up of new ways of thinking and acting. In doing so, we argue that current approaches are based on a narrow range of rational-technical approaches which do not give sufficient recognition to the fact that much of the work is uncertain and variable, and that it is crucial to have a curiosity about each individual offender's unique world in order to engage with her or him and collaboratively construct possibilities for change, thus moving towards resisting the invitations for crime. It is recognized that an offender's 'local' knowledge is as, or more, important than knowledge which has been derived from the 'scientific' research and which has been disseminated and embedded in a variety of new systems and service packages.

Such an approach proceeds from an understanding that negative and problem-saturated discourses associated with the notion of offenders can have the effect of blocking any change and fail to give sufficient recognition to the occasions where offenders have resisted entering into criminal activity and when they have a wider range of strengths than is often given sufficient attention. Understanding why people stop offending is as important as exploring why people offend in the first place, so that talk about safety is equally as important as talk about risk. Similarly, an ability to work with relationships is as, if not more, important than the ability to classify and categorize offenders for the purposes of allocating them to various punishment, surveillance and treatment facilities. The ability to be careful and sensitive in the use of language and, in particular, being positive and future-oriented, and drawing upon the offender's own phrases and metaphors, are central to this process. A detailed discussion of the offender's best hopes and aspirations in working with the particular service and thereby developing relevant goals and descriptions of what the future might hold, including not engaging in crime and not being the subject of the attention of criminal justice agencies, is seen as central. This detailed discussion requires an identification of where key elements of this future vision are currently present in current behaviour and relationships. In addition, a detailed examination of the exceptions to offending behaviour is required, not only in relation to what happened, but also in relation to how certain invitations to offend were resisted and how others in the wider social and community network responded to this.

In doing so, it is important to recognize and to discuss how difficult resistance can be and thereby identify the wider support networks that can be drawn upon in order to enable the offender to engage in this process. Such an approach, while informed by certain theoretical approaches and skills, is crucially attitudinal. In emphasizing the positive and the constructive it is important to believe in the offenders' ability to work out how to achieve what they want and to overcome any obstacles. In the process, it is important to see any relapses as being a sign of an ability to make progress rather than simply as a sign of failure. Identifying and talking about how previous progress was made, so that this can be built on in the future, is a crucial element of the work.

Such an approach has implications not only for the direct work with offenders themselves, but also for the well-being of practitioners and for the way practitioners relate to their wider organizational contexts. Constructive practice is less stressful for practitioners and less likely to lead to burn-out and other health problems for three reasons: first, the responsibility for making progress is shared by the offender, whose responsibility-taking and efforts at self-control begin to grow – every client becomes a potential collaborator against crime; second, supporting people against the invitations to commit crime and building up their strengths is a less stressful relationship than endless personal confrontations; third, since a relationship takes a little time to develop, going slowly for the first few meetings and focusing on wants and strengths, showing more interest in what is okay than in what is not okay, is free from the pressure to make a quick impact – the paradox is that going slowly here can make for more rapid progress.

With regard to the wider organizational contexts, it has been demonstrated that the single most important characteristic of highly effective workers in public service settings is that they are almost always seen as team players (Bricker-Jenkins 1997). They are always ready to give help and support, and are able to ask for assistance and advice when they need it. Helping to create and sustain the workplace as a 'learning environment' has been identified as a significant element of their team work. They are often involved in peer consultation and supervision, together with the teaching of new recruits. In order to maintain and sustain their morale it is important that they are not only concerned with a narrow focus on day-to-day practice. They are also engaged in improving policy more generally, as well as work relationships and working conditions; in effect, they take responsibility and are supported for expanding their jobs to change and develop the contexts of their day-to-day work. A major problem with recent developments is that much of the organizational context has gone in exactly the opposite direction whereby frontline practitioners have been disempowered and their own 'local knowledge' has not been taken seriously. This is clearly a major challenge for those who want to engage in what we call constructive work with offenders.

References

Alaszewski, A., Harrison, L. and Manthorpe, J. (eds) (1998) *Risk, Health and Welfare*. Buckingham: Open University Press.

Bauman, Z. (1993) *Postmodern Ethics*. Cambridge: Polity Press.

Bauman, Z. (1995) *Life in Fragments*. Oxford: Blackwell.

Berger, P. and Luckman, T. (1967) *The Social Construction of Reality: A Treatise in the Sociology of Knowledge*. New York: Doubleday.

Billig, M. (1987) *Arguing and Thinking: A Rhetorical Approach to Social Psychology*. Cambridge: Cambridge University Press.

Bricker-Jenkins, M. (1997) 'Hidden treasures: Unlocking strengths in the public social services.' In D. Saleebey (ed.) *The Strengths Perspective in Social Work Practice* (2nd edition). New York: Longman.

Burr, V. (2003) *Social Construction* (2nd edition). London: Routledge.

Cann, J., Falshaw, L., Nugent, F. and Friendship, C. (2003) *Understanding What Works: Accredited Cognitive Skills Programmes for Adult Men and Young Offenders*. Home Office Research Findings 226. London: Home Office.

Carter, P. (2003) *Managing Offenders, Reducing Crime: A New Approach*. London: Home Office.

Chapman, D. and Hough, M. (1998) *Evidence Based Practice: A Guide to Effective Practice*. London: Home Office.

Copas, J. (1995) 'On using crime statistics for prediction.' In M. Walker (ed.) *Interpreting Crime*. Oxford: Clarendon.

Cordess, C. (2002) 'Building and nurturing a therapeutic alliance with offenders.' In M. Murran (ed.) *Motivating Offenders to Change*. Chichester: Wiley.

crimereduction.gov.uk (2004) Last update: 16 September 2003. Available at www.crimereduction.gov.uk/workingoffenders3.htm#no1 (accessed 1 November 2004).

De Shazer, S. (1985) *Keys to Solutions in Brief Therapy*. New York and London: Norton.

De Shazer, S. (1991) *Putting Differences to Work*. New York and London: Norton.

De Shazer, S. (1994) *Words Were Originally Magic*. New York and London: Norton.

De Shazer, S. (2001) Personal communication.

Downes, D. and Morgan, R. (2002) 'The skeletons in the cupboard: The politics of law and order at the turn of the millennium.' In M. Maguire, R. Morgan and R. Reiner (eds) *The Oxford Handbook of Criminology* (3rd edition). Oxford: Oxford University Press.

Falshaw, L., Friendship, C., Travers, R. and Nugent, F. (2003) *Searching for 'What Works': An Evaluation of Cognitive Skills Programmes*. Home Office Research Findings 206. London: Home Office.

Farrall, S. (2002) *Rethinking What Works with Offenders: Probation, Social Context and Desistance from Crime*. Cullompton: Willan Publishing.

Farrall, S. (2004) 'Supervision, motivation and social context: what matters most when probationers desist?' In G. Mair (ed.) (2004) *What Matters in Probation*. Cullompton: Willan Publishing.

Farrington, D.P., Gallagher, B., Morley, L., St Ledger, R.J. and West, D.J. (1986) 'Unemployment, school leaving and crime.' *British Journal of Criminology* 26, 4, 335–56.

Friendship, C., Blud, L., Erikson, M. and Travers, R. (2002) *An Evaluation of Cognitive Behavioural Treatment for Prisoners*. Home Office Research Findings 161. London: Home Office.

Gergen, K.J. (1999) *An Invitation to Social Construction*. London: Sage.

Gorman, K. (2001) 'Cognitive behaviourism and the Holy Grail: the quest for a universal means of managing offender risk.' *Probation Journal* 48, 1, 3–9.

Hacking, I. (1999) *The Social Construction of What?* London: Harvard University Press.

Holt, P. (2002) 'Case management: Shaping practice.' In D. Ward, J. Scott and M. Lacey (eds) *Probation: Working for Justice* (2nd edition). Oxford: Oxford University Press.

Home Office (1990) *The Victim's Charter*. London: HMSO.

Home Office (1992a) *Three Year Plan for the Probation Service, 1993–1996*. London: HMSO.

Home Office (1992b) *National Standards for Supervision in the Community*. London: HMSO.

Home Office (1995) *National Standards for the Supervision of Offenders in the Community*. London: Home Office.

Home Office (1996a) *Three Year Plan for the Probation Service, 1996–1999*. London: HMSO.

Home Office (1996b) *Protecting the Public: The Government's Strategy on Crime in England and Wales*. London: HMSO.

Home Office (1996c) *The Victim's Charter: A Statement of the Rights of Victims of Crime*. London: HMSO.

Home Office (1998a) *Inter-Agency Work with Potentially Dangerous Offenders and Risks/Needs Tools*. London: Home Office Special Conferences Unit.

Home Office (1998b) *Effective Practice Initiative: National Implementation Plan for the Supervision of Offenders*. Probation Circular 35/1998. London: Home Office.

Home Office (2000) *National Standards for Supervision in the Community*. London: HMSO.

Home Office (2004a) *Reducing Crime, Changing Lives*. London: Home Office.

Home Office (2004b) *Learning and Skills for Offenders in Wales: Targets and Funding 2004–05*. Probation Circular 30/2004. London: Home Office.

Husserl, E. (1975) *Ideas*. New York: Macmillan.

Jenkins, A. (1990) *Invitation to Responsibility: The Therapeutic Engagement of Men who are Violent and Abusive*. Adelaide, South Australia: Dulwich Centre Publications.

Kemshall, H. (1998) *Risk in Probation Practice*. Aldershot: Ashgate.

Kemshall, H., Holt, P., Bailey, R. and Boswell, G. (2004) 'Beyond programmes: Organisational and cultural issues in the implementation of What Works.' In G. Mair (ed.) (2004) *What Matters in Probation*. Cullompton: Willan Publishing.

Kemshall, H., Parton, N., Walsh, M. and Waterson, J. (1997) 'Concepts of risk in relation to organizational structure and functioning within the personal social services and probation.' *Social Policy and Administration* 31, 3, 213–32.

Lipsey, M.W. (1995) 'What do we learn from 400 research studies on the effectiveness of treatment with juvenile delinquents?' In J. McGuire (ed.) *What Works: Reducing Offending. Guidelines from Research and Practice.* Chichester: John Wiley and Sons Ltd.

Lords Hansard (2004) 3 March. Available at www.parliament.the-stationery-office.co.uk/pa/ld199900/ldhansrd/pdvn/lds04/text/40303w03.htm (accessed 2 November 2004).

Losel, F. (1995) 'The efficacy of correctional treatment: A review and synthesis of meta-evaluations.' In J. McGuire (ed.) *What Works: Reducing Offending. Guidelines from Research and Practice.* Chichester: John Wiley and Sons Ltd.

Lynch, M. (1998) 'Towards a constructivist genealogy of social constructionism.' In I. Velody and R. Williams (eds) *The Politics of Constructionism.* London: Sage.

Mair, G. (2004) 'The origins of What Works in England and Wales: A house built on sand?' In G. Mair (ed.) (2004) *What Matters in Probation*. Cullompton: Willan Publishing.

Martinson, R. (1974) 'What works? Questions and answers about prison reform.' *The Public Interest* 35, 22–54.

Maruna, S. (2000) 'Desistance from crime and offender rehabilitation: A tale of two research literatures.' *Offender Programs Report* 4, 1–13.

Maruna, S. (2001) *Making Good: How Ex-convicts Reform and Rebuild their Lives.* Washington, DC: American Psychological Association.

Maruna, S., Immarigeon, R. and LeBel, P.T. (2004) 'Ex-offender reintegration: Theory and practice.' In S. Maruna and R. Immarigeon (eds) *After Crime and Punishment: Pathways to Offender Integration.* Cullompton: Willan Publishing.

McGuire, J. and Priestley, P. (1995) 'Reviewing "What Works": Past, present and future.' In J. McGuire (ed.) *What Works: Reducing Offending. Guidelines from Research and Practice.* Chichester: John Wiley and Sons Ltd.

McIvor, G. (1992) 'Intensive probation: Does more mean better?' *Probation Journal* 39, 1, 2–6.

McIvor, G. (2004) 'Getting personal: Developments in policy and practice in Scotland.' In G. Mair (ed.) *What Matters in Probation*. Cullompton: Willan Publishing.

McIvor, G., Jamieson, J. and Murray, C. (2000) 'Study examines gender differences in desistance from crime.' *Offender Programs Report* 4, 5–9.

McNeill, F. (2003) 'Desistance-focused probation practice.' In W.H. Chui and M. Nellis (eds) *Moving Probation Forward.* Harlow: Pearson Education Limited.

Miller, G. (1997) *Becoming Miracle Workers: Language and Meaning in Brief Therapy.* New York: Aldine de Gruyter.

Miller, W.R. and Rollnick, S. (1991) *Motivational Interviewing.* New York: The Guilford Press.

Milner, J. and O'Byrne, P. (2002) *Assessment in Social Work* (2nd edition). Basingstoke: Palgrave/Macmillan.

National Probation Directorate (2004) *Performance Report 13 – August 2004.* London: National Probation Directorate.

National Probation Service (2001) *A New Choreography: An Integrated Strategy for the National Probation Service for England and Wales.* London: NPS.

Nellis, M. and Chui, W.H. (2003) 'The end of probation?' In W.H. Chui and M. Nellis (eds) *Moving Probation Forward.* Harlow: Pearson Education Limited.

O'Hanlon, B. (1993) 'Possibility theory.' In S. Gilligan and R. Price (eds) *Therapeutic Conversations.* New York: Norton.

O'Hanlon, B. and Beadle, S. (1994) *A Field Guide to Possibilityland.* Omaha: Possibility Press.

O'Hanlon, B. and Weiner-Davis, M. (1989) *In Search of Solutions.* New York: Norton.

Parker, H. (1976) 'Boys will be men: Brief adolescence in a down-town neighbourhood.' In G. Mungham and G. Pearson (eds) *Working Class Youth Culture*. London: Routledge.

Parton, N. (1996) 'Social work, risk and the blaming system.' In N. Parton (ed.) *Social Theory, Social Change and Social Work*. London: Routledge.

Parton, N. (2002) 'Postmodern and constructionist approaches to social work.' In R. Adams, L. Dominelli and M. Payne (eds) *Social Work: Themes, Issues and Critical Debates*. Basingstoke: Palgrave/Macmillan.

Parton, N. (2003) 'Rethinking *professional* practice: The contributions of social constructionism and the feminist "ethics of care".' *British Journal of Social Work* 33, 1, 1–16.

Parton, N. and O'Byrne, P. (2000) *Constructive Social Work: Towards a New Practice*. London: Macmillan.

Pitts, J. (1992) 'The end of an era.' *Howard Journal* 31, 133–49.

Potter, J. and Wetherell, M. (1987) *Discourse and Social Psychology: Beyond Attitudes and Behaviour*. London: Sage.

Prochaska, J.O. and DiClemente, C.C. (1994) *The Transtheoretical Approach: Crossing Traditional Boundaries of Therapy*. Malabar, FL: Krieger Publishers.

Raynor, P. (2003) 'Research in probation: from "Nothing Works" to "What Works".' In W.H. Chui and M. Nellis (eds) *Moving Probation Forward*. Harlow: Pearson Education Limited.

Raynor, P. and Vanstone, M. (1997) *Straight Thinking on Probation (STOP): The Mid-Glamorgan Experiment*. Probation Studies Report 4. Oxford: Centre for Criminological Research.

Ross, R.R., Fabiano, E.A. and Ross, R.D. (1986) *Reasoning and Rehabilitation: A Handbook for Teaching Cognitive Skills*. Ottawa: University of Ottawa.

Saleebey, D. (ed.) (1997) *The Strengths Perspective in Social Work Practice* (2nd edition). New York: Longman.

Sampson, R.J. and Laub, J.H. (1993) *Crime in the Making: Pathways and Turning Points through Life*. London: Harvard University Press.

Schutz, A. (1962–6) *Collected Papers* (3 volumes). The Hague: Martinus Nijhoff.

Shotter, J. (1993) *Conversational Realities: Constructing Life through Language*. London: Sage.

Spencer, J. and Deakin, J. (2004) 'Community reintegration: For whom?' In G. Mair (ed.) *What Matters in Probation*. Cullompton: Willan Publishing.

Taylor, C. and White, S. (2000) *Practising Reflexivity in Health and Welfare: Making Knowledge*. Buckingham: Open University Press.

Trotter, C. (1999) *Working with Involuntary Clients*. London: Sage.

Velody, I. and Williams, R. (eds) (1998) *The Politics of Constructionism*. London: Sage.

White, M. (1990) *Re-Authoring Lives: Interviews and Essays*. Adelaide, South Australia: Dulwich Centre Publications.

White, M. (1993) 'Deconstruction and therapy.' In S. Gilligan and R. Price (eds) *Therapeutic Conversations*. New York: Norton.

White, M. and Epston, D. (1990) *Narrative Means to Therapeutic Ends*. New York: Norton.

Worrall, A. (1997) *Punishment in the Community: The Future of Criminal Justice*. London: Longman.

Chapter 2

Collaborative and Constructive Frontline Practice with Offenders in a Climate of 'Tough Love' and 'Third Way' Politics

Bill Jordan

This chapter is about how the political culture underlying recent criminal justice policy can be put to constructive use in work with offenders. It considers how the cultural resources available in a climate of 'tough love', and the social relations which prevail under a 'Third Way' regime, might be mobilized for collaborative, positive practice. It takes as its background the developments outlined in the introduction, and asks how some of the themes and narratives of the Blair government – choice, enterprise, property, investment, human and social capital, social cohesion – can contribute to better practice at the front line.

I shall not argue that the current political climate is specially propitious for constructive practice in criminal justice. It is one in which the tough elements in the Third Way formula are far more prominent than the loving ones (Jordan with Jordan 2000). The UK government has at times opportunistically manipulated fears on crime and security to gain support from citizens made insecure and fearful in part by its economic programmes. It has also tried to gain political capital by fostering hostility to 'welfare cheats' and 'bogus asylum seekers'. Its restrictive policies in the fields of income maintenance and immigration have reinforced suspicions and resentments against poor people and minority ethnic populations (Jordan and Düvell 2003, ch.4).

However, I shall argue that the broader context of policy programmes does present opportunities for constructive practice. The government has redefined the terms of citizenship, and the relationship between itself and citizens, under a 'New Social Contract' (Department of Social Security 1998, p.80). In this, individuals are expected to be autonomous, 'independent' and active, and above all to avoid being a burden on taxpayers. They are required to develop themselves to their full potential, as economic and social beings, through projects for self-realization (Jordan 2004, chs 2 and 3; Rose 1996, 1999). In return, the government undertakes to reward hard work and initiative, and to provide incentives and opportunities for enterprise.

This new contract has both a social-psychological and an economic dimension, and each of these gives some scope for constructive practice. In terms of psychology, the contract emphasizes that citizens make themselves through their choices. They take responsibility for managing their developmental trajectories in their 'projects of self'. This includes education and training, and building up their skills and capabilities, as well as accumulating property and establishing close relationships. All this is in line with the principles of constructive work.

However, at the centre of any such approach must be a core of identity and self-esteem (Cruikshank 1994, 1996); each citizen must value themselves sufficiently to invest in the 'human capital' of these forms and a portfolio of material assets. The difficulty for practitioners in the current political culture is to nurture this core, when government ministers and the media refer to offenders as 'yobs', 'thugs', 'animals' or 'scum'. In order to gain access to the status of citizen, and hence a foot on the ladder of programmes for self-development, offenders must overcome these stereotypes, which promote self-loathing rather than empowerment. It is a rhetoric which revives the political philosophy of the early modern period, when the founders of liberal individualism linked unequal property to government by consent, and described those who used violence, fraud or theft against this regime as 'wild beasts', deserving cruel punishment (Locke 1698, secs.3, 93). Because criminal justice is again (as in that era) at the centre of the social contract, practitioners are required to engage directly with these issues (Jordan 2003).

The economic dimension of self-realization is linked with the psychological one. All are expected to demonstrate that they are trying to make an economic contribution, to avoid dependence and to be enterprising. The New Deals and other welfare-to-work programmes emphasize an active search for self-reliance through employment or self-employment (Department of Social Security 1998, pp.26–80). In a business-minded environment, every citizen must be accountable for their adaptability and innovation; passivity and security are not approved (Doheny 2004).

In an ironic way, New Labour's often unconvincing efforts to be enterprise-friendly can sound like a prospectus for the Delboy Trotters and Arthur Daleys of this world. The line which separates entrepreneurialism from crime is often blurred; criminals can display many of the characteristics (misplaced optimism, self-deception, faulty risk assessment) of marginal business people. The challenge for practitioners is to pick up some of the positive themes of Third Way economic programmes – energy, an active posture, taking opportunities – and reframe offenders' thinking in these terms.

The difficulty is that offenders often operate in very unpromising economic territory – deprived districts, depressed regions – and have very little start-up capital. During the 1980s and 1990s, crime grew (along with begging, hustling and prostitution) as part of an overall expansion of 'informal economic activity' in such neighbourhoods (Jordan and Travers 1998). Deserted by the market and the state, these areas' economic vacuum was filled by various kinds of petty trading, drug dealing and rackets. I shall argue that an imaginative approach is required, if practitioners are to help offenders reorientate themselves towards the formal economy, including small business initiatives.

Finally, New Labour is increasingly aware of a third dimension of citizenship, which transcends individualism and enterprise. Since the intercommunal violence in Bradford, Burnley and Oldham in the summer of 2001, there has been increasing concern about rivalry and resentment between ethnic groups in deprived areas (Home Office 2002a). This has sparked a search for 'bridging social capital' (Leonard 2004; Putnam 2000, pp.27–9), and a set of new initiatives for 'civil renewal' (Blunkett 2003) and 'community cohesion' (Blunkett 2004). Practitioners now must balance challenging racism and violence with the constructive tasks of community-building. Many offenders are strongly embedded in systems of interdependence, constructed around kinship, parochial tradition, loyalty and self-defence. Great skill is needed to draw out the positives in these forms of belonging and turn them to good account.

Cultural resources, resistance and constructive work

The first step in my analysis is to show that the dominant ideology of official discourse – deployed by the government in policy documents, law and press releases – can enter the culture and practices of poor, marginal, excluded and deviant groups in society, as resources for survival, resistance and (occasionally) as means to reduce the power of those with authority over them. I shall then go on to suggest ways in which frontline workers with such groups can help them deploy these for more reliable and sustainable purposes, and make more constructive links with mainstream society.

Researchers in the UK and abroad have noted that 'outsiders' and subordinates in all societies have mobilized official rhetoric and recycled it to their purposes, often using it to justify actions which are unorthodox or illegal. Historically, for example, those claiming poor relief were able to use the Laws of Settlement (which were supposed to limit claims of assistance, by requiring them to be made in the pauper's 'parish of origin') as a means of free public transport. By insisting they were born somewhere where they heard there was work, Irish labourers in particular were able to get a free ride to this destination (Thompson 1963, p.478).

The American anthropologist James C. Scott has elaborated his researches in Malaysia (Scott 1985) into a theory of how transformed discourses of power are turned against the authorities, and combined with unorthodox practices, to forge 'weapons of the weak'. He gives many examples of this subversive process in his study of how power has been resisted through the ages, not so much by direct opposition and organized revolt as by using the very narrative elements and frameworks in the dominant ideas of economic, political or religious elites against them (Scott 1990).

When I and my colleagues studied how British claimants of income support made decisions about what employment to take, we found that they used much of the rhetoric of the (then) Thatcher administration to reinterpret its policies and rules. In justifying what emerged as the common practice of doing bits of undeclared cash work while claiming, they relied on discourses of hard work and family responsibility – Thatcherite themes – as legitimations, rather than seeking to criticize the dominant ideology or challenge her regime. For example, Mr Bow, the father of three children, with a wife who also did undeclared work, explained why he was unable to come off benefits and take the scraps of low-paid formal employment then available for unskilled workers like himself.

> *Mr Bow*: 'Cause with these jobs here they only last about, maybe 2 weeks, see, and it's, I can't actually sign off the dole… 'Cause if I sign off the dole I'm gonna go all through the rigmarole of signing on and all this lot and […] when you re-sign on…you're like 2 weeks in arrears […] No, it wouldn't be worthwhile, so…I just takes a chance of finding a bit of work […]. 'Cause the moneywise here – the money on social security, it's not great, you can't, you know I, my wife can't live on it, she's always arguing all the time 'cause she haven't got the money, she ha'n, can't go to the shop

and get this and get that. [...] But that's the only way: it's either that or go
out pinching. Now if I go out pinching, I'm in prison! (Jordan *et al.* 1992,
pp.239–42)

Like other claimants on a deprived council estate, Mr Bow adopted the
identity of a hard-working family man, living by the standards of a
self-respecting breadwinner, in an economic environment made up of
below-subsistence, insecure employment and shoddy benefits administration. Even his hobby, hunting by night with dogs, was framed in terms of
the regulations for income support, rather than directly challenging them.

> *Mr Bow:* I got four...well four dogs, they're all curled up see. I go out
> hunting with 'em. That's the only, that's me, you know, that's the enjoy-
> ment I get [...] I used to go out now about 3 or 4 times [...] a week, see [...]
> Yeah, yeah, rabbits. Rabbits, hares, foxes, deer, or you know that's...well
> it's...ain't s'posed to some of the things but...most of it I, I get it all [...]
> You know, on an average night there'll be 15, 20 rabbits, that's maybe,
> that's what, 20 pound i'n it. [...] It's like...social security, if they found out
> I was [...] rabbits, selling 'em [...] But if I go out rabbiting or...go out, it's
> me dogs do the work, see... And that money don't go into me wife's...or
> me, it goes back into food for the animals. (Jordan *et al.* 1992, pp.315–16)

Such re-interpretations of official discourses and rules were familiar to me
from my earlier experiences, both as a probation officer (Jordan 1970), and
as an activist in a benefit claimants' movement (Jordan 1973). They picked
up specific elements in the rhetoric of power and its legitimations, and used
them as resources in the narratives of unorthodox strategies, such as Mr
Bow's. The art of successful practice in probation seemed to lie in challenging those aspects of these strategies which were illegal and unsustainable,
while developing the positive, optimistic, energetic and survival-oriented
features of the stories. In the claimants' union, we did the same thing collectively, turning individual strategies for informal economic activities (which
were against the rules) into schemes such as vegetable-growing and fund-
raising, which were within them (because collective, and openly pursued).
We also gave people the security of mutual support, both for claiming their
full entitlements, and for challenging the fairness of some of the regulations
(Jordan 1973, 1994). The goal was not to accept mainstream standards
compliantly, but to reach a critical co-existence with them, in which a distinctive identity was asserted, and the injustices built into some aspects of
power relations were debated.

My argument in this section has been that the cultural resources from
the current political ideology and policy discourses are not optional
elements in practice. They inevitably enter the exchanges between offenders

and practitioners, because they frame all relationships between the public and officials. My colleagues and I were surprised, when researching irregular immigrants who were working without proper immigration status, to find that they, too, picked up these cultural resources of the host country. When we compared the accounts of Polish irregular workers in the UK, Germany, Italy and Greece, we found that each group's discourses and practices reflected the political and social institutions of the host nation, partly because of self-selection in Poland (Jordan 2005). UK interviewees were attracted by work opportunities in a competitive economy and spoke of their contribution to the prosperity of London, in particular of behind-the-scenes workers in this underground sector (Düvell and Jordan 2005). German interviewees were experts in networking and sustaining relationships of patronage and dependence with citizens and settled co-nationals, which they needed to survive in this far more regulated economy (Cyrus and Vogel 2005). Italian and Greek interviewees were mainly women, and from more depressed regions of Poland; they sought work as live-in carers for elderly citizens and deployed a rhetoric of care and exploitation (Psimmenos and Kasamati 2005; Triandafyllidou and Kosic 2005). If irregular migrants, many of whom could barely speak the host country's language, could pick up and use these cultural resources so distinctively (re-interpreting for their own strategic purposes), this indicates their importance in transactions between service users and officials (Jordan 2005).

New Labour rhetoric as a cultural resource

The next step in my analysis is to show that Third Way policies and discourses do supply distinctive materials for constructive practice. My starting point is that the Clinton administration in the US and the Blair government in the UK were consciously building on their Reagan–Bush and Thatcher–Major neo-liberal legacies, rather than seeking to make radical breaks with them (Blair 1998; Jordan 1998; Waddan 1997). They sought to re-interpret social democratic values and political traditions in the light of the more individualistic culture which their predecessors had fostered and the privatization of much of the public infrastructure. They aimed to improve incentives to take low-paid work (for example, through tax credits) rather than to raise the wages of unskilled workers; to consolidate a tougher, more conditional regime of benefits administration, balanced by more training and welfare-to-work counselling (Department of Social Security 1998); and to implement socially conservative measures to foster traditional family, kinship and community bonds (Driver and Martell 1997; Etzioni 1993), while clamping down on crime.

However, New Labour also adopted a more positive and future-oriented approach in relation to poverty and social exclusion, promising to lift millions out of disadvantage and provide pathways into the mainstream for those who had been pushed to the margins of society by the policies of the Conservatives. Typical of this new spirit was the pledge in the Department of Social Security White Paper, *A New Contract for Welfare* (1998), that the responsibilities of individuals who can provide for themselves and their families must always be matched by a responsibility on the part of government to provide opportunities for self-advancement (p.31). It is easy to imagine Mr Bow endorsing (in principle at least) the statements that all citizens should 'seek training or work where able to do so', 'take up the opportunity to be independent if able to do so', 'give support, financial or otherwise, to their children and other family members', 'save for retirement where possible', and 'not [...] defraud the taxpayers' (p.80) – the bases of the New Contract – even if he might have put a different spin on all of them.

Furthermore, the Third Way innovation in citizenship and governance was not simply to emphasize that responsibilities must balance rights, but to develop a whole new rhetoric of self-development and self-realization, in which individuals owed it to themselves to fulfil their potential, through their own projects, commitments and choices. Instead of exercising surveillance over them, policing their performance of citizenship and demanding compliance, government set out to enable and empower them to govern, develop and monitor themselves (Foucault 1988). This new rhetoric was visible in many ministerial statements, press releases and policy documents.

> People should be encouraged to solve their own problems in part because they know from their everyday lives what the core of the problem is, and how to engage in the best way in solving the challenge; but also because tackling your own problems is a vital part of growing as a person, a source of confidence and self-respect. (Blunkett 2003, p.1)

This new approach has been described as using 'ethical techniques of self' (Rogers 2004); it was first manifested, in a clearly identifiable way, in certain US programmes, which identified self-esteem and self-reliance as fundamental to the success of welfare-to-work and inclusion programmes (Cruikshank 1994). This led to the Clinton administration embracing measures which tried to persuade disadvantaged citizens that governance was 'something we do to ourselves, not something done to us by those in power' (Cruikshank 1996, p.253). This style and many of these programmes were adopted by New Labour as it sought to develop a programme for empowerment and inclusion of poor and disadvantaged people (Rose 1996, 1999).

The discourses of self-improvement and self-realization were, of course, borrowed from a culture which was already prevalent among mainstream citizens in the US and UK. During the neo-liberal era, they had been persuaded to rely more on their own resources, as public benefits and services were cut back and a more competitive, rivalrous environment created. This applied to striving for positional advantage in the housing market, in choice of schools for their children (Jordan, Redley and James 1994) and in accumulating property rights of all kinds (shares, savings, private or occupational pensions), as well as developing their 'human capital' through training and promotion at work. None of these options was open to poor people, who relied more on state support, public services and communal mutuality; who were less mobile; and hence who often became mired in concentrations of disadvantage, as more able and resourceful people move to better districts (Jordan 1996; Jordan with Jordan 2000, ch.7).

However, the positive aspects of these innovations do supply some elements which are potentially valuable for constructive practice. The views that individuals' inner resources are the most important keys to their futures, that they can take responsibility and control their actions and that the future can be shaped by planning and discussion are all aspects of Third Way thinking which are also elements of constructive practice. Implicit also in New Labour's programme is the idea that people who are disadvantaged can 'turn round' their lives by constructing more positive futures, and telling themselves and others more optimistic stories about their capacities and aspirations.

Indeed, one of the more surprising features of Third Way social policy is the faith placed in counselling and personal advice – for example, in the New Deals for Young People, the Long-Term Unemployed and Lone Parents (Department of Social Security 1998, p.28). It is an anomaly of New Labour programmes that social work is seen as a very limited, circumscribed branch of this activity, confined to assessing risks and rationing resources in child protection and social care (Department of Health 1998); but many of the profession's skills, insights, values and approaches are given high-profile roles in flagship initiatives (Jordan with Jordan 2000, ch.1). Furthermore, both new agencies for the most intractable and complex issues (such as the National Asylum Support Service of the Home Office) and new programmes of key importance for policy goals (such as Sure Start and the Children's Fund) owe much to social work methods and analyses. Hence there are sometimes more opportunities for constructive work in agencies which have been deliberately kept separate from public sector social work (i.e. local authority social services departments) than in those departments themselves. The earlier separation of social work from probation may therefore be seen as advantageous for the latter in some ways.

Above all, the potential for constructive practice, using Third Way resources, lies in the strong message that self-stories are not determined by economic or social circumstances, but can be rewritten (Parton and O'Bryne 2000, p.87). The most challenging task is to reframe stories of resistance to disadvantage and exclusion through rule-breaking and rule-bending (such as Mr Bow's) into stories of resistance to crime and of offenders taking control over their lives, and to steer them towards other forms of enterprising activities. It is to the broader background of such reconstructions that I turn in the next section.

Deprived communities, the informal economy and constructive practice

If frontline work with offenders is to be more effective, it needs to go further than building on the future orientation of Third Way rhetoric, and encouraging individuals to revalue their inner resources and reconstruct their narratives of their lives. It must also recognize their local expertise, their place in their communities and the context in which these plans are to be implemented. New Labour has a number of programmes and policies in relation to economic regeneration, community building and social cohesion, which are of relevance to these aspects and offer cultural resources for constructive methods.

Communities and community development were themes of the Blair government's programmes from the time it took office. The New Deal for Communities, the Social Exclusion Unit and the Single Regeneration Budget were among the main instruments of community reconstruction which focused on deprived districts (Jordan with Jordan 2000, chs 5 and 7). However, here again the government chose to make links with business and the voluntary sector, rather than with social work and the Probation Service, in tackling such issues as homelessness, truancy, drug abuse and the decay of communities, and to use a combination of economic measures (Ginsburg 1999) and authoritative interventions, rather than starting with social regeneration. They used these programmes to improve the physical infrastructure for businesses, to get homeless people and drug-dealing off the streets, and – through the Employment Zones and Action Teams – to increase participation in the formal economy.

These approaches have been only partly successful; poverty, inequality and squalid conditions persist in many such districts, as do all the social problems addressed. To give just one example, homeless people have been cleared into various kinds of shelter or hostel, so they are no longer as visible; but homelessness itself has doubled in the past seven years, with an estimated 500,000 individuals and families now in temporary accommodation (BBC Radio 4 2004). This reveals the need for approaches which start from social needs, and mobilize the energies of those most affected, to solve their own problems collectively. In relation to homelessness, the Emmaus Community (which was founded by a French cleric, a wartime resistance hero) adopts this approach; it creates communities where homeless 'companions' not only live together, but work for the benefit of their common unit, on projects like furniture recycling (Jordan with Jordan 2000, pp.111–13). In this way, the community adopts a constructive method of self-development, and rewrites narratives of despair as cooperative self-sufficiency and heroic resilience.

The Emmaus movement is classified as a Social Enterprise (Department of Trade and Industry 2003, p.48). This is defined as 'a business with primarily social objectives whose surpluses are principally reinvested for the purpose in the business or in the community' (p.2). However, the fact that the government department involved is separate from those with responsibilities for health, education, social care and the environment, and is concerned to 'make social enterprises better businesses' (p.10), is very limiting. It has meant that government policy is led by aims such as improving efficiency and competitiveness, rather than the social concerns which are supposed to inspire such enterprises.

Furthermore, the whole New Labour strategy on regeneration has failed to develop constructive measures to deal with the 'informal economy' of which crime is a part. This underground sector flourished and expanded under Conservative administrations because of the impact of market forces that they released on marginal businesses in declining industries, depressed regions and less able entrepreneurs. As a result, not only the cash economy of undeclared transactions of all kinds, but also a whole universal network of unrecorded activities, came to coexist with the formal economy, especially in deprived districts. Williams and Windebank (1999) found that most 'paid informal work' took place among kin, friends and neighbours as part of systems of exchange and strengthened bonds between members. However, there existed a hard core of criminal activities within this sector.

Recent research has focused on the issue of how those who have come to rely on informal activities of all kinds (undeclared cash work, informal businesses and illegal trading in undocumented goods) can be enabled to make the transition into the formal economy. This is clearly of special relevance to frontline work with offenders; it involves the constructive effort to reframe much illegal activity as enterprise, and to divert criminal activity into legitimate business. One recent publication provided case studies of how a new micro-finance agency, Street UK, has supplied credit to people (some of whom were offenders) who had been operating for years in the informal economy (Capisarow and Barbour 2004). They insist that this has allowed a transition mechanism for individuals 'who wish to build an income-generating scheme into a fully-fledged business' (p.30). They argue that the benefits rules should be changed, to enable rather than penalize such transitions.

They also contend that the informal economy itself makes a valuable contribution to the life of deprived communities. They see it as 'a means of encouraging affordable mutual service provision in a community, which builds its social capital and reduces community residents' individual difficulties' (Capisarow and Barbour 2004, p.30). This leads into the second aspect of Third Way policy in relation to communities – the social relations they sustain and the attempt to transform these through programmes of intervention.

When New Labour came to power, its leaders spoke glowingly of community as a source of support, strength and responsibility. Tony Blair insisted: 'I have no doubt that the breakdown of law and order is intimately linked to the breakup of a strong sense of community. And the breakup of community is in turn, to a crucial degree, consequent on the breakdown of family life' (Blair 1996, p.68).

This explains the emphasis placed on 'building social capital' in deprived districts – attempting to establish norms of trust, reciprocity and cooperation, both between officials and residents, and among community groups. However, these efforts tended to ignore the crucial distinction between 'bonding' and 'bridging' social capital (Putnam 2000, pp.27–9). This differentiates between ties which bond members with similar values, commitments, resources and goals, and links which build trust between heterogeneous members of a wider, diverse 'community of communities', bridging their differences. For instance, the deprived Protestant and Catholic communities of West Belfast have large supplies of bonding social capital, and flourishing informal systems of cooperation (Leonard 1994); what is lacking is bridging social capital, to create trust and reciprocity between them.

The distinction was made painfully clear to the New Labour government in the intercommunal riots in Bradford, Burnley and Oldham in 2001, and led to a new theme and set of initiatives within the Third Way programme – community cohesion (Blunkett 2003, 2004; Home Office 2002a). The reports on the riots recognized that there was longstanding rivalry between white and Asian residents of deprived districts in these and other northern English towns, and resentment had been fuelled by BNP agitators. Local authority housing policies had allowed what amounted to segregation between these communities and government policies had done little to challenge either the decay or the conflict.

The response from the Home Office has been to give far more prominence to grass-roots community development programmes and community cohesion, for instance through Connecting Communities grants, with 75 new projects to build bridges between groups (Blunkett 2003, p.21). It is also to place far more emphasis on the 'integration of new arrivals' (p.23) – a shift from the negative stance of the White Papers on immigration of the earlier period (Home Office 1998, 2002b), and the rhetoric of 'bogus asylum seekers' and 'swamping'.

However, it is a challenge for frontline practitioners to translate these new discourses of community cohesion and bridging social capital into constructive practice. These districts have been neglected for decades, first under the Conservatives, and then New Labour. Minority ethnic citizens and new immigrants alike, along with white communities, have come to rely on close-knit circuits of mutual protection, sustained by fierce loyalty and sometimes by violent enforcement of conformity. These bonds of locality, faith and kinship are often sustained by a 'blood and guts code' of conduct, which defines itself by opposition to officialdom, to other racial groups and to other neighbourhoods (Jordan with Jordan 2000, chs 2 and 7) – much as in the rivalry between deprived communities in Northern Ireland.

Hence practitioners must tread warily. On the one hand, there is genuine expertise, loyalty and mutuality in these communities; many offenders contribute substantially to networks of support and protection. On the other, this is often used in exclusive, hostile or aggressive ways, directed at other groups and communities or to scapegoat members of their own. To reconstruct these as narratives of survival, solidarity and active citizenship, and to build projects which bridge hostilities and fears, should be a task of practice with offenders, as well as community development work.

Conclusion

There is much that is positive, forward-looking and optimistic in Third Way thinking, above all its discourses of empowerment through the mobilization of capacities and potentials. However, particularly in its first term, New Labour's social policies were strongly directed against benefit fraud, crime and illegal immigration, using rhetoric which was full of negativity and punitive intent. In its determination to display continued commitment to private property values, individual independence and enterprise, and the ethos of the business sector, the government denounced the people involved in these activities, as well as the activities themselves. Taken together with the trends in criminal justice and penal policy identified in the introduction, and above all with the massive rise in the prison population, this has constrained the cultural resources available for constructive practice.

Even more crucially, government rhetoric on empowerment, inclusion and social justice has not been matched by implementation. The poorest and most marginal citizens remain outside the mainstream of organized life. Survey evidence has revealed that, among men in social class V born in 1970, far more had been arrested (over 45%) than were members of any kind of organization (less than 2%), including trade unions (Bynner and Parsons 2003, figs. 10.16 and 10.9). This reflected a massive increase over the percentage of those born in 1958 of this class who had been arrested by the age of 30 (from 15%), and a massive decline in those who were members of an organization among that cohort (from 18%). Social inclusion and empowerment have not been achieved by Third Way programmes.

In terms of cohesion and bridging social capital, also, the evidence is that poor and marginal communities have become more isolated and homogeneous, as more resourceful residents have moved out to escape from their social problems (Dorling and Thomas 2004). The community cohesion agenda has been more than cancelled out by the choice agenda, which enables better-off citizens to switch and shift, and to move to districts with better amenities and services (Jordan 2004, chs 5 and 6).

So practitioners face three difficulties in terms of the cultural and political context, and the economic situation of offenders. Although the new discourses of citizenship are future-oriented and self-developmental, those of criminal justice deal in negative stereotypes and retributive punishment. Poor and marginal people have predominantly negative experiences of the state, with heavy involvement with the police and little participation in civil society. And community development approaches to building more cohesive communities are offset by policies which promote the flight of educated and better-off residents from disadvantaged districts, as has also occurred in the US (Oliver 1999; Orbell and Uno 1975).

As the editors outline in their introduction, the response of the criminal justice system in general, and the Probation Service in particular, has been discouraging. The heavily structured programmes for 'challenging' offending behaviour, using cognitive-behavioural methods in groups, have had at best unconvincing results. In this chapter, I have argued that it would be possible to adopt far more constructive methods, in work with individuals and community action groups, deploying cultural resources from New Labour's own programmes.

Fortunately, there is still sufficient diversity in the Probation Service for these traditions to have remained alive. Thoughtful practice, based on an overview of the ideological, structural and cultural context, and reflection on everyday interactions with offenders, is still possible (see for instance Elliott 2001). The service has seen many changes in fads and fashions from theory, its management and the Home Office since I was a practitioner in the 1960s and 1970s. The basis for constructive approaches has survived these in reasonable shape, despite much of this effort.

What will perhaps be most difficult is to create the overall ethos in which constructive practice can flourish, within the present institutional order of criminal justice. While current individualist ideology does provide resources for such practice, and especially for narratives of self-development and change, it also breeds insecurity, anxiety and defensiveness. The reliance on property holdings, bank credit and competitiveness as the material basis for projects of self leads to paranoia about crime, and demands for vengeance. Too little attention is paid to creating an overall context of cooperation and sharing, in which conviviality and membership are given their due value.

Crime rates are not the products of individual characteristics alone; they are largely the outcome of social relations and cultural conditions. In the affluent countries generally, and specifically in the US and UK, successful policies for economic growth have *not* led to greater subjective well-being; both rich and poor remain no happier (on self-reported scales) than their counterparts were in the 1970s (Frey and Stutzer 2002; Kahneman, Diener and Schwartz 1999; Layard 2003). Many commentators put this phenomenon of 'stalled well-being' down to rivalry and excessively competitive relationships. Constructive practice might seek to reduce the impact of these factors on disadvantaged offenders, by recognizing and valuing their cheerfulness, optimism and friendship skills, rather than constantly confronting them over their failures and weaknesses.

References

BBC Radio 4 (2004) *News.* 13 December.

Blair, T. (1996) *Speech to Labour Party Conference.* October.

Blair, T. (1998) *The Third Way: New Politics for the New Century.* London: Fabian Society.

Blunkett, D. (2003) *Active Citizens, Strong Communities: Progressing Civil Renewal.* London: Home Office.

Blunkett, D. (2004) 'New challenges for race equality and community cohesion in the twenty-first century', speech to the Institute for Public Policy Research. London, 7 July.

Bynner, J. and Parsons, S. (2003) 'Social participation, values and crime.' In E. Ferri, J. Bynner and M. Wadsworth (eds) *Changing Britain, Changing Lives: Three Generations at the Turn of the Century.* London: Institute of Education, University of London.

Capisarow, R. and Barbour, A. (2004) *Self-Employed People in the Informal Economy – Cheats or Contributors? Evidence, Implications and Policy Recommendations.* London: Street UK/ Community Links.

Cruikshank, B. (1994) 'The will to empower: Technologies of citizenship and the war on poverty.' *Socialist Review* 23, 4, 29–55.

Cruikshank, B. (1996) 'Revolutions within: Self-government and self-esteem.' In A. Barry, T. Osborne and N. Rose (eds) *Foucault and Political Reason.* London: UCL Press.

Cyrus, N. and Vogel, D. (2005) 'Managing access to the German labour/market: How Polish (im)migrants relate to German opportunites and restrictions.' In F. Düvell (ed.) *Illegal Immigration in Eroupe: Addressing the Illegal Immigration Dilemma.* Basingstoke: Palgrave.

Department of Health (1998) *Modernising Social Services: Promoting Independence, Improving Protection, Raising Standards.* Cm 4169. London: Stationery Office.

Department of Social Security (1998) *A New Contract for Welfare.* Cm 3805. London: Stationery Office.

Department of Trade and Industry (2003) *Social Enterprise: A Strategy for Success.* London: Stationery Office.

Doheny, S. (2004) 'Responsibility and welfare: In search of moral sensibility.' In H. Dean (ed.) *The Ethics of Welfare: Human Rights, Welfare and Responsibility.* Bristol: Policy Press.

Dorling, D. and Thomas, B. (2004) *People and Places: A 2001 Census Atlas of the UK.* Bristol: Policy Press.

Driver, S. and Martell, L. (1997) 'New Labour's communitarianisms.' *Critical Social Policy* 13, 3, 27–46.

Düvell, F. and Jordan, B. (2005) 'Documented and undocumented workers in the UK: Changing environments and shifting strategies.' In F. Düvell (ed.) *Illegal Immigration in Europe: Beyond Control.* Basingstoke: Palgrave.

Elliott, N. (2001) *Working with Structural and Ideological Change: An Example from Practice.* Social Work Monographs No.186. Norwich: University of East Anglia.

Etzioni, A. (1993) *The Spirit of Community: The Re-invention of American Society.* New York: Touchstone.

Frey, B. and Stutzer, A. (2002) *Happiness and Economics: How the Economy and Institutions Affect Human Wellbeing.* Princeton, NY: Princeton University Press.

Foucault, M. (1988) 'Technologies of the self.' In L. Martin (ed.) *Technologies of the Self.* London: Tavistock.

Ginsburg, N. (1999) 'Putting the social into urban regeneration policy.' *Local Economy* May, 17–28.

Home Office (1998) *Fairer, Faster and Firmer: A Modern Approach to Immigration and Asylum.* Cm. 4018. London: Stationery Office.

Home Office (2002a) *Community Cohesion: Report of the Independent Review Team* (Chaired by Ted Cantle). London: Stationery Office.

Home Office (2002b) *Secure Borders, Safe Haven: Integration with Diversity in Modern Britain.* London: Stationery Office.

Jordan, B. (1970) *Client–Worker Transactions.* London: Routledge and Kegan Paul.

Jordan, B. (1973) *Paupers: The Making of the New Claiming Class.* London: Routledge and Kegan Paul.

Jordan, B. (1994) 'Framing claims and the weapons of the weak.' In G. Drover and P. Kerans (eds) *New Approaches to Welfare Theory.* Aldershot: Edward Elgar.

Jordan, B. (1996) *A Theory of Poverty and Social Exclusion.* Cambridge: Polity.

Jordan, B. (1998) *The New Politics of Welfare: Social Justice in a Global Context.* London: Sage.

Jordan, B. (2003) 'Criminal justice, social exclusion and the social contract.' *Probation Journal* 50, 3, 198–210.

Jordan, B. (2004) *Sex, Money and Power: The Transformation of Collective Life.* Cambridge: Polity.

Jordan, B. (2005) 'Poles apart: Each EU country gets the migrants it requires.' In F. Düvell (ed.) *Illegal Immigration in Europe: Beyond Control.* Basingstoke: Palgrave.

Jordan, B. and Düvell, F. (2003) *Migration: The Boundaries of Equality and Justice.* Cambridge: Polity.

Jordan, B. with Jordan, C. (2000) *Social Work and the Third Way: Tough Love as Social Policy.* London: Sage.

Jordan, B. and Travers, A. (1998) 'The informal economy: A case study in unrestrained competition.' *Social Policy and Administration* 32, 3, 292–306.

Jordan, B., James, S., Kay, H. and Redley, M. (1992) *Trapped in Poverty? Labour-Market Decisions in Low-Income Households.* London: Routledge.

Jordan, B., Redley, M. and James, S. (1994) *Putting the Family First: Identities, Decisions, Citizenship.* London: UCL Press.

Kahneman, D., Diener, E. and Schwartz, N. (eds) (1999) *Well-being: The Foundations of Hedonic Psychology.* New York: Russell Sage Foundation.

Layard, R. (2003) *Happiness: Has Social Science a Clue?* Lionel Robbins Memorial Lectures, London School of Economics, 3–5 March.

Leonard, M. (1994) *Informal Economic Activity in Belfast.* Aldershot: Avebury.

Leonard, M. (2004) 'Bonding and bridging social capital: Reflections from Belfast.' *Sociology* 38, 5, 927–44.

Locke, J. (1698) *Second Treatise of Government* (ed. P. Laslett). Cambridge: Cambridge University Press.

Oliver, J.E. (1999) 'The effects of metropolitan economic segregation on civic participation.' *American Journal of Political Science* 43, 186–212.

Orbell, M. and Uno, T. (1975) 'A theory of neighbourhood problem solving: Political action *vs* residential mobility.' *American Political Science Review* 66, 471–89.

Parton, N. and O'Byrne, P. (2000) *Constructive Social Work: Towards a New Practice.* Basingstoke: Macmillan.

Psimmenos, I. and Kasamati, K. (2005) 'Albanian and Polish undocumented workers' life stories: Migration paths, tactics and indenties in Greece.' In F. Düvell (ed.) *Illegal Immigration in Europe: Beyond Control.* Basingstoke: Palgrave.

Putnam, R.D. (2000) *Bowling Alone: The Collapse and Revival of American Community.* New York: Simon and Schuster.

Rogers, R. (2004) 'Ethical techniques of self and the "Good Jobseeker".' In H. Dean (ed.) *The Ethics of Welfare: Human Rights, Dependency and Responsibility.* Bristol: Policy Press.

Rose, N. (1996) *Inventing Ourselves: Psychology, Power and Personhood.* Cambridge: Cambridge University Press.

Rose, N. (1999) 'Inventiveness in politics.' *Economy and Society* 28, 3, 470–88.

Scott, J.C. (1985) *Weapons of the Weak: Everyday Forms of Peasant Resistance.* Princeton, NJ: Princeton University Press.

Scott, J.C. (1990) *Domination and the Arts of Resistance: Hidden Transcripts.* New Haven, CT: Yale University Press.

Thompson, E.P. (1963) *The Making of the English Working Class.* Harmondsworth: Penguin (1980 edition).

Triandafyllidou, A. and Kosic, A. (2005) 'Polish and Albanian workers in Italy: Between legality and undocumented status.' In F. Düvell (ed.) *Illegal Immigration in Europe: Beyond Control.* Basingstoke: Palgrave.

Waddan, A. (1997) *The Politics of Social Welfare: The Collapse of the Centre and the Rise of the Right.* Cheltenham: Edward Elgar.

Williams, C.C. and Windebank, J. (1999) 'Empowering people to help themselves: Tackling social exclusion in poor neighbourhoods.' Leicester: Department of Geography, Leicester University.

Chapter 3

The Offender as Citizen

Socially Inclusive Strategies for Working with Offenders within the Community

Marilyn Gregory

This chapter will seek to explore the ways in which practice with offenders could contribute to the development of a constructive citizenship for individuals who have committed offences. It will analyse the way in which the concept of citizenship is used within criminal justice policy and consider how it is reflected within criminal justice practice, focusing particularly on the National Probation Service in England. It will be argued that current probation practice is at odds with the government's own understanding of citizenship because it has removed its focus from the community and largely abandoned efforts to help offenders to re-engage with their communities. Policy changes are suggested which would refocus practitioners' energies toward local communities and the active re-engagement of probationers as constructive citizens.

What is citizenship?

'Citizenship' could be narrowly conceived as indicating membership of a particular nation state, as in British citizenship or Irish citizenship. For the purposes of this discussion, we need to examine the wider meaning of the concept, which tells us something about the relationship between the individual and their community and how that is regulated or managed by the state. This will involve an examination of the nature of that relationship, how it is conceived of and translated into social policy.

Within the literature, citizenship is a contested concept. The emphasis upon citizenship as a *status*, which brings with it civil, political and social rights, denotes the liberal perspective. From this standpoint, the contribution made by the individual to his or her community does not affect their status as an equal citizen. One does not have to contribute in order to enjoy full citizenship. Where citizenship is seen as a *practice*, a civic republican or communitarian position is taken. Here, citizenship requires the acceptance of responsibilities and duties toward the wider community, as well as the enjoyment of rights (Dwyer 2004; Lister 1990; Plant 1988).

Most conceptions of citizenship imply equality of status between individuals, following the authoritative contribution of T.H. Marshall: 'Citizenship is a status bestowed upon those who are full members of a community. All those who possess the status are equal with respect to the rights and duties with which that status is endowed' (Marshall and Bottomore 1992, p.18). Although Marshall notes that the rights and duties are not governed by any universal principle, he suggests that societies create an ideal toward which individuals should strive in their quest for 'a fuller measure of equality, an enrichment of the stuff of which the status is made and an increase in the number of those on whom the status is bestowed' (Marshall and Bottomore 1992, p.18). Equality here was predicated on the existence of paid work, family support and the provisions of the welfare state (Roche 1992). The current debate frames this as the ability to achieve 'social inclusion'.

In order for individuals to achieve social inclusion, they need to be in possession of what is now termed 'social capital'. The main aspects of social capital have been identified by the Office for National Statistics as: 'citizenship, neighbourliness, trust and shared values, community involvement, volunteering, social networks and civil and political participation' (Office for National Statistics 2003, pp.19–27). In his book on the Third Way, Giddens sees the concepts of social inclusion and citizenship as inextricably linked:

> the new politics defines equality as inclusion and inequality as exclusion…inclusion refers in its broadest sense to citizenship, to civil and political rights and obligations that all members of a society should have… It also refers to opportunities and to involvement in the public space. (1998, pp.102–3)

Citizenship is a key concern of New Labour social policy. Dwyer notes that policy-makers repeatedly focus upon the role of the state in addressing public welfare needs, as well as individual rights and responsibilities (Dwyer 2004). Issues of social exclusion and how it can be addressed are central, as is evident from the work of the Social Exclusion Unit, the government's commitment to racial equality and the teaching of citizenship in schools (Faulkner 2004).

In his paper on civil renewal, David Blunkett sets out the government's understanding of citizenship, firmly rooted in the civic republican/communitarian tradition. He looks at the relationship between citizenship and democracy, the balance between individual freedom and civic duty, and the role of the state in providing public protection and social control. He proposes the setting up of 'community courts' to encourage participation and ownership of the criminal justice process by local communities, as well as a new Centre for Active Citizenship. His view is that civil renewal 'must form the centrepiece of the government's reform agenda for the coming years' (Blunkett 2003a, p.1).

The White Paper *Justice for All* (Home Office 2002) also envisages a more active role for the public in the criminal justice process (Faulkner 2004). The logic of this approach should be the encouragement of active citizenship and social inclusion for all citizens, including those who have committed offences, but an understanding of citizenship as encompassing equality has been abandoned in *Justice for All*. This is justified when we are told that the White Paper's 'single clear priority' is 'to balance the criminal justice system in favour of the victim' (p.14). The need for such a balancing appears to be premised upon the idea that any protections or privileges for offenders in the system are necessarily to the detriment of victims. But as Tonry (2004) points out, the criminal justice system is not some zero-sum game in which every good for an offender leads to harm for a victim. On the contrary, victims, many of whom may at other times in their lives be offenders, have an interest in a criminal justice system that is fair and just for all.

Offender, not citizen

There was a time when offenders were treated more like citizens who had gone wrong and needed support to return, as it were, to the fold. The legal requirement on a probation officer was to 'advise, assist and befriend' an individual whose citizenship was recognized when they were asked to consent to the making of the order. What has changed? That mode of social work (for probation work was social work at the time) has elsewhere been referred to as a 'clinical mode' (Gregory and Holloway 2005). It developed within the prosperous, relatively secure society in the two decades following the Second World War. There was confidence in, and acceptance of, the welfare state and its role in people's lives. With that came a commitment to full citizenship for most people. It was a period of consensus politics within a framework of relatively well-paid work, the mixed economy, the family and a legal system which was perceived to be free and fair (Young 1999). At a time like this, the population enjoys what Giddens (1990) has called 'ontological security'; that is, they can simply *be* without a high level of insecurity about crime, or the future, or day-to-day risks to themselves or their family. During such a period of relative security, the individual with the problem, be they for example mentally ill, a member of a 'problem family' or an offender, is someone who, being the exception to the rule, simply reinforces other people's ontological security. The prevailing discourse is positivist, in which the social work client's behaviour is seen as *determined* by social or psychological factors. Talk is of 'is', 'does' and 'causes' (Bruner 1986, quoted in Parton and O'Byrne 2000, p.47). The state's role is rehabilitative in relation to such people. The social work task is therefore a clinical one, to diagnose and to treat, to enable the individual to be returned to society's fold. There is empathy and warmth for the individual, who is to be *included* not *excluded*. This welfare consensus was accepted by some to the extent that the welfare state's existence was seen as necessary; however, from a number of different, though intersecting positions, feminists, anti-racists, socialists, disabled activists and other new social movements sought to challenge the scope, extent and equity of welfare provision (Clarke 2004).

Socio-economic changes in the following decades which contributed to the loss of faith in the rehabilitative ideal underpinning the welfare state are well documented. Hobsbawm (1994, p.403) remarks that 'The history of the 20 years after 1973 is that of a world which lost its bearings and slid into instability and crisis'. The damage to the post-war optimism and the belief that the welfare state would provide a safety net against poverty, ill health and other social ills is irretrievable. Young (1999) sees these two decades, the 1980s and 1990s, as the development of what he terms 'the exclusive society'. Against a background of economic recession, encompassing a massive rise in structural unemployment, a move from Fordist to post-Fordist modes of production, the development of primary and secondary labour markets, and downsizing (Hutton 1995), social features develop which have a significant impact on social policy approaches to the poor, who become deviant, an 'underclass'. The concomitant loss of stable lifelong career expectations, with accompanying anxiety and insecurity amongst the better-off, contribute to a lack of tolerance of deviance. At the same time the gap between income groups widens, leading to a more acute experience of relative deprivation, at the same time as voracious consumerism is encouraged in all sectors of society, contributing to a rise in consumer crime amongst the poorest. This takes place alongside a steady rise in individualism and the disaggregation of community and family ties (Gregory and Holloway 2005).

In these circumstances, Garland (2000) considers that governments in Britain and the US have engaged in two strategies: 'preventive partnership' and 'punitive segregation'. The first is a way of spreading the responsibility for crime control to the wider society, to the 'responsible citizens' – the shopkeepers, business people and community members – engaging them in partnerships to take preventive action against crime and redefining the roles of criminal justice agencies such as the police and the Probation Service (p.348). It is an approach which focuses less on crime causation and more upon the management and processing of offenders. The second is a 'tough on crime' stance including harsher penalties, fewer opportunities for early release, harder prison conditions and a move away from treating young offenders as children and toward treating them as criminals, as in the case of the killers of James Bulger.

Turning its attention toward so called 'anti-social behaviour' amplifies the offending of younger people and exacerbates intolerance, whilst diverting attention away from any increases in more serious crimes. Punitive segregation is an expressive policy stance – victims become representatives of the wider public, and the assumption is that they want to see criminals punished harshly. All of these developments increase anxiety about crime and anti-social behaviour and widen the gulf between citizens (the law-abiding, responsible kind) and *others*, that dangerous underclass who are responsible for the graffiti, the criminal damage, the burglary and other similar offences which contribute to the loss of ontological security.

Garland believes that this helps us to understand why penal-welfare professionals have failed to protest strongly enough against the harsher regimes that they now help to administer. Their status as baby boomers – the first generation to enjoy the benefits of the welfare state – their middle-class education with its liberal, rehabilitationist stance toward crime, and their ability to live in relatively crime-free neighbourhoods, enabled them to distance themselves from crime and criminals and thereby adopt a 'civilized' approach to it.

Developments of the last few decades have undermined this in a number of ways. Criminal justice was not a party-political issue prior to the 1970s. An unspoken consensus appeared to exist between the major parties that crime was politically neutral and something either party would have to tackle once in government. As crime began to rise throughout the 1970s this changed, so that by the time of the 1979 election campaign crime, linked with public disorder, was a major campaigning platform (Downes and Morgan 1994). With this politicization of crime has come the desire of governments to reassert their own power to punish rather than, as previously, leaving the treatment and rehabilitation of offenders to the professional experts. In the case of probation officers this has included not only changes to the legislation underpinning their work but also fundamental changes to their professional status, which has moved from that of social worker to 'case manager'. Welfare professionals' judgement is eschewed in favour of actuarial prediction tools, and their power to challenge and resist these developments has diminished. The loss of ontological security may also have undermined welfare professionals' civilized approach to crime and criminals as, from the 1960s onwards, they began to experience some forms of crime – such as car theft, burglary and robbery – as a normal social fact, especially when that crime is refracted through mass media moral panics (Young 1999). This leaves them more likely in Garland's view actually to support more punitive penal strategies.

Wider cultural adaptations on behalf of individual citizens, households and private organizations include a plethora of security measures from alarms and locks to CCTV and private police in our shopping malls and city centres. All of this contributes to the actual and ideological separation of 'decent' citizens from the dangerous others.

Welfare no more

In this climate of punitive segregation, criminal justice professionals turn their attention away from the communities in which their 'clients' live, and toward programmes designed to manage the behaviour of individuals. Communities harden themselves against offenders, rather than making provision for their reacceptance. 'Offender' becomes an all-encompassing identity and by implication a 'citizen' is law abiding (or a victim). A 'new penology' develops whose task is managerial not transformative. Its task is to regulate and manage risky populations, providing estimates of the risk posed by individual offenders based upon actuarial calculations using data from large populations. Information gathering is carried out using increasingly structured and prescribed tools and proformas, and the influence of clinical judgement is restricted. Public protection is the stated justification for these strategies. An irony of the system is that recidivism, though still important, is not as crucial as enforcement, which becomes a goal in its own right. Therefore, failures of probation or parole ironically become a kind of success, in that they indicate system efficiency (Feeley and Simon 1992).

The impact of these developments upon the UK Probation Service is well documented (Goodman 2003; Harris 1996; May 1991). The injunction to 'advise, assist and befriend' probationers has been abandoned and the probation officer, no longer trained as a social worker, has a job which focuses upon the assessment of risk, the enforcement of legal sanctions, the challenging of offending behaviour and case management (Goodman 2003). Kemshall suggests that the assessment of risk is the core business of the Probation Service 'supplanting ideologies of need, welfare or indeed rehabilitation' (1998, p.1). Though some have suggested that rehabilitation has seen a revival, this has been limited mainly to treatment within cognitive-behavioural groupwork programmes. There has been, and continues to be, an explicit use of language as a way of achieving these changes and of representing them publicly, both inside and outside the service. Mumby (1993) suggests that there is a battle for power over meanings, with the politically powerful seeking to dominate and 'fix' those meanings. From as early as the White and Green Papers preceding the 1991 Criminal Justice Act, there has been a flood of punitive terminology into the probation arena, flushing out the former language of social work and rehabilitation. The Association of Chief Officers of Probation in its 1988 paper *More Demanding Than Custody* appeared to be vying with the Home Office in the use of more punitive terminology than was used in the White and Green Papers (ACOP 1988, in Gregory and Holloway 2005). The language which characterizes and actively constitutes the work of the Probation Service has been deliberately changed to make the service appear more punitive. In *Joining Forces to Protect the Public: Prisons – Probation*, this was made clear:

> It is important that the names, language and terminology used by the services should give accurate and accessible messages about the nature and aims of the work… On the probation side, some of the terms used have been criticised, for example because: they are associated with tolerance of crime (e.g. probation which can be seen as a conditional reprieve and inconsistent with 'just deserts' or even a rigorous programme aimed at correcting offending behaviour). (Home Office 1998, para. 4.14)

The same paper went on to consider renaming the service and it narrowly missed being renamed the 'Community Punishment and Rehabilitation Service', becoming instead the 'National Probation Service', but, six years later, is likely to become part of a joined-up prison and probation agency and called 'The National Offender Management Service'. The reality with which we are presented by this crime-infused discourse is one in which offenders cannot be seen as citizens; neither can they be seen as individuals making progress toward a better way of life. The National Offender Management Service needs offenders to manage and, in so doing, the status of offender is confirmed over and over. An individual made the subject of a Community Rehabilitation Order will be referred to as an offender in person, they will see the word 'offender' on notices and official documents and they will be required to sign their name against the title 'offender' on various documents used during the course of supervision, and even for referrals made during the pre-sentence report preparation stage.

The language of probation methodology is also illustrative of the way the service has responded to these changing socio-political conditions. 'What works?' was a legitimate question in the mid-1970s, in the wake of Martinson's now infamous article suggesting that 'nothing works' in the treatment of offenders (Martinson 1974). Martinson was in fact never so unequivocal and was really saying something more along the lines of most things don't work very well, but some things work with some people in some circumstances (Cohen 1985). This and the fact that Martinson also included imprisonment in the category of failed measures didn't stop the slogan 'nothing works' being applied chiefly to rehabilitative social-work-based measures that had till then been used with both adult and young offenders, to the deep demoralization of a whole generation of probation and social workers. 'What works?' became the quest for measures that could be proved to 'work'. Mair (2004) documents the development in Canada of cognitive-behavioural treatment programmes, coupled with evaluative research that claimed to demonstrate their effectiveness in reducing recidivism. A concomitant development was the use of meta-analysis as a research technique, comparing data from large collections of previous studies to establish a statistically significant claim that one kind of treatment was more effective than others. This, it was confidently asserted, was cognitive-behavioural treatment (McGuire and Priestley 1995). Cognitive-behavioural packages were marketed with an entrepreneurial zeal never previously witnessed within UK criminal justice. Bearing in mind that most practitioners were provided with this information via uncritical 'effectiveness' training events, conferences or workshops prior to being asked to implement a particular programme already purchased by their service, it is unsurprising that many accepted the idea of a 'proven' effective treatment package. 'What works' was no longer a question but, as Mair notes, became more akin to an orthodoxy (Mair 2004). Significantly, the question mark is dropped, and the unwritten prefix is [*This* is] what works. Hard evidence of the efficacy of accredited programmes instituted on the basis of these claims remains elusive, and ambitious targets for putting offenders through them have been halved (Gorman 2001; Gorman *et al.* this volume, ch. 1). Academic researchers have begun to turn their interest to a broader view of success in terms of interventions with offenders, encompassing the concept of desistance from crime (Farrall 2002, 2004; Maruna 2001; Maruna, Ummarigeon and LeBel 2004).

The offender as citizen

I have argued that citizenship is a concept central to most aspects of social policy, but that in the current climate, criminal justice policy denies the citizenship of those who have committed offences and confirms them in their status as offenders. This section goes on to argue that prioritizing citizenship and supporting people to return to active membership of society would encourage desistance from crime. The principles of constructive practice are consistent with this approach and, as already noted, there is a growing body of evidence that a positive relationship between worker and offender supports desistance from crime (Farrall 2002, 2004; Maruna 2001; Maruna *et al.* 2004). This section develops the outline of a fully blown constructive Probation Service. Perhaps this is 'pie in the sky' but all that is really suggested is that social policy includes *the offender as a citizen*.

Central to constructive practice is the centrality of language, talk, narrative and meaning. The approach would eschew the language of punishment, risk and behaviour management and replace it, through dialogue with service users, with that of inclusion and active citizenship. This is because the approach views such dialogue as central to the helping relationship. The language must be generative, forward-looking and about possibilities for action and change.

An initial step is to reclaim some of the key policy and practice terminology. 'Probation' itself is crucial. In its dictionary meaning there is a notion of 'testing the character or abilities of a person in a certain role' which implies a time scale, a temporary period and a goal to strive towards, in succeeding in proving one's abilities. This implies a dynamic, a process in which someone is moving forward, is changing for the better. It infers capability on the part of the person to make those changes and this necessarily involves some form of commitment on their part to the process. Ideally, this would involve an individual in consenting to the order being made, as used to happen in the past. However, even with an imposed order, there is the possibility for negotiation about the kind of work to be done during its currency. The role of the professional helper in this process is a 'client centred' one. It is based upon the relationship between the helper and the helped, and fundamentally regards them as equals. The basis of the work is a negotiation which assumes that the helped person knows themselves and their local community better than the helper does, and understands what they need in order to make progress toward a crime-free life. The communication between the parties to the relationship is central; there is a shared search for meaning and understanding (Jordan 1979). The early understanding of 'probation' is retrieved here: the court is 'putting someone on probation' in order to see if they can achieve something – giving them a chance. My own experience of court practice is that magistrates frequently still see probation (although it is no longer called this) as just that, and use such phraseology in their comments to defendants when making a *community rehabilitation order.*

The understanding of 'citizenship' within a constructive form of practice would be a civic republican one; that is encompassing rights and responsibilities with an assumption of equality. Crucially, the offender within the helping relationship would be given the respect due to a fellow citizen. The task of the helper would be the encouragement of a full and active citizenship, and this could not be achieved without addressing the barriers to social inclusion faced by the majority of offenders. There may be some way to go before this could be achieved because of the gulf created between an offender and the community by their behaviour, and also because there may be particular personal difficulties such as drug or alcohol addiction, debt, mental health problems, poor social functioning and so on. These problems need to be addressed before an individual will be ready to engage positively with their community.

Two aspects of the civil republican tradition of thought set out by David Blunkett in his paper on civil renewal are particularly pertinent to this relationship:

- 'That enduring and genuine citizen participation in public life requires education for citizenship, including the development of the habits, skills and knowledge needed for active engagement in the community.

- 'Likewise that active citizens must cultivate civic virtues, including commitment to the common good; the free acceptance of duty and obligation and patriotism in its best sense of loyalty to community and shared values.' (2003a, p.4)

The meaning of 'constructive practice' here would encompass its link to the theoretical perspectives of social construction and narrative work as well as the common understanding of construction as in building, or putting together (Parton and O'Byrne 2000). In so doing it acknowledges the findings of Barry (2000, and this volume, ch.10) and Howe (1993) that recipients of social work interventions value the dialogue that takes place between themselves and their social worker, especially when they feel they have genuinely been heard. With offenders, the building required is in large part *rebuilding.* They need to rebuild relationships with their families and communities, which have almost always been damaged by their offending. A constructive approach would also seek to help them toward a position where they can take part in the rebuilding of their communities, as active citizens. As we have seen, the literature on citizenship widely acknowledges that citizenship implies equality, and active citizenship requires social inclusion; therefore the basis of that rebuilding has to be access to the social capital needed to achieve social inclusion.

A constructive approach fits more comfortably with the principles of restorative justice than it does with conventional justice. Unlike conventional justice, which confers the power to deal with offenders upon the state, restorative justice places the responsibility for the resolution of conflict caused by offending firmly within the remit of all members of the community affected by it, including those with links to the offender as well as the victim and their connections. There is a collective ethos and collective responsibility. It seeks to restore respect and dignity to the victim, to enable the offender to take responsibility for their behaviour and to enable the offender to take control and make reparation for what they have done (Strang and Braithwaite 2000). It is clearly an approach that treats all parties affected by an offence as equal citizens, and it prioritizes narrative and dialogue in searching for solutions.

Would a constructive approach to work with offenders mean being 'soft' on them? Is it rewarding offending to encourage inclusion? I would answer no to both these questions, and argue that, on the contrary, there is evidence that achieving access to social capital supports desistance from offending and that probation intervention can be the medium through which this access can be achieved. Unfortunately, although the earliest proponents of cognitive-behavioural programmes acknowledged the need to address the social context of offending, the vast majority of the 'what works' literature bases the success or otherwise of probation supervision on reconviction rates alone (Rex 1999). When a broader view of effectiveness is taken, the success of probation supervision in encouraging desistance can be seen. Rex documents the value that probationers place upon their relationship with their probation officer, whom they still regard as helpful (Rex 1999). Farrall (2002) demonstrates that it is changes in their social circumstances that most often enable offenders on probation to desist from crime; and the probationer's own social networks are often better than statutory services in solving some of the obstacles which prevent that desistance. A key task for probation therefore is supporting the individual to remain in the community where they can achieve positive changes to their social circumstances, which will facilitate desistance. He notes numerous examples from his study in which probation officers took active steps, through their supervisory relationship with the probationer, to link them with various forms of social capital, such as families and community agencies and services. On this basis, probation can, and does, 'work'.

A constructive approach would regard supporting offenders to achieve active citizenship as the key task of the Probation Service. There is already official acknowledgement of the strengths of the Probation Service in achieving this:

> And the correctional services have a part to play in making offenders more active citizens themselves…the National Probation Service also has a significant track record in encouraging community involvement and in particular is encouraging greater involvement through the enhanced Community Punishment Scheme. (Blunkett 2003b, p.31)

However, as practitioners are aware, the focus of the service over the past decade or more has been away from communities and toward cognitive treatment aimed at changing the behaviour of individuals. Probation offices have moved away from local sites and into city centres, work is office based, officers do not engage with or support the probationer's family as they once did, probation officers are no longer members of committees of community or charitable organizations and, very important, the basis of the relationship between worker and probationer has been undermined by compartmentalizing tasks so that the probationer is likely to see numerous different people during the course of his or her contact with the service, and therefore does not form a relationship with anyone as a result. A series of interviews which I carried out with newly qualified and experienced probation officers during 2003 (Gregory, unpublished) has revealed the frustrations experienced by workers who feel that their professional training and expertise is no longer valued by the organization. The following comment, 'There is no culture of encouraging professional development, no valuing of expertise and experience', is representative of a theme which emerges through the 30 interviews. This, and the loss of the centrality of the relationship as the cornerstone of work with probationers, came up time and again as issues which led to feelings of demoralization and futility in the work. One officer puts it like this:

> When I came in there was still some optimism – but now the Probation Service is fully incorporated into the punishment system, and I feel much more fatalistic about it now. The value base it has now is not intrinsic to the service but is carried by its existing workforce. The big thing is when you sit down with a client there isn't a two-way process where you adjust your position and learn, and maybe in a dialogue with you, they learn as a consequence of that. They are seen as flawed from the start. This reminds me of something I read when I was doing my dissertation about Aristotle's notions about practice in interacting with other people. He talked about *techne* and *phronesis*. *Phronesis* is about getting into a reflexive relationship

with another personality and working it out together. *Techne* is about technically rational technique, and that is the approach we are heading for. (Gregory, unpublished)

Within a constructive approach, the community role of the Probation Service would be expanded, in order for the service to make an impact upon offenders' abilities to desist from offending and begin to engage as active citizens.

We know that the majority of offenders come from less advantaged communities, and will therefore have reduced access to social capital (Farrall 2002; Mair and May 1997). Their own skills and abilities (i.e. their human capital) will be diminished as a result. Many of the groupwork programmes into which the Probation Service has placed its energy in the past few years address the deficits in human capital by addressing offenders' cognitive or educational abilities. We have seen also that probation workers do work in ways that link probationers with various forms of social capital. However, entrenched socio-economic difficulties such as urban decay and high unemployment in the communities in which offenders live require interventions which address the longer-term impact of the loss of social capital (Shover and Henderson 1995). Farrall (2002) notes the development in Surrey and Inner London Probation Services of schemes aimed at developing local employment opportunities to meet the needs of those on probation (p.220).

A constructive Probation Service would expand these kinds of initiatives, but would also involve itself in community regeneration on a larger scale under the auspices of already existing government policy initiatives such as the Single Regeneration Budget or New Deal for Communities. As the remit of such schemes includes crime reduction, it makes perfect sense that the Probation Service is involved in the spirit of 'joined-up government'. By involvement, it is not suggested that the service takes part only at higher management level or similar, but that probationers should be supported to engage actively in development projects themselves, whether this be as part of a community rehabilitation order (or its equivalent) or as part of a community team which provides some of the regenerative labour on such a scheme. This would enable the restorative justice principles already underpinning some aspects of probation practice to be extended, because those who have offended against their local communities would have to take an active role in the rebuilding of those communities. There is scope for the development of restorative community conferences as part of such rebuilding, so that victims and their supporters, and the offender and their supporters, can have a say in the nature and extent of the offender's reparation. The

Community Court, which has just begun to sit in Liverpool, is a small but significant step in the right direction. Building on these developments, a constructive Probation Service would work towards reducing the gulf between offenders on probation and their communities, thus benefiting not only the individual victim and offender, but also the wider community.

Conclusion: Constructive practice within a constructive Probation Service: What would it look like?

A constructive Probation Service would be a community-based agency whose remit would be the development of safer communities and the rehabilitation of offenders through restoration of active citizenship. The service would have close links with other community bodies, both statutory and non-statutory. It would be a key contributor to the development of economic regeneration within local communities affected by urban decay and high crime. Its governance would include representatives of its local community, victims, ex-offenders and current service users.

A strong emphasis of the constructive Probation Service's work would be dialogue with its local community. As such its staff would be involved in a variety of ways with the work of other local organizations, and community members, victims and ex-offenders would be involved in the development and management of the service itself. The purpose of this dialogue would be to ensure that any regenerative schemes in which the service involved itself would be in accordance with the needs and wishes of the local community. Crucially, such schemes would aim to provide probationers with opportunities to improve their human capital by improving their knowledge or practical skills, and at the same time enable them to make reparation to their community by the work they contributed to the schemes. There would be positive encouragement for ex-offenders, once their desistance from offending was secure, to support schemes by providing mentoring for subsequent probationers.

Another key area of work would be the service's relationship with the courts. This would be very similar to the traditional role of the service, carrying out pre-sentence assessments on offenders and providing the court with the full range of community-based sentencing options. Pre-sentence assessments would in every case involve dialogue and negotiation either with direct victims, or with representatives of the community affected by the offending. The views of the defendant on how they see the solution to their current difficulties would also be sought. Pre-sentence reports would explore the full socio-economic circumstances of the defendant as well as addressing offence analysis and risk management.

Every community sentence would contain a restorative element and would seek to address the personal and social problems of the probationer in order to enable them to make a positive contribution to a scheme benefiting their local community. This element would clearly build upon existing community service (community punishment) schemes. Whenever possible, links to permanent employment or training would be established during the currency of the order.

The basis of all the work within a community sentence would be the relationship between the probationer and their key probation worker. That relationship would be one of negotiation and dialogue and would emphasize the probationer's local knowledge and awareness of his or her needs in solving current difficulties. Progress during, and at the end of, the sentence would be reviewed through dialogue with the probationer which would evaluate development in all aspects of their life, not solely by taking account of offending behaviour. The emphasis would be building on strengths, expanding gaps in offending, decreasing relapses, repeating successful past solutions. The probationer would be encouraged to keep a log of progress which would include his or her own thoughts about solutions, times when lapses have been avoided, positive contributions to work or relationships that have been made. It would also contain witness testimony from other members of the community who are aware of any progress. These might include workers at an agency where the probationer is working or volunteering, family members, friends or neighbours. The probationer's views on the usefulness of the community sentence from their point of view would also be sought.

A constructive Probation Service would value highly the professional skill and expertise of its workforce and would endeavour to provide a learning environment in which constructive dialogue between professionals is valued. Such an environment allows for mistakes, and the learning which can result from them. Reflective practice is encouraged and is the basis for the supervision of practice, in contrast to the current emphasis upon meeting of corporate targets. Individual workers' contributions to the development of policy based upon their own expertise within professional practice would be welcomed in such a learning organization.

A programme of research would be put in place to evaluate the work of a constructive Probation Service. Such research would take account of available statistical evidence on the broad socio-economic status of the communities in which the work takes place. It would also consider criminal statistics, both self-report studies and reconviction data. These would provide context but would not be the sole sources of evidence. Of key importance would be the views of both probationers and probation workers about how the work of the service impacted on the lives of probationers in terms of improved access to social capital and desistance from offending. Other measures would include the health of the organization and its success as a learning organization, and its role as part of a wider partnership of agencies concerned with community redevelopment. Research would use both quantitative and qualitative methods. In this way it should be possible to measure the 'success' on a number of different levels, using data from a wide range of sources and providing a realistic and detailed picture of work within a community-based organization.

References

Association of Chief Officers of Probation (1988) *More Demanding Than Custody.* London: ACOP.

Barry, M. (2000) 'The mentor/monitor debate in criminal justice: What works for offenders.' *British Journal of Social Work* 30, 575–95.

Blunkett, D. (2003a) *Civil Renewal, A New Agenda.* London: Home Office.

Blunkett, D. (2003b) *Active Citizens, Strong Communities.* London: Home Office.

Clarke, J. (2004) *Changing Welfare, Changing States: New Directions in Social Policy.* London: Sage.

Cohen, S. (1985) *Visions of Social Control.* Cambridge: Polity Press.

Downes, D. and Morgan, R. (1994) 'Hostages to fortune? The politics of law and order in post-war Britain.' In M. Maguire, R. Morgan and R. Reiner (eds) *Oxford Handbook of Criminology.* Oxford: Clarendon Press.

Dwyer, P. (2004) *Understanding Social Citizenship, Themes and Perspectives from Policy and Practice.* Bristol: Policy Press.

Farrall, S. (2002) *Rethinking What Works with Offenders.* Cullompton: Willan.

Farrall, S. (2004) 'Social capital and offender reintegration: Making probation desistance focused.' In G. Mair (ed.) *What Works in Probation.* Cullompton: Willan.

Faulkner, D. (2004) 'Taking citizenship seriously.' *Criminal Justice* 3, 3, 90–9.

Feeley, S. and Simon, J. (1992) 'The new penology: Notes on the emerging new criminal law.' In D. Nelken (ed.) *The Futures of Criminology.* London: Sage.

Garland, D. (2000) 'The culture of high crime societies.' *British Journal of Criminology* 40, 347–75.

Giddens, A. (1990) *The Consequences of Modernity.* Oxford: Polity Press.

Giddens, A, (1998) *The Third Way: The Renewal of Social Democracy.* Cambridge: Polity Press.

Goodman, A. (2003) 'Probation into the millennium: The punishing service?' In R. Matthews and M. Young (eds) *The New Politics of Crime and Punishment.* Cullompton: Willan.

Gorman, K. (2001) 'Cognitive behaviouralism and the Holy Grail: The quest for a universal means of managing offender risk.' *Probation Journal* 48, 1, 3–9.

Gregory, M. (unpublished) Interviews with probation officers in 2003.

Gregory, M. and Holloway, M. (2005) 'Language and the construction of social work.' *British Journal of Social Work* 35, 1, 37–53.

Harris, R. (1996) 'Telling tales: Probation in the contemporary formation.' In N. Parton (ed.) *Social Theory, Social Change and Social Work.* London: Routledge.

Hobsbawm, E. (1994) *The Age of Extremes.* London: Michael Joseph.

Home Office (1998) *Joining Forces to Protect the Public: Prisons – Probation: A Consultation Document.* London: Home Office.

Howe, D. (1993) *On Being a Client: Understanding the Process of Counselling and Psychotherapy.* London: Sage.

Hutton, W. (1995) *The State We're In.* London: Jonathan Cape.

Jordan, B. (1979) *Helping in Social Work.* London: Routledge and Kegan Paul.

Kemshall, H. (1998) *Risk in Probation Practice.* Aldershot: Ashgate.

Lister, R. (1990) *The Exclusive Society: Citizenship and the Poor.* London: CPAG.

Mair, G. (2004) 'The origins of What Works in England and Wales: A house built on sand?' In G. Mair (ed.) *What Works in Probation.* Cullompton: Willan.

Mair, G. and May, T. (1997) *Offenders on Probation.* London: Home Office.

Marshall, T.H. and Bottomore, T. (1992) *Citizenship and Social Class.* London: Pluto Press.

Martinson, R. (1974) 'What works? Questions and answers about prison reform.' *The Public Interest* 35, 22–54.

Maruna, S. (2001) *Making Good: How Ex-Convicts Reform and Rebuild Their Lives.* Washington, DC: American Psychological Association Books.

Maruna, S., Immarigeon, R. and LeBel, T. (2004) 'Reintegration and restorative justice: Towards a theory and practice of informal social control and support.' In S. Maruna and R. Immarigeon (eds) *After Crime and Punishment: Pathways to Offender Re-integration.* Cullompton: Willan.

May, T. (1991) *Probation: Politics, Policy and Practice.* Buckingham: Open University Press.

McGuire, J. and Priestley, P. (1995) 'Reviewing "What Works": Past, present and future.' In J. McGuire (ed.) *What Works: Reducing Reoffending.* Chichester: Wiley.

Mumby, D.K. (1993) 'Introduction.' In D.K. Mumby (ed.) *Narrative and Social Control.* Newbury Park, CA, and London: Sage.

Office for National Statistics (2003) 'Investing in each other and the community: The role of social capital.' *Social Trends* (33rd edition), 19–27.

Parton, N. and O'Byrne, P. (2000) *Constructive Social Work: Towards a New Practice.* London: Macmillan.

Plant, R. (1988) *Citizenship, Rights and Socialism.* London: Fabian Society.

Rex, S. (1999) 'Desistance from offending: Experiences of probation.' *Howard Journal of Criminal Justice* 38, 4, 366–83.

Roche, M. (1992) *Rethinking Citizenship: Welfare Ideology and Change in Modern Society.* Oxford: Polity Press.

Shover, N. and Henderson, B. (1995) 'Resistance, crime and male persistent thieves.' In H. Barlow (ed.) *Crime and Public Policy, Putting Theory to Work.* Oxford: Westview Press.

Strang, H. and Braithwaite, J. (eds) (2000) *Restorative Justice: Philosophy to Practice.* Aldershot: Ashgate.

Tonry, M. (2004) *Punishment and Politics.* London: Willan.

Young, J. (1999) *The Exclusive Society.* London: Sage.

Chapter 4

Constructing Safety

A Collaborative Approach to Managing Risk and Building Responsibility

Michelle Hayles

The decline of rehabilitative optimism

Risk as an organizing principle in health, social welfare and criminal justice is now a familiar and well-documented part of practice reality (see for example Alaszewski, Harrison and Manthorpe 1998; Kemshall 1998, 2002; Kemshall *et al.* 1997; Nash 1999; Parton 1996). The preoccupation with risk that is a characteristic of our times (Beck 1992; Giddens 1990, 1991) permeates the human services and nowhere more so than in the field of criminal justice where it manifests itself in legislation, policy and practice that subordinate the traditional concern for justice to a growing demand for public security. The heightened sense of insecurity across the globe following the events of 11 September 2001 has added momentum to an already existing readiness, particularly in the US and UK, to relinquish established commitment to due legal process in favour of preventive measures (Dworkin 2002; Hudson 2001, 2003; Kennedy 2004). Terrorism may be the most high-profile threat to our sense of security but the category of the 'dangerous' extends well beyond its boundaries. Not only are those who pose a risk of serious physical or psychological harm, such as violent or sexual offenders, seen as a threat to public security but also increasingly those whose anti-social or nuisance behaviour is seen as contributing to the fear of crime (Garland 2001; Holloway and Jefferson 1997).

In this culture of fear (Furedi 1997; Glassner 1999) optimism about the potential for offenders to change has been a major casualty. The trust that is required to give someone another chance is difficult to exercise in a climate in which the public's right to security is paramount and where culpability may attach not only to the offender who commits a further offence but also to the organization or individual who fails to predict or prevent it. No matter how ardently the risk analyst strives to persuade us that risk assessment is a purely scientific process, risk assessment takes place within a cultural context that has at its heart a concern with the distribution of blame (Douglas 1992). In such a context, pessimism may seem a sensible precautionary response. A stark example of such pessimism in the UK is our willingness to incarcerate large numbers of young people on the basis of their risks to the community when the rates of self-harm and suicide suggest that it is they who bear the greater risk (Nacro 2003).

Where rehabilitative optimism continues to reside it tends to be largely in mainstream practice where the 'what works' movement has generated a range of cognitive-behavioural programmes of intervention that hold out the hope that offending can be prevented by changing offenders' thinking patterns. Even here, however, practice has not been unaffected by the tendency to adopt a precautionary principle that shifts 'the emphasis from proof and evidence to fears of "what if"' (Kemshall 1998, p.278). In the arena of 'public protection', where the level of harm that may be inflicted by 'potentially dangerous offenders' is high, practice ambitions have tended to be at their most restricted and pessimistic (Maguire *et al.* 2001; Robinson 2002). Official guidance has tended towards caution, for example referring to the work as being 'almost always about prevention and damage limitation rather than cure' (HMIP 1997, p.231). The inception of allegedly more sophisticated systems of risk assessment and risk management in the form of multi-agency public protection panels appears to have done nothing to instil greater optimism. According to Kemshall and Maguire (2001) references to 'rehabilitation' and 'resettlement' are rarely heard in these fora, even from probation officers. Such is the cultural pessimism surrounding 'public protection' that there is a tendency even for positive research findings to be interpreted in such a way as to reinforce existing negative beliefs. In relation to sex offenders, for example, any findings that reconviction rates are low compared to other types of offending (for example, Hood *et al.* 2002) tend to be construed as unrepresentative of the 'real' rate of offending and confirmation of the stereotype of the sex offender as cunning and able to escape prosecution (Hudson 2003).

The rise of risk technology

An integral part of the developing risk discourse in criminal justice has been the transition from risk assessment as an interpersonal 'clinical' process to one guided by technical assessment tools. Initial risk of custody scales (for example, Bale 1987), largely used to ensure the proper targeting of alternatives to custody, were swiftly succeeded by predictors focused on risk of reconviction (Humphrey, Carter and Pease 1992). Building on these earlier efforts, the Home Office commissioned work on a reconviction predictor that could be used more routinely by Probation Services, which has since become known as the Offender Group Reconviction Scale (OGRS) (Copas, Ditchfield and Marshall 1994). OGRS has been significant in establishing an actuarial element in work with offenders, promoting a shift from the traditional concern with the unique circumstances of individuals to a more actuarial or 'insurance' approach in which offenders are increasingly dealt with according to classificatory group. In this 'new penology' (Feeley and Simon 1992) rehabilitation of individuals has become subordinate to the management of offender groups classified according to levels of risk.

Criticized for their reliance on 'static' factors (such as criminal history), which tend to over-predict and are not amenable to change (Beaumont 1999; Hudson 2003), these actuarial tools have been superseded by assessment tools that attempt to integrate 'dynamic' factors (such as employability and attitudes). According to supporters, these 'third-generation' risk-need instruments (Bonta 1996) have overcome the problems of the earlier examples and, by identifying areas that can be worked on, construct a 'transformative' rather than 'fixed' risk subject for intervention (Hannah-Moffat 2002). First used widely in the Canadian penal system, this type of combined tool has now been adopted in the UK, the principal example being the Offender Assessment System (OASys) produced by the Home Office (Home Office 2002).

Leaving aside the continuing debate about the applicability of these new tools to the less routine, more serious 'public protection' offences, the key point for this discussion is their preoccupation with inventories. The human exchange between worker and offender is largely reduced to a process of data collection aimed at identifying offending-related factors. These factors are used to locate the offender within a particular classificatory risk matrix and to indicate issues for attention. The reduction of the offender's unique human story to a catalogue of components, however, offers little insight into the meaning of offending within the offender's life as a whole or into personal desires, goals and ambitions, strengths and solutions. Moreover, the reduction of assessment to a technical process largely exempts the practitioner from the moral dilemma of false positives (Hudson 2003). Predictions of re-offending generally carry both the possibility of false negatives and of false positives: that someone who is not predicted to offend does – the false negative – and that someone who is predicted to offend does not – the false positive. The false negative is of concern to potential victims and practitioners alike because of the harm that may be inflicted on the person or upon professional reputation. The false positive, on the other hand, most affects the offender since it usually entails restriction of liberty. Traditionally practitioners have also interested themselves in the false positive, seeking to balance the necessary protection of potential victims with the rights of individual offenders. The conversion of risk assessment into a technical process distances practitioners from the implications of the false positive. 'Accuracy' ceases to refer to correct prediction of re-offending; it describes proper completion of the assessment tool. Accountability becomes a matter of meeting organizational requirements. As long as practitioners comply with the technical requirements of the risk assessment process (complete the forms correctly), they have fulfilled their professional responsibilities.

Supporters of the shift towards a more technical approach to risk assessment assert, with some justification, that the traditional process was variable, overly subjective and too reliant upon the experience and expertise of the individual practitioner (HMIP 1995). They contend that the use of assessment tools supports professional judgement by ensuring that all relevant issues are covered, all appropriate questions asked. What this argument fails to appreciate adequately, however, is that greater reliance upon technical instruments leads to increasingly technicist practice. Assessment tools begin to determine rather than guide the process; human exchanges are perceived as insufficiently reliable or 'scientific' and decisions arising from human negotiations are viewed as somehow less trustworthy than decisions based upon the attribution of scores. The human interaction is mediated through the technology, distancing practitioner and offender from each other: the practitioner feels decreasing responsibility for the practice outcome; the offender has little reason, therefore, to engage meaningfully with the practitioner. Put simply, there is no personal investment for either of them in the process.

'Dangerization' and the loss of trust

Drawing upon the work of Beck (1992) and Giddens (1990, 1991) criminologists have sought to explain how the preoccupation with risk that is a general characteristic of late modernity has shaped current responses to crime and to work with offenders. Garland (2001) outlines the development of criminological thought since the 1970s as one in which issues of social deprivation have been replaced by issues of control, and where the depiction of the individual offender has relied increasingly on dehumanizing language that portrays the offender as 'alien', as 'predator', as 'other'. The public agenda is concerned with the distribution and control of risks rather than economic inequalities, an environment in which 'the values of the unsafe society displace those of the unequal society' (Ericson and Carriere 1994, p.103). Irrespective of actual crime rates, fear of crime has become a key concern, to the extent that perfectly legal behaviour, such as adolescents gathering on street corners, has become part of the perceived crime problem. This process of 'dangerization' is one in which perceptions of the world are increasingly defensive, constructed as they are through 'categories of menace' where optimism becomes subordinate to fear and anxiety (Lianos and Douglas 2000, p.267).

Clear and Cadora (2001) argue that it would be misguided to view the contemporary criminal justice concern with risk as new in itself, but that what is new is the shift towards its control. Risk control seeks to eliminate the uncertainty and ambiguity inherent in the concept of risk by privileging public security over the liberty and rights of the individual. This shift manifests itself in legislation and policies that erode traditional rights such as the 'right to silence' and the 'doli incapax' provision for young people, that change rules of evidence in favour of the prosecution and that make increasing use of preventive detention (Hudson 2001, 2003; Kennedy 2004). Few voices are raised in opposition. So pervasive are the arguments in favour of 'public protection' measures that virtually everyone, including professionals in the criminal justice arena, has been 'socialized by the ethos of our time' into accepting their validity (Tonry 2001, p.171).

As Hudson (2003) points out, the social contract is essentially a trade-off between liberty and security. The key question is, what is the optimum balance between the two principles? Citizens may have a right to protection but permanent security can only be achieved at the cost of liberty, of individual autonomy. Trust is a key component of civic culture; it has an intimate relationship with risk. Where complete control of risk exists, individual autonomy is fatally undermined and trust becomes redundant since 'trust which is demonstrated only in the absence of risk is not in fact demonstrated' (Caddick and Watson 1999, p.66). In the shift towards risk control, not only does policing become more pervasive and penal sanctions more restrictive, but civic culture also becomes less tolerant and less capable of trust (Young 1999). Rather than signifying a failure to accommodate differences, the phrase 'zero tolerance' becomes a bold assertion of the value of control and an affirmation of social exclusion. In such a climate, the option of reintegration, of full return to the community fold, is increasingly restricted since it entails trusting the offender and, by its very nature, trust allows for the possibility that the offender may fail.

Control undoubtedly has a part to play in relation to offenders who pose a serious risk of harm to the community, but reliance upon it leads to the alienation and brutalization of individual offenders with little compensatory benefit to the community as a whole in terms of an enhanced sense of security. The 'safety paradox' (Lianos and Douglas 2000, p.274) is the vicious cycle set up when safety is divorced from social relations. Control leads to increasing demands for predictability and certainty, which in turn lead to an increased sense of vulnerability and danger. This generates further demands for control. The demand for safety cannot be satiated. In the practice environment this phenomenon is illustrated by the growing call on resources as the number of cases referred to multi-agency public protection panels increases, and by the tendency for some panels to be 'swamped on occasion by too many cases' (Maguire et al. 2001, p.vi).

The shift towards risk control is accompanied by an inexorable devaluing of the more interpersonal strategies for assisting offenders to rebuild responsibility and trust. In their discussion of 'dangerization', Lianos and Douglas (2000) argue that automated environments (for example, turnstiles, credit cards, passwords) are replacing the need for personal trust and that social control is being moved out of the sphere of personal interaction into an arena where the social processes of value reproduction and reinforcement are unable to take place. In work with offenders, the increasing emphasis on assessment instruments and technological strategies for risk management, such as electronic monitoring, similarly move the focus of practice from the exploration and negotiation of values to exchanges based largely on identifying right or wrong responses, ticked or not ticked boxes, high or low risk categories. In such a context, risk assessment and risk management become separated from their interpersonal context, divorced from their relationship with the social bonds of trust.

Traditionally offenders were seen as having served their time when their punishment expired and thus, in theory at least, were eligible for re-entry into the community. The risk discourse, however, operates to differentiate the included from the excluded much more permanently. In law and penal policy, we are steadily moving towards a position in which those now deemed a risk are assumed always to pose a risk, whatever they do. Not only is this a means for effecting the lasting social exclusion of an ever-expanding group of offenders, it is also a recipe for exacerbating the very risks that we seek to control, by establishing a growing pool of alienated, resentful individuals who have no investment in rejoining the community from which they have been barred.

Risk control may seem compelling, appearing as it does to promise security, but its costs are high both in economic terms and in terms of the damage, largely unacknowledged, that is done to civic society. Imprisonment may be a popular control strategy but it is expensive, generally only temporary and has a tendency to produce unintended negative consequences. Despite the apparent public willingness to commit large sums to the running of existing institutions and to the building of new prisons, the money thus spent can only assure public safety for the period in which offenders are incarcerated. Outcomes in terms of reconviction are generally poor, and particularly negative in the case of young males (Nacro 2003). Recent governmental efforts to emphasize resettlement (Social Exclusion Unit 2002) constitute recognition of the damage wrought upon civic society by the social exclusion of offenders.

Securing gains or avoiding losses

The current dominant framework for practice with offenders is the risk-need model (Andrews 1995; Andrews and Bonta 2003; McGuire 2000). Instrumental in its approach, it is focused almost exclusively on attempting to identify, and then alter or manage, those characteristics of offenders' lives that are seen to give rise to the risk posed by the offending behaviour. Legitimate targets of intervention tend to be restricted to those factors ('criminogenic needs' or 'dynamic risk factors') that have been shown to be statistically associated with offending and that are deemed amenable to change. Programmes of intervention based on cognitive-behavioural approaches are generally identified as those most compatible with the achievement of the practice objective, combined with elements of other practice theory, in particular Prochaska and DiClemente's model of change (Prochaska and DiClemente 1984), Miller and Rollnick's work on motivational interviewing (Miller and Rollnick 1991) and Trotter's work on engaging involuntary clients (Trotter 1999).

Apart from a passing nod to the contributions of Miller and Rollnick and Trotter, who emphasize the importance of engaging and motivating the client, much of the work currently undertaken with offenders pays little genuine deference to their personal goals and ambitions. In an ethos of concern for actual and potential victims, this may seem acceptable, if not laudable, but the model has significant weaknesses. It constructs a practice environment focused primarily on offenders' shortcomings in social competence and psychological functioning and concerned largely with negative goals (reductions or absences of behaviour). Even if one accepts that offenders pose a risk because of their social and psychological deficits, it is hard to see how, in such a context of personal deficiency, they can be expected to know what to do to cease harmful behaviour without much greater attention being paid to the identification and construction of positive alternatives. In *Signs of Safety*, an exposition of an approach to child protection practice, Turnell and Edwards (1999) assert that practitioners are much more accustomed to thinking in terms of what they expect to stop than focusing on what positive behavioural objectives they expect to be achieved. As the authors comment, 'it is hard to work towards *not doing* something without providing something else to fill the vacuum' (p.141).

In similar vein, but from a perspective of work with sexual offenders, Ward and Stewart (2003) criticize the risk-need model for its underpinning assumption that the complexity of offenders' lives can be disaggregated into factors to be treated, as if the individual were no more than the sum of discrete and quantifiable components. In their 'good lives' approach Ward and Stewart accept that the primary aim of intervention is to reduce offending but argue that this is best achieved by taking a more 'constructive and holistic approach to rehabilitation' (p.23), one which is not simply about teaching offenders to minimize their chances of imprisonment but about giving them the necessary conditions to lead better lives. In this endeavour, they argue, 'it is fruitless to base treatment on problems alone, a positive vision is needed' (p.24).

In seeking this 'positive vision' it is argued here that the language of 'constructing safety' has more to offer than the current emphasis on 'risk management'. This is not merely a matter of semantics. From the perspective of social constructionism, the change of language fundamentally transforms the nature of the activity (Parton and O'Byrne 2000). Rather than treating the offender as an object of criminal justice strategies, which risk management implies, constructing safety offers a collaborative endeavour to which the offender can contribute. Rather than focusing on the absence of negative behaviour, it promotes the presence of positive behaviour. Instead of exclusion, it proposes a model based on cooperation and the possibility of inclusion.

The concept of framing within decision-making theory supports this argument. Framing explains how individuals may be risk seeking or risk averse dependent upon the way in which they make sense of decision-making contexts, whether they perceive themselves as being within a zone of losses or, alternatively, of gains (Kahneman and Tversky 1972). In applying this theory to the field of professional practice within social work and criminal justice, Strachan and Tallant (1997) argue for the involvement of the offender in the process of risk assessment and risk management, suggesting that 'assessors of risk should be working towards a model in which self-management of risk by the service-user is paramount' (p.24). Knowing whether individuals consider themselves to be in the zone of gains, when they are likely to be risk averse, or in the zone of losses, when they are likely to be more risk seeking, is helpful in understanding how offenders may be viewing their situation and the options available to them. Theoretically complex though framing may seem, these ideas are embedded in our culture, reflected in maxims such as 'one might as well be hanged for a sheep as for a lamb' (the zone of losses and risk-seeking behaviour), and 'a bird in the hand is worth two in the bush' (the zone of gains and risk-averse behaviour). The advantage of using the language of 'constructing safety' is that linguistically it helps to maintain focus on the zone of gains, supporting risk-averse rather than risk-seeking behaviour.

Narratives of desistance

The transition from risk management to the construction of safety involves a major paradigm shift, but there are signs that the move may be beginning. A significant indicator of the changing environment is the revival of interest in the subject of desistance (for example, Farrall 2002; Maruna 2001; Maruna and Immarigeon 2004; McNeill 2003). The desistance literature turns the spotlight from internal, cognitive deficiencies onto those factors that may play a key role in interrupting an individual's attachment to criminal behaviour. In his study of probation supervision, Farrall (2002) concludes that if practice were to become desistance focused, rather than offence focused, it would have a broader mandate to assist offenders in areas that in the recent past have been marginalized such as family relationships. Drawing upon the concept of social capital, Farrall (2004) explores the implications of a desistance focus for practitioners attempting to foster offender reintegration into the community. He concludes that this would probably entail a retreat from the almost exclusive emphasis on individual decision-making and cognitive processes that has been the hallmark of the recent cognitive behavioural era in favour of greater recognition of offenders' social context.

The corollary of his argument is that the negative goal of repression of anti-social behaviour would be reframed as the more positive objective of strengthening the offender's investment in conformity. Whilst the change of emphasis in practice from repairing deficiencies to enhancing resources is to be welcomed, the desistance project still largely retains the positivist preoccupation with the identification of factors associated with offending that can be targeted generally, paying insufficient attention to contexts and processes (Pawson and Tilley 1997; Smith 2004). Expertise remains in the hands of the researchers seeking to catalogue those factors and with the practitioners mandated to 'treat' the offender in accordance with that knowledge. The offender's role in this scenario remains a 'bit part', primarily as a recipient of the knowledge and expertise of others. Apart from the ownership of 'motivation', the offender contributes little.

In his analysis of the accounts of ex-offenders, however, Maruna (2001) highlights the power of personal narrative in desistance. He identifies two types of narrative: the 'condemnation' script of those who remain active offenders and the 'generative' script of those who manage to give up their criminal activities. Desistance is not primarily associated with improved consequential thinking, decision-making and problem-solving – the developed rational narrative beloved of the cognitive-behavioural model. On the contrary, it is the desisters who arguably are guilty of cognitive distortion in their inflated sense of control over their lives and their ambitions for the future. It is they who succeed in finding ways of rewriting the narratives of their lives so that they become stories of overcoming offending rather than succumbing to criminality. These are active 'resisters', not mere 'desisters'.

In this process of narrative reconstruction, language plays a key part. Maruna (2001) describes being admonished by a focus group of offenders for using the term 'rehabilitation'; the offenders prefer the word 'recovery'. 'Recovery', like 'going straight', locates agency differently. This is what ex-offenders do; it is not what practitioners or researchers do. As the study illustrates, ownership of change needs to rest with the person who struggles to resist the temptation to offend, whether that urge is towards dishonesty or towards violence, whether at the 'low' or 'high' end of the risk spectrum.

The term 'desistance' is generally used in the criminological literature to define a termination point in a criminal career but, as Maruna (2001) notes, this assumes that offending is a stable trait, that the 'criminal career' is a steady occupation. In reality, of course, desistance occurs all the time, sometimes for short periods, sometimes for longer. 'Offence- focused' practice, however, treats offending as if it were a stable trait that primarily defines the individual; it perceives and responds to the individual through a negative lens of criminality, of anti-social or 'dangerous' behaviour, of deficiencies and weaknesses. Practice is thereby trapped in a paradox, seeking to promote positive changes in behaviour, whilst at the same time casting the offender ever more firmly in a criminal narrative.

Constructing safety with offenders

The model of practice being advanced here draws on constructive approaches, such as solution-focused and narrative therapies, contending that these are compatible with a focus on constructing safety and address many of McNeill's (2003) conclusions about the characteristics of a more desistance-focused practice. The primary change to practice generated by the adoption of such a model with offenders would be the much greater emphasis on the development of solutions, alternative behaviours and 'resistance' stories. The identification and reinforcement of capabilities and strengths would assume greater prominence than the assessment of problems and deficits.

Before considering the model in more detail, it is worth addressing two of the most common accusations levelled at constructive approaches: first that they are naïve and second that they are only appropriate for offenders who pose a low risk of harm, not for those deemed 'high risk'. In relation to the charge of naïveté, and without underestimating the harm that offenders may inflict on others, it is worth reflecting upon the unintended consequence that the risk narrative has had upon practice in generating pessimism and undermining belief in the possibility of change. It should not be assumed, in other words, that pessimism equates with realism, or that optimism equates with naïveté. It is also worth emphasizing that looking for strengths and resources is not the same as naïve acceptance of what an offender says. Examples of practitioners willingly convinced by offenders reciting, as if from a script, what they have learned or what has changed are not confined to any one model of intervention. Naïveté is naïveté; and the best protection from it is painstaking questioning, probing, testing and verification – irrespective of the model of intervention.

In relation to the second accusation, it is important to acknowledge that the rhetoric of risk is not the same as taking protective action; the assessment of an offender as 'high risk' is not synonymous with managing that risk. In order to protect potential victims, offenders need to be assisted to manage themselves in order to reduce their threat to others. This may take time and may not always prove possible. Other protective measures will almost certainly need to be in place as offenders work to provide evidence that they can be trusted to manage their behaviour. As Jenkins (1990) points out in relation to his work with violent and abusive men, the criminal justice system has an important role to play in holding an offender in the process of change while the motivation towards personal responsibility is taking place and in monitoring the offender's achievement of attitudinal and behavioural change in order to protect victims. Fuller descriptions of constructive approaches applied to 'high risk' behaviours can be found elsewhere (see, for example, Jenkins 1990; Milner and O'Byrne 2002; Turnell and Edwards 1999).

One of the key ideas in constructive approaches is that of utilizing 'exceptions'. Offenders, however persistent, have many examples of situations in which they have been tempted to commit an offence, whether because of peer pressure, financial circumstances, arguments with a partner, boredom, too much alcohol…and have resisted! These exceptions to criminality open up opportunities to discover, not what causes the particular individual to commit an offence but, more important, what are the features of that individual's resistance to offending. Most practitioners can give their interpretations of the causes of an offender's behaviour, even if the form of that analysis varies according to theoretical preference. They may also know about periods when a particular individual did not offend and would be able to surmise the reason for that gap in criminality. Rarely, however, will they be able to provide a detailed account of the story of resisting criminal activity. This is because the focus on offending behaviour runs counter to an exploration of exceptions. In asserting the need to establish offending-related factors and 'treat' offenders through standardized packages of intervention, the current model of practice is poorly equipped to utilize the offender's unique knowledge and expertise in how to 'go straight'.

The power of 'exceptions' is that they maintain focus on the non-offending narrative, on the times when behaviour is positive. For many offenders and practitioners this is a difficult process because it contradicts the problem-saturated narrative of current practice. It feels odd. Desistance from offending, however, generally requires more than a sudden termination of criminal activity. For some offenders it may be just that, a dramatic conversion; but it is more often a process of amplifying other activities, other bonds and connections, so that offending loses its significance and is squeezed out. Constructive practice suggests that the non-offending story needs to be drawn carefully; goals need to be negotiated in detail so that progress, however small, can be identified and affirmed, so that success can be reinforced and amplified.

In the majority of criminal justice settings, practitioners have adopted something of a didactic role with offenders, becoming treatment or programme 'experts'. Within a constructive perspective, practitioners relinquish that image in order to adopt a more collaborative stance. The development of a genuine belief in offenders as experts on their own lives is challenging in an environment that now has a pervasive, negative view of offenders' capabilities. The temptation to slip back into the role of expert, to offer solutions, to be the person who puts others 'back on track' can be immensely seductive. For practitioners who work within a constructive framework, expertise is pooled in a collaborative process: offenders bring the expertise on their lives and what works for them; workers bring their understanding of the processes that mobilize change. Where workers carry statutory responsibility, their enforcement and public protection roles are made clear to offenders and collaboration is offered within that context.

Co-constructing hope

Constructive approaches share an interest in the power of language and narrative to transform experience. Practitioners working in this way need to have acute listening skills and the ability to utilize the language of offenders effectively in order to assist them to 're-author' their lives (White 1995). This is different from overlaying the offender's narrative with a professional interpretation: the activity is one of co-authoring, not translation. Michael White proposes that 'we live by the stories that we have about our lives, that these stories actually shape our lives, constitute our lives, and that they "embrace" our lives' (1995, p.14). In many cases these 'stories' or 'narratives' are unhelpful or downright destructive to self and to others. The purpose of intervention within this framework is to explore different ways of living and thinking and encourage individuals to reconstruct their personal narratives in a more positive way. As White argues, 'there is always a stock of alternative stories about how life might be' and the role of the practitioner working with an offender is to assist that individual to find the available alternative stories and 'to step more into those stories' (p.19).

Language is crucial not merely as a technical tool of communication but also as the means by which we daily construct our personae in the eyes of others and ourselves. This understanding of the role of language has been expounded upon in the philosophical works of Wittgenstein (1968) and Derrida (1978), in de Shazer's descriptions of solution-focused practice (de Shazer 1985, 1988, 1994) and in the narrative therapy texts of White (1989, 1995) and White and Epston (1990). This understanding of the role of language is why constructive approaches place such emphasis on concepts like 'solution talk' (Furman and Ahola 1992). 'Solution talk' is more than a mechanism for accessing an offender's strategies for achieving goals; though valuable in this respect, it is also a process by which the writing of a narrative of competence, ingenuity and resourcefulness begins. Where the offender is a serious risk to others, it begins the process of building responsibility and constructing safety. Focusing on times when harmful behaviour was resisted (exceptions) and the ways in which that was achieved (solution talk) provides an entry point into an alternative script. It makes explicit, but without counterproductive confrontation, that there is personal agency, that harmful behaviour does not 'just happen', is not the inevitable result of past experiences or trauma. It indicates that what can be achieved once can be achieved again; that the offender has the competence to control harmful behaviour and to be something other than abusive.

In his exposition of practice with men who are violent towards partners and sexually abusive to children, Jenkins (1990) describes how abusive men tend to be well practised in abdicating responsibility for their behaviour and pushing others, whether workers or partners, into filling the vacuum. He identifies the range of ways in which workers are lured into taking responsibility for the abuser: they give advice, challenge and confront, provide rational arguments against the violence, try to break down denial. Compelling though these responses may seem in a risk-sensitive environment, they all serve to reinforce a narrative in which the worker carries the concern for the behaviour, not the rightful owner. Jenkins argues that seeking causal explanations for violence and abuse can have the same effect; becoming woven into a narrative that places abusers at the mercy of influences over which they have no control – whether those influences are psychological and developmental, interpersonal or socio-cultural. Instead of 'causes', he frames them as 'restraints to responsibility', inviting abusers to identify and then challenge them as impediments to their ability to take responsibility. This powerful change of language constructs a conversation that has personal responsibility as its starting point and allows for the development of goals and strategies focused upon ways of taking responsibility.

In any discussion of risk, the issue of denial is likely to arise. Much of the work with offenders deemed to be 'high-risk' or 'dangerous' takes as its working premise that full acknowledgement of responsibility is a sine qua non for effective intervention and that its absence aggravates risk. The value of acknowledging culpability is a belief deeply embedded in Western cultural traditions, in criminal justice processes and in practice with offenders, but elevating the issue of denial to such a position of primacy has a number of serious drawbacks. Overcoming 'denial' may become a goal in itself for the worker, obscuring the primary purpose, which is to construct safety. Debating the issue of 'denial' may create oppositional dynamics between the worker and the offender in which dominance becomes the primary goal of each individual. A vicious cycle may also be set in motion if the offender attempts to cooperate by giving a 'right answer', only to find that the worker is not convinced of its veracity. In these circumstances, the worker may become more distrustful, the offender less willing to cooperate. Finally, assumptions of 'denial', 'lack of motivation' and 'pre-contemplation' can all too easily become strategies for blaming the offender for lack of progress. Turnell and Edwards (1999) argue for maintaining an open mind on this issue, allowing room for the possibility of other routes to safety that do not require a full confession of culpability.

Practitioners working with 'dangerous' offenders are often clear about what behaviour should stop but articulation of what the future will look like in its absence and how that future will be achieved are often assumed to take care of themselves. For a different future to be constructed, it has to be articulated in detail with attainable goals. Constructive approaches often use scaling questions to identify a continuum along which progress can occur. 'Safety' and 'danger' exist on a continuum and the task is to encourage individuals to adopt behaviours that move them towards the 'safety' zone and embed them incrementally into a narrative of self-management and personal responsibility. The preoccupation with risk often results in too little time for building safety and responsibility. Maintaining a focus on safety, looking for signs of it and establishing concrete goals in relation to it uses available time to shape positive changes in behaviour. Examples of signs of safety scales can be found in several texts and are useful aids to maintaining a focus on constructing safety (for example, Milner and O'Byrne 2002; Parton and O'Byrne 2000; Turnell and Edwards 1999).

Concluding thoughts on risk and safety

The risk discourse has operated to differentiate the excluded from the included, the 'safe' from the 'dangerous', 'them' from 'us', and has muted the discussion of values in work with offenders. Cloaked within the guise of scientific objectivity and technical accuracy, the risk discourse lulls us into a false sense of security, into a belief that we can dispense with the challenge of complexity and uncertainty, that we can create security without the ambiguity of trust.

The reality is much more complex. Let us consider rape as an illustration. A consensus almost certainly exists that the rapist is a 'dangerous' offender because of the harm that rape inflicts at both the physical and psychological level. Peculiarly low conviction rates for rape, however, suggest that we are not unequivocal in our condemnation. As Andrea Dworkin (1981, 1987) controversially argued, our cultural narrative of masculinity so entwines sexuality and violence that to make simple assertions that rape is an aberration is to deny the ambiguity of its cultural context. Rape is at the extreme end of a spectrum of thought and behaviour in relation to sexuality and aggression on which men (and women) negotiate and enact their individual and shared personal stories. To assert that the rapist exists outside that spectrum may provide reassurance to the rest of us about our individual 'normality', but does little to assist the rapist to occupy a more acceptable place on it and become less 'dangerous'. Very few, if any of us, are wholly harmless or wholly 'dangerous'. We are a composite of individual and cultural narratives in which our relationship with 'dangerousness' and, indeed, altruism shifts according to time and context. Humans are not 'dangerous' or altruistic but 'dangerous' and altruistic. To focus on offenders' 'dangerousness' to the exclusion of all else misses the opportunity to discover the building blocks of safety. We need to work with the complexity of offenders' stories, acknowledging and managing potential harm but also building upon their capacity for responsibility and self-management.

New and potent ways need to be found of expressing the idea that offenders 'are people worth doing business with' rather than 'people we do business to' (Turnell and Edwards 1999, p.32). There are encouraging signs that some parts of the community are finding ways of doing just that. One such example is the government-backed experimental project for supporting sex offenders in the community, Circles of Support and Accountability (Home Office 2003; Quaker Peace and Social Witness 2004). Adopted from Canada, the initiative involves volunteers providing support to high-risk sex offenders in the community's midst, whilst holding them accountable for their behaviour. Such initiatives actively demonstrate optimism about the possibility of change while maintaining a realistic approach to potential harm.

Practitioners working with 'dangerous' offenders have traditionally managed this tension and can continue to do so. Coercion and control have always been part of this work and statutory power is rightfully exercised to prevent situations of continuing or escalating danger. Nonetheless, there is an important choice to be made in working with the risk that offenders pose. Is power to be transparently exercised within an optimistic commitment to collaboration and with a view to constructing safety, building responsibility and achieving reintegration? Is it, on the other hand, to be exercised within a pessimistic framework that privileges perceptions of danger and assumes that little can be achieved beyond monitoring and surveillance? These are not issues that can be resolved by greater reliance on the technologies of practice; they are moral questions about our view of those we choose to call 'offenders' and the human stories each of us chooses to inhabit.

References

Alaszewski, A., Harrison, L. and Manthorpe, J. (eds) (1998) *Risk, Health and Welfare.* Buckingham: Open University Press.

Andrews, D. (1995) 'The psychology of criminal conduct and effective treatment.' In J. McGuire (ed.) *What Works: Reducing Offending.* Chichester: Wiley.

Andrews, D. and Bonta, J. (2003) *The Psychology of Criminal Conduct* (3rd edition). Cincinnati, OH: Anderson.

Bale, D. (1987) 'Using a "risk of custody" scale.' *Probation Journal* 34, 4, 127–31.

Beaumont, B. (1999) 'Risk assessment and prediction research.' In P. Parsloe (ed.) *Risk Assessment in Social Care and Social Work.* London: Jessica Kingsley Publishers.

Beck, U. (1992) *Risk Society.* London: Sage.

Bonta, J. (1996) 'Risk-needs assessment and treatment.' In A. Harland (ed.) *Choosing Correctional Options that Work.* London: Sage.

Caddick, B. and Watson, D. (1999) 'Rehabilitation and the distribution of risk.' In P. Parsloe (ed.) *Risk Assessment in Social Care and Social Work.* London: Jessica Kingsley Publishers.

Clear, T. and Cadora, E. (2001) 'Risk and community practice.' In K. Stenson and R.R. Sullivan (eds) *Crime, Risk and Justice.* Cullompton: Willan Publishing.

Copas, J., Ditchfield, J. and Marshall, P. (1994) *Development of a New Risk Predictor Score.* Research Bulletin 36. London: Home Office.

de Shazer, S. (1985) *Keys to Solutions in Brief Therapy.* New York and London: Norton.

de Shazer, S. (1988) *Clues: Investigating Solutions in Brief Therapy.* New York and London: Norton.

de Shazer, S. (1994) *Words were Originally Magic.* New York and London: Norton.

Derrida, J. (1978) *Writing and Difference.* London: Routledge.

Douglas, M. (1992) *Risk and Blame: Essays in Cultural Theory.* London: Routledge.

Dworkin, A. (1981) *Pornography: Men Possessing Women.* London: The Women's Press.

Dworkin, A. (1987) *Intercourse.* London: Martin Secker and Warburg.

Dworkin, R. (2002) 'The real threat to US values.' In the *Guardian,* Saturday Review, 9 March, 3.

Ericson, R. and Carriere, K. (1994) 'The fragmentation of criminology.' In D. Nelken (ed.) *The Futures of Criminology.* London: Sage.

Farrall, S. (2002) *Rethinking What Works with Offenders.* Cullompton: Willan Publishing.

Farrall, S. (2004) 'Social capital and offender reintegration: Making probation desistance focused.' In S. Maruna and R. Immarigeon (eds) *After Crime and Punishment.* Cullompton: Willan Publishing.

Feeley, M. and Simon, J. (1992) 'The new penology: Notes on the emerging strategy of corrections.' *Criminology* 30, 4, 449–75.

Furedi, F. (1997) *Culture of Fear: Risk-Taking and the Morality of Low Expectation.* London: Cassell.

Furman, B. and Ahola, T. (1992) *Solution Talk: Hosting Therapeutic Conversations.* New York and London: Norton.

Garland, D. (2001) *The Culture of Control.* Oxford: Oxford University Press.

Giddens, A. (1990) *The Consequences of Modernity.* Cambridge: Polity Press.

Giddens, A. (1991) *Modernity and Self-Identity.* Cambridge: Polity Press.

Glassner, B. (1999) *The Culture of Fear.* New York: Basic Books.

Hannah-Moffat, K. (2002) 'Criminogenic need and the transformative risk subject: The hybridizations of risk/need in penality.' Paper presented at the British Criminology Conference UK, Keele University.

HMIP (Her Majesty's Inspectorate of Probation) (1995) *Dealing with Dangerous People: The Probation Service and Public Protection.* London: Home Office.

HMIP (1997) 'Risk management guidance.' In *The Assessment and Management of Risk.* London: Home Office/Association of Chief Officers of Probation.

Holloway, W. and Jefferson, T. (1997) 'The risk society in an age of anxiety: Situating fear of crime.' *British Journal of Sociology* 48, 2, 252–66.

Home Office (2002) *Offender Assessment System, OASys.* User Manual, V. 2. London: Home Office.

Home Office (2003) *Restorative Justice: The Government's Strategy.* London: Home Office.

Hood, R., Shute, S., Feilzer, M. and Wilcox, A. (2002) 'Sex offenders emerging from long-term imprisonment: A study of their long-term reconviction rates and of parole members' judgement of their risk.' *British Journal of Criminology* 42, 2, 371–94.

Hudson, B. (2001) 'Punishment, rights and difference: Defending justice in the risk society.' In K. Stenson and R.R. Sullivan (eds) *Crime, Risk and Justice.* Cullompton: Willan Publishing.

Hudson, B. (2003) *Justice in the Risk Society.* London: Sage.

Humphrey, C., Carter, P. and Pease, K. (1992) 'A reconviction predictor for probationers.' *British Journal of Social Work* 42, 2, 67–72.

Jenkins, A. (1990) *Invitations to Responsibility.* Adelaide: Dulwich Centre Publications.

Kahneman, D. and Tversky, A. (1972) 'Subjective probability: A judgement of representativeness.' *Cognitive Psychology* 3, 430–54.

Kemshall, H. (1998) *Risk in Probation Practice.* Aldershot: Ashgate.

Kemshall, H. (2002) *Risk, Social Policy and Welfare.* Buckingham: Open University Press.

Kemshall, H. and Maguire, M. (2001) 'Public protection, partnership and risk penality: The multi-agency risk management of sexual and dangerous offenders.' *Punishment and Society* 3, 2, 237–64.

Kemshall, H., Parton, N., Walsh, M. and Waterson, J. (1997) 'Concepts of risk in relation to organizational structure and functioning within the personal social services and probation.' *Social Policy and Administration* 3, 3, 213–32.

Kennedy, H. (2004) *Just Law.* London: Chatto and Windus.

Lianos, M. and Douglas, M. (2000) 'Dangerization and the end of deviance.' *British Journal of Criminology* 40, 261–78.

Maguire, M., Kemshall, H., Noaks, L., Wincup, E. and Sharpe, K. (2001) *Risk Management of Sexual and Violent Offenders: The Work of Public Protection Panels.* Police Research Series, Paper 139. London: Home Office.

Maruna, S. (2001) *Making Good: How Ex-Convicts Reform and Rebuild their Lives.* Washington DC: American Psychological Association.

Maruna, S. and Immarigeon, R. (eds) (2004) *After Crime and Punishment.* Cullompton: Willan Publishing.

McGuire, J. (2000) 'Explanations of criminal behaviour.' In J. McGuire, T. Mason and A. O'Kane (eds) *Behaviour, Crime and Legal Processes: A Guide for Legal Practitioners.* Chichester: Wiley.

McNeill, F. (2003) 'Desistance focused probation practice.' In W.H. Chui and M. Nellis (eds) *Moving Probation Forward.* Harlow: Pearson Education.

Miller, W.R. and Rollnick, S. (1991) *Motivational Interviewing: Preparing People to Change Addictive Behaviour.* New York: Guilford Press.

Milner, J. and O'Byrne, P. (2002) *Brief Counselling: Narratives and Solutions.* Basingstoke: Palgrave.

Nacro (2003) *Counting the Cost: Reducing Child Imprisonment.* London: Nacro Publications.

Nash, M. (1999) *Police, Probation and Protecting the Public.* London: Blackstone Press.

Parton, N. (1996) 'Social work, risk and "the blaming system".' In N. Parton (ed.) *Social Theory, Social Change and Social Work.* London: Routledge.

Parton, N. and O'Byrne, P. (2000) *Constructive Social Work.* Basingstoke: Macmillan.

Pawson, R. and Tilley, N. (1997) *Realistic Evaluation.* London: Sage.

Prochaska, J.O. and DiClemente, C.C. (1984) *The Transtheoretical Approach: Crossing Traditional Boundaries of Therapy.* Homewood 111: Dow Jones-Irwin.

Quaker Peace and Social Witness (2004) *Criminal Justice Work.* Factsheet. QPSW: Religious Society of Friends in Britain.

Robinson, G. (2002) 'Exploring risk management in probation practice.' *Punishment and Society* 4, 1, 5–25.

Smith, D. (2004) 'The uses and abuses of positivism.' In G. Mair (ed.) *What Matters in Probation.* Cullompton: Willan Publishing.

Social Exclusion Unit (2002) *Reducing Re-offending by Ex-prisoners.* London: Office of the Deputy Prime Minister.

Strachan, R. and Tallant, C. (1997) 'Improving judgement and appreciating biases within the risk assessment process.' In H. Kemshall and J. Pritchard (eds) *Good Practice in Risk Assessment and Risk Management, 2.* London: Jessica Kingsley Publishers.

Tonry, M. (2001) 'Unthought thoughts: The influence of changing sensibilities on penal policies.' *Punishment and Society* 3, 1, 167–82.

Trotter, C. (1999) *Working with Involuntary Clients.* London: Sage.

Turnell, A. and Edwards, S. (1999) *Signs of Safety: A Solution and Safety Oriented Approach to Child Protection Casework.* New York and London: Norton.

Ward, T. and Stewart, C.A. (2003) 'Good lives and the rehabilitation of sexual offenders.' In T. Ward, D.R. Laws and S.H. Hudson (eds) *Sexual Deviance: Issues and Controversies.* Thousand Oaks, CA: Sage.

White, M. (1989) *Selected Papers.* Adelaide: Dulwich Centre Publications.

White, M. (1995) *Re-Authoring Lives: Interviews and Essays*. Adelaide: Dulwich Centre Publications.

White, M. and Epston, D. (1990) *Narrative Means to Therapeutic Ends*. New York and London: Norton.

Wittgenstein, L. (1968) *Philosophical Investigations*. Oxford: Blackwell.

Young, J. (1999) *The Exclusive Society*. London: Sage.

Chapter 5

The Constructive Use of Courtroom Skills and Enforcement to Achieve Client Cooperation and Change

Geoff Kenure

Whilst there are clear constraints upon the opportunity for constructive work with defendants in the court setting, such opportunity does exist, and can be used effectively. The defendant in court is often in, what is for them, a crisis of varying degree. Crisis theory in social work, building on psychiatric models, has long emphasized the value of working within a crisis scenario: 'a relatively minor force, acting for a relatively short time, can switch the balance' (Caplan 1961, p.293). In other words, work in a crisis can often be proportionately more productive than working at other times. 'The initial contact in a crisis situation is an important one. The person is most often under considerable tension and stress and will be very sensitive to the reactions of the intervener' (Romano 1990, p.49). As we approach the centenary of the Probation Service in England and Wales, the climate and opportunity for constructive work with defendants in court has rarely been better. This chapter suggests that court work, having declined to a point where it was perceived as a mechanistic low-level information-processing role, has moved forward to a growing acceptance such that the court worker can use their skills in the interface with the court system and also in constructive work with defendants. Of special significance is the value of the court worker as a vehicle for engendering and sustaining the compliance of defendants with court orders. This issue is highlighted together with the opportunities for constructive dialogue with defendants both generally and especially in the enforcement process (which impacts on compliance). It is postulated that compliance in particular, and court intervention in general, can be enhanced by focused work which encourages and motivates defendants.

The development of court work

The original probation officers in 1907, who in many cases had been Police Court Missionaries, did much of their work in the environs of the local magistrates' courts. That location, and the fact that their employers were the local magistrates, gave the Probation Service a 'court-centred' approach. After the 1925 Criminal Justice Act, the organization of the service developed, and working space for probation staff was increasingly obtained away from court buildings. The Probation Rules of 1949 required Probation Committees to provide 'office accommodation for every Probation Officer appointed to its Area' (Home Office 1949, para 29). So began the inexorable drift of the Probation Service away from its 'court-centred' origin, both physically and organizationally, a drift that arguably reached its apogee in 2001 when, with the creation of Probation Boards, the service formally lost its last vestige of direct management from local justices.

The drift in management links between the service and courts was mirrored in the way that case supervisors became distanced from court work. This was a differential experience dependent upon the location of the officer; in rural areas probation staff still service small courts as one of their many duties. But from the 1970s onwards in urban areas specialist staff have been provided to service courts. This derived from the advent in the Probation Service of what might be called 'managerialism'. As managers looked for cost effectiveness, they divined that court attendance interrupted the supervisory and report-writing functions, and so used specialist personnel to facilitate the non-attendance of most staff at courts. Like all specialisms it increasingly led to the de-skilling of non-specialist staff, who lost touch with the operation of courts. In some places this has resulted in staff operating with limited cognizance of the legal framework in which they supervise defendants and/or of court practice – both crucial issues in report writing and dealing with defendants who are due to appear before court. This de-skilling has been acknowledged by the National Probation Directorate who felt the need in 2004 to circulate a document *Working with Court (Advice on Court Procedures)* (Macgregor 2004) written at such a simplistic level that it would have been basic knowledge to all trained probation staff appointed before 1985.

Originally the probation officer carried a large number of varied duties. In the 1974 *Probation Officers Manual* there are 43 listed 'Mandatory and

Non Mandatory Duties' (Jarvis 1974, pp.28–30). Interestingly, none of these refers to court work or enforcement, as at that time these responsibilities were seen as part of managing the supervision of offenders. Well into the 1970s there were many officers who regularly undertook this full range of duties, including, for example, family worker, youth/child worker, matrimonial worker group worker, mental health worker, accommodation/employment finder, addictions worker, counsellor, welfare rights worker, and case supervisor. Most of these responsibilities have gone on to become 'specialisms' (and even in some cases 'Services') in their own right, but court work has never achieved such status.

Almost in denial of the court-based origin of the Probation Service, managers felt the only function of court staff was to get 'results' and be a conduit for passing low-level information to and from the courts. One has to be sceptical about the assertion that 'The service's contribution to the work of the courts has always been a priority' (Sanders and Senior 1993, p.89) since a contemporary Home Office inspection report opined that the Probation Service had 'experienced a movement away from the courts' (Probation Inspectorate 1993, para 1.2). There were some very dedicated court staff but, because many managers perceived court work as low priority, courts became a useful location for placing staff who were proving difficult to maintain or locate within other teams because of their health or attitudes. This management view coincided with the expansion of probation assistants (later probation services officers) and led to an increased use of inexperienced staff in the court role. It is difficult to imagine a commercial enterprise consciously staffing its 'shop or sales force' either with people who were difficult to employ in the 'factory', or with people who had a limited knowledge of the 'factory processes' or the 'product'. Indeed it is of great credit to many probation services officers who were thrown in at the deep end with little training or support that they managed to survive and develop and do such a good job.

The courtwork role

The role of the probation worker in a court setting is multifaceted. Just pursuing the shop and factory analogy, clearly there is a role for court officers in 'buying' and 'selling' to those in the market, including sentencers, defendants and other court users. Similarly they get orders for the factory and do the sales service; also it is important that they feed back to the factory about the marketplace issues. Feedback when the courts have complained or complimented the factory is done well. The compliment is passed on so that a colleague may have some reward for work that has been well received. The complaint is often sent with extra gusto because the court worker has probably experienced 'pain' inflicted by being told off in public and now can pass on some of that to the person causing the blunder or failure.

Perhaps court workers are less mindful about feeding back on issues from defendants and other court users. One example is the defendant who is in employment. Supervision requirements clearly indicate that appointments should 'not disrupt the working hours of an employed person' (National Probation Directorate 2002, para C 8). This is further strengthened by S 217(2) of the Criminal Justice Act 2003, which requires a Responsible Officer to take account of the work requirements of the offender. Yet often a court worker will struggle to obtain a 'first appointment' outside working hours. Where offices/teams fail to provide such systems, court staff should challenge this through the management chain. This will help avoid future non-constructive brokerage by the court officer between the team and the defendant, in which the latter may feel pressurized. In such cases the defendant may experience the event as one which undermines the order at its start.

In court, as in the analogy of sales, first impressions count. On arrival in the court precincts workers should be in role. They interact as representatives of the service and should avoid behaviour which portrays the service as uninterested or inefficient. For example, the reading of newspapers should be reserved for the staff room or a break, casual conversations in courtrooms with other professional staff and users should be tempered in the presence of members of the public, conversations about last night's social activities may be offensive to defendants or make the worker appear shallow or careless, and disparaging comments about the judge or justices can undermine the whole process of justice. Approaches from all should be dealt with in a courteous and helpful or informative manner. One never knows whom one may later have to engage for professional purposes.

The return of constructive opportunities in court work

Constructive court work declined and became a functional operation focusing on results and simple information processing. However, in the 1990s that began to change and one catalyst was the arrival of a wholly new element to court work, namely Bail Information.

A Home Office initiative in 1987 built on work done 20 years earlier by the Inner London Probation Service and the Vera Institute. In eight pilot areas, with cooperation between the Probation Service, police and the newly established Crown Prosecution Service (CPS), a Bail Information

Scheme (BIS) was tested out. Such schemes were, and remain, designed to provide factual and verified information to assist the CPS when considering the issue of bail. A probation worker (that is, independent from police and defence) attends the cells to see those arrested overnight who fall within set criteria. With the defendant's agreement, an interview takes place focusing on factors likely to stand in favour of bail, for example accommodation, employment, community ties and so on. After interview the worker attempts to verify these factors by phoning people who may verify the defendant's assertions. The subsequent report focuses on positive verified factors, except where a public protection issue has been unearthed, in which case this will be reported to the CPS and other relevant agencies.

Self-evidently this work is highly focused and yet constructively outcome directed. BISs led to a re-awakening of the idea of an opportunity for constructive work in courts and provided satisfaction to those working in them who immediately saw the outcomes of their work on bail decisions. Some established court staff may have been initially wary of this new element – especially as it involved new techniques and an early start to see prisoners before court. However, in a significant number of cases the CPS prosecutor changed the police application from one of remand in custody to conditional or straight bail. Where the prosecutor is unmoved, the information is available to courts through the defence solicitor, to whom a copy is given. As a consequence the direct outcome of intervention could very quickly be seen and those workers involved became motivated and enthusiastic.

From the pilots in 1987, BISs quickly expanded and, by 1992, of 53 probation areas, 39 had schemes. 'The overall impact of bail information has been shown to reduce the number of defendants remanded in custody without compromising public safety' (Home Office 2000, para 2.2) and from 2000 comprehensive BISs were to be provided in all probation areas (Home Office 2000, para 1). Bail Information was soon followed by the Specific Sentence Report (SSR), another highly focused piece of innovative court work; a wider focus, but a short-term, discrete piece of work nonetheless.

The Criminal Justice Act 1991 provided that Pre-Sentence Reports (PSRs) should be considered before passing sentence in most cases where a community penalty or imprisonment were being considered. Within a year the judiciary's opposition to what they felt to be restrictions on their discretion had become public and led to section 40 of the Criminal Justice and Public Order Act of 1994, which provided greater discretion for courts to sentence without a PSR. There were fears that this would lead to courts returning to requesting unstructured pre-1991 'standdown' reports, where court staff received limited briefing from the court, and were frequently offered no information and given little time to make enquiries. A group of court staff in Bradford, West Yorkshire, felt that to return to the old 'standdown' would be to sacrifice the gains of the 1991 Act. They devised a set of 'ground rules' by which 'standdowns' could be operated. The court should provide a focus by specifying the sentence it was considering and then allow a minimum period (up to one hour) and provide the probation worker with specific information, namely CPS details of the offence(s) and the defendant's previous convictions. Only where these conditions were met would the 'immediate' service be provided.

The original Specific Sentence Enquiries adopted by courts throughout West Yorkshire in 1994 came to the attention of the Home Office two years later, and three years after that they were rolled out across England and Wales with the title changed by substituting the word 'Report' for 'Enquiry'. 'West Yorkshire Probation Service, amongst others, have been pioneering the use of SSRs and their own monitoring seems to indicate that SSRs are no less favourable than PSRs in terms of the outcome of resulting orders' (Home Office 1999, para 4). As a result of changes driven by the introduction of the Criminal Justice Act 2003, the need for a separate SSR and PSR is giving way to a concept of reports on a continuum: Fast Delivery reports, with the features of the SSR, and Standard Delivery reports, with the full PSR. The National Implementation Guide for the Criminal Justice Act 2003 (Home Office 2005b) suggests that the targeting of report type will now attempt to ensure that all offenders have their reports allocated to the appropriate process: Fast Delivery for low-risk cases and Standard Delivery for medium- to high-risk cases, thereby acknowledging that, in the latter cases, there is greater need for detailed assessment and more complex storytelling.

Development of the BIS and SSRs provided a new impetus to the court worker role and hard on the heels of the SSR came a burgeoning of 'enforcement' work. The 'National Standards for Supervision of Offenders in the Community', first introduced in 1992 (subsequently revised, most recently Home Office 2005a), had gradually been refined and targets were set to check comparative differences between areas.

This led to the attachment of financial incentives where targets were met and penalties when not. Proving that community sentences were tough was a political imperative and thus the enforcement of orders assumed a high profile, eclipsing the importance of compliance. This led to increased numbers of cases being returned to court. Court staff were responsible for this prosecution work and so increasingly dealt with offenders who were often in conflict with the Probation Service who had brought them back to court. The service still has targets for those who fail the exacting enforcement rules, for example a return to court on a second missed appointment. However, there has been a shift of emphasis from only having targets based on enforcement (failure) to a new set of targets based on encouraging compliance (success). It is hoped that the compliance management initiative (National Probation Directorate 2004) will redress the one-sided imbalance which has held sway since the mid-1990s. Indeed with the creation of the National Offender Management Service (NOMS) in 2004, an organization which is designed to weld together the operation of the Prison and Probation Services, compliance is likely to be a significant issue. The more defendants are enabled and encouraged to comply with community orders, the less likely they are to be in breach, and consequently the less likely they are to go to prison for failing to comply.

Interestingly, there is an argument as to whether probation court staff should act as prosecutor in enforcement cases. Arguably, since 1991, when community orders were made into punishments in their own right, prosecutions for breach could have passed to the CPS – especially where there was likely to be a revocation and re-sentence. The CPS claim never to have had sufficient resources to take on this role, so it is left to probation staff, people untrained in the law or advocacy. Despite a breach not being an offence it is arguable that probation staff prosecuting in court should assume the full responsibility of a prosecutor and have regard to *The Code for Crown Prosecutors* (Crown Prosecution Service 2000).

Indeed, the National Standards requirement for breach action to be taken no later than the second unacceptable absence (Home Office 2005a) is not consistent with the rules of the CPS. These rules provide first for a review of evidence and the application of two tests:

1. the 'Evidential Test' requiring prosecution to be based upon there being 'enough evidence to provide a "realistic prospect of conviction"' (Crown Prosecution Service 2000, para 5.1)

2. the arguably more significant 'Public Interest Test', which quotes the classic statement on public interest by Lord Shawcross, Attorney General in 1951: 'It has never been the rule in this country [that offences] must automatically be the subject of prosecution' (Hansard 1951, Vol. 483, column 681).

There is clearly an argument for probation staff, who are being asked to act as prosecutors, to assess cases against these tests.

Facing constraints...

There are constraints upon engaging in constructive work with defendants in court settings.

Time limitation

The court worker is always under pressure of time. Courts are busy places often with a large daily throughput of cases and limited probation staff resources. That has in the past been used to suggest that there is little point in attempting constructive work at court. However, the advent of Bail Information and SSRs has challenged this and brought a number of new concepts to constructive work in courts that are of enduring value. Whilst any attempt at constructive intervention needs time, it can be achieved by limiting and focusing the scope of the work to be done and by the management of such time as is available.

Staff availability

Many variables affect court staffing numbers, including the local management view of the relative importance of court work, and ability to respond to differential levels of demand. Courts organize in blocks of work, some of which require more probation staffing than others. Court managers should attempt to provide staff when they are most likely to be needed and workers need to be disciplined managers of their own time. The geographical location of staff can affect how work is planned. Courts with probation offices within the court building may enable all court staff to be available. In many cases, however, 'reinforcements', if any, are in other locations some time and distance away.

Working environment

Court arrangements vary greatly in terms of the availability of interview space. Both workers and managers have a duty to try to obtain sufficient privacy for work like SSRs, whilst being reasonable in their expectations, as often court buildings have limited available space.

Unrealistic demands

Both courts and defendants can be unrealistic in their expectations. If workers can meet appropriate demands they should attempt to do so, but they have to assess whether and how the demand may be met. Where it is beyond the worker involved, support should be sought from colleagues/

managers, but where the demand cannot be met the reasons should be given.

Social work interviewing models

In days when most staff did court duty, interview techniques relied on putting the defendant at ease and creating a working relationship. Court interview time was seen as inadequate for those older social work interview models. This was another factor in court work being seen as of limited constructive value.

...seeking opportunities

These constraints were used to justify the idea that a court worker could do little to assist in the 'constructive' work of the service. But the advent of Bail Information, SSRs and the burgeoning of enforcement challenged that view and brought with them a new generation of staff, keen to engage in focused constructive work. Once you move court workers' mindset away from the fatalism of 'there are so many constraints in this job that there is little I can do', to the freedom of 'despite the constraints there are some bits of constructive work I can achieve', then the door begins to open and the opportunities appear.

Justice

The saying 'justice delayed is justice denied' is a useful motivator for the principled court worker and encourages the attitude of getting matters finalized today. It also means doing all that can be reasonably done to ensure that natural justice takes its course whenever possible.

Whole system thinking

So often there are events within the criminal justice system that unnecessarily give work to other parts of the system, and sometimes the court worker can intervene to prevent this. An example may be where a Bail Information enquiry is not made and a defendant who may have been bailed is remanded in custody.

Service integrity

The service which the worker represents, whilst part of the criminal justice system, nevertheless has its own remit. The court worker is there to be a 'gatekeeper' or, in more commercial parlance, a customer service advisor. Therefore staff must represent the service not just at the easy times where one is saying 'yes' but also on the tougher occasions where the defendant, or the court (or others), need telling 'no' because they are asking one to go outside one's remit.

Some practical court worker principles may thus be postulated within these broader concepts of justice, whole system thinking and service integrity:

- Do it today. This meets the justice issue and has the cost advantage to the court team of having the case handled only once.

- Do not create more work for the service. Wider service costs are saved by not letting work be put off, for example an SSR saves the much longer time needed to prepare a PSR.

- Avoid unworkable cases. Another resource loss is in cases or work that are self-evidently unworkable or inappropriate to the service from the outset.

These three principles have a very useful application to all work and are particularly helpful in the field of enforcement.

Ingredients for turning constraints into opportunities

Focus on outcome

To achieve constructive work within the constraints of normal court work requires a clear focus on outcome. In every human interaction there are liable to be digressions from the focus of the contact, but the worker must keep the outcome goal in mind. Opportunity to 'chat' may only be indulged once the outcome has been achieved.

Controlling approach

Ensuring focus needs a controlling approach. This does not mean an overbearing or arrogant approach. It involves being businesslike in manner, conveying a sense of purpose, having confidence in role, smiling and being polite. However, once at the point where the interview can start, stick to your outline 'script' and drive the process towards the outcome focus.

Simple and clear explanation of focus

Workers need to understand for themselves the outcome focus and then to prepare their own thinking about it. This can then be developed into a 'script', whereby the nature of the contact, its parameters, exceptions and outcome focus, can be explained succinctly. Only when this focus is reduced to its main points and presented in a way that defendants can understand are workers able to impart their dedication to outcome focus to the defendant.

Use of self- and positive engagement

The worker with the positive 'can do' approach will often find that the defendant responds by mirroring their approach and actively contributes to the outcome focus.

Direct questioning

Because of time limitations in this outcome-focused approach, questions need to be direct; for example 'do you take drugs?' may lead to a slow introduction to the answer, whereas 'what drugs do you take?' invites a more precise statement, or a denial.

Negotiation skills

Because focused work is of a speedy nature, there is a danger some defendants may misunderstand what is happening and why. In such circumstances the worker needs to be able to negotiate the defendant back to the focus by reiterating from the outline script or by allowing time to explain in an area where the defendant has become lost.

Available time

There is a preliminary need to establish the available time for the contact. These constraints need to be communicated to the defendant in a sensitive way. Clearly the defendant may feel there is 'all day' for their case, so the worker must impart an understanding that whilst the defendant's views are important, this is a 'headline' operation with tight time limits.

Space to work

Time may be affected by access to interview space, but there needs to be a private location where the defendant can talk freely. Also it is useful for the worker to develop techniques to get the defendant on his or her own; for example, by explaining to the significant other that there is a need to see the defendant alone, but that later they may be involved. Alternatively, it may be felt that the significant other should be present to start with, but in that case techniques for politely excluding them later on are needed.

Court work opportunities to engender defendant cooperation and change

As indicated at the beginning of this chapter, the court worker is dealing with a defendant in a crisis situation. Thus, the worker is intervening in the defendant's life at a potentially sensitive and significant moment. In this context we can see the court worker having a critical and potentially impacting role to play. This exists in all court work interventions and even the most mundane (to the worker) can be highly significant to the defendant. It is more obvious when the court worker is dealing with an SSR, for example. However, the impact of a court worker in dealing with apparently less significant matters should not be underestimated. Explaining the practicalities of how an order will get started or the process of the PSR can alleviate anxieties and therefore make defendants feel more positive about the way they approach the period of contact with the service. It is now particularly important given that such great emphasis has been placed on compliance, and the court worker can contribute to a positive start.

Thus the helpfulness and demeanour of the worker, within the focus of the task in hand, are important motivational experiences for the defendants. Similarly, dealing with relevant supporters in a like manner provides positive reinforcement to the defendant's own impressions.

Court worker role in constructive enforcement and compliance

Historically the concept of 'compliance' predates the concept of 'enforcement'. 'The Probation Officer shall endeavour to ensure compliance with the requirements of the probation order' (Home Office 1949, p.13). This has been reinforced over time, for example the title of Probation Circular 1/1997 *Enforcing Community Sentences: Ensuring Compliance, Dealing with Breach* (Home Office 1997). But as the Probation Service tried to relocate itself within the post-1991 Criminal Justice Act 'punishment' imperative, the focus emphasized enforcement over compliance. This was compounded by standards which focused on reacting to failures rather than encouraging compliance. Thus, no later than on the second 'unacceptable absence' (National Probation Directorate 2002, para D 21) breach action is to be initiated at court. Service targets were set, encouraged by financial rewards for hitting them. This was to ensure rigorous enforcement and the spotlight fell on this aspect whilst compliance remained in the shadow. However, after seven or so years of focus on enforcement, the National Probation Service (NPS) realized that the stick of enforcement may have led to less compliance because so many defendants experienced breach proceedings during the course of their orders. 'Approximately 45% of offenders on community penalties have two or more unacceptable absences' (National Probation Directorate 2004, para 2); in other words, almost half those under supervision should have breach proceedings.

Thus the recent focus on compliance whereby 'attention also needs to be given to reducing the number of offenders who need enforcement action' (National Probation Directorate 2004, para 2) is overdue. Whilst continuing commitment to robust enforcement is evident in precursors to the new National Standards (Home Office 2005a, para GS9), mechanisms are now in place for rewarding the achievement of compliance targets. This emphasis is likely to encourage more constructive working relationships between probation staff and some defendants. It also helps court staff to be 'compliance focused', helping defendants through the enforcement process and back into compliance whenever possible.

Enforcement is central to the punishment element of an order and is the consequence of failing to abide by its terms. It is that part of the process of supervision which reminds defendants when they have breached the boundaries and, used constructively, is a formal means of admonishing the defendant in the hope of securing compliance. Using the process as positively as possible can keep defendants on board and motivated; the opposite is true when the process is handled negatively.

Working creatively to influence the defendant into a positive start to a community penalty is a first step towards encouraging compliance with an order. Unfortunately, the next time the court worker sees that defendant may well be in an enforcement situation. It is the nature of the work that workers are confronted with the failures whilst the successes are less often seen. It follows therefore that being judgemental about the defendant's 'failure' is neither necessary nor helpful.

For most people being summoned to appear before a court is a stressful experience. There may be some for whom it is inconsequential, but they are only a tiny minority. What is more, they may come to court with a demeanour that seems to express carelessness or arrogance, or they may put on an act of contrition to get themselves a better outcome. Similarly, the defendant who is mortified to be before the court may try to hide his or her fear by adopting a careless or arrogant manner. It is rarely possible to discern which is which. Therefore the starting point must be to expect that the defendant is anxious or concerned about the court appearance. Making that assumption, until clearly shown to be wrong, allows the court worker to start contacts with defendants in a positive manner.

So the constructive approach to enforcement work reflects the overall aim of supervision, namely compliance, and it involves a mindset of:

- being non-judgemental about a defendant's demeanour or reputation

- being dedicated to getting the order completed wherever possible

- being clear about the strict rules but encouraging compliance.

From this starting point the following constructive opportunities arise for a court worker dealing with an enforcement case; they do suggest that the worker needs to focus on pragmatism and creativity as he or she approaches defendants and their cases before the court.

Dialogue

Take every opportunity for dialogue with defendants. Sometimes they are in the cells having been arrested on warrant and contact has to be via solicitors. However, before a breach hearing or during an adjournment, take the opportunity to see those waiting who have no solicitor. In court when the bench are out, or after the case, use the opportunity to talk to the defendant in an encouraging way; point out their errors but also, crucially, how they can be rectified.

Know the enforcement law

Being able to think on one's feet is aided by knowledge of the law on enforcement. Fortunately this is easily referenced as it forms only a short section of Acts of Parliament. For easy reference on the law on breaching community orders made on offences committed after April 2005, refer to the Criminal Justice Act 2003, Schedule 8. Prosecutors should insist upon the availability of this type of material to them in the workplace and should become familiar with it.

Continue orders whenever possible and practicable

Most defendants want to get on and complete their orders. Those who have not engaged at all or who have repeatedly been breached quickly on more than one occasion need to have those facts put before the court. However, whenever a defendant is asking for a further chance a court worker should look pragmatically and creatively at that request.

Accepting limited pleas

Sometimes defendants feel that they have reasonable excuses for some misses (even though they have not provided proof to their supervisor) and dropping some allegations or amending them to failure to bring proof in time may make them feel better about pleading guilty. Getting a plea to anything is usually preferable to a trial. Any breach is recorded on their record and they will get a punishment, but they feel they have been heard, and that may aid their re-engagement with the order.

Give credit for work done (and put in context)

One of the most important factors for the defendant is to hear the prosecutor acknowledge in open court their achievements as well as their failings: for example, 'The defendant has admitted this breach, Your Worships, but to his/her credit...' Many defendants will have made efforts and these should be recognized. In 'Unpaid Work' one can state the hours worked out of the total. In 'Supervision Requirements' the number of contacts since the order was made alongside the number expected by National Standards at that stage of the order gives the court a quantification of compliance level. Finally, some defendants' compliance level may be affected by their circumstances (drug addiction, mental health, and so on) and this should also be acknowledged.

Suggest alternatives where current order not working/impractical

Looking at information in a case and making the necessary pre-court enquiries may lead to an unworkable order being replaced by an appropriate alternative; for example 'Unpaid Work', where there have been health problems, may be replaced by a 'Supervision Requirement'.

Use court appearance to engender encouragement

Once the court event is over the prosecutor can encourage compliance by emphasizing the positives in the case before arranging the next contact with the officer.

Summary

This chapter has attempted to show that court intervention and dialogue can be productive in encouraging compliance with orders both at the outset and during enforcement. These specialist workers need a good knowledge base, familiarity with the work of the Probation Service, and to be sufficiently empowered with its authority to make judgements in the quick-fire arena of the courts. They should also be confident in appearance and approach so as to make a positive personal impact on defendants. Such workers also need to be able to focus on the outcomes of the particular job in hand, to have a clear idea about that outcome focus and have an outline 'script' to aid focused questioning. In enforcing orders they will be pragmatic but compliance oriented; in other words, they will look to continue orders whenever possible and deal with the enforcement process in a way that impacts on the defendant as positively as possible.

Tailpiece

In an accident or serious illness you may recall the doctors and nurses by whom, over time, you were treated. You may also clearly remember the helpful paramedic who dealt so calmly and positively with you as the ambulance took you on that stressful journey into the unknown. The paramedic knows the full range of the work but is only required to focus, and focus quickly, on the main issues by providing an intervention upon which others with more time and facilities can build. A good court worker will be that paramedic, making a constructive start to the defendant's experience in passing through this particular 'treatment'.

References

Caplan, G. (1961) *An Approach to Community Mental Health*. New York: Grune and Stratton.

Crown Prosecution Service (2000) *The Code for Crown Prosecutors*. London: Crown Prosecution Service Communications Branch.

Hansard (1951) *House of Commons Debates, Volume 483, column 681*. 29 January. London: Home Office.

Home Office (1949) *Probation of Offenders Rules*. Statutory Instrument 1328 Part IV 29. London: Home Office.

Home Office (1997) *Enforcing Community Sentences: Ensuring Compliance, Dealing with Breach*. Circular 1/1997. London: Home Office.

Home Office (1999) *Pre Sentence Reports and Specific Sentence Reports*. Probation Circular 85/1999. London: Home Office.

Home Office (2000) *National Standards for the Supervision of Offenders in the Community*. London: Home Office.

Home Office (2005a) *National Standards*. Circular 15/2005. London: Home Office.

Home Office (2005b) *National Implementation Guide for the Criminal Justice Act 2003 Community Sentence Provisions.* Annex A Circular 25/2005. London: Home Office.

Jarvis, F.V. (1974) *Probation Officers Manual* (2nd edition). London: Butterworths.

Macgregor, J. (2004) *Working with Court (Advice on Court Procedures) Paper.* London: National Probation Directorate.

National Probation Directorate (2002) *National Standards for the Supervision of Offenders in the Community.* London: National Probation Directorate.

National Probation Directorate (2004) *Managing Compliance and Enforcement of Community Penalties.* Probation Circular 43/2004. London: National Probation Directorate.

Probation Inspectorate (1993) *Bail Information; Report of Thematic Inspection.* London: Probation Inspectorate, Home Office.

Romano, A.T. (1990) *Taking Charge; Crisis Intervention in Criminal Justice.* New York: Greenwood Press Publishers.

Sanders, A. and Senior, P. (1993) *Probation Service Manual* (5th edition). London: PAVIC Publications.

Chapter 6

Constructing a Convincing Narrative

The Art of Persuasive Storytelling within the Tight Constraints of Formal Pre-Sentence Assessments for the Criminal Courts

Kevin Gorman

In 1978, Barbara Wootton, a former member of the Streatfeild Committee, identified an implicit but key function of pre-sentence court reports when she asserted that 'they transform a "case" into a human being' (cited in Harris 1992, p.146).

Since then, however, such reports have contributed to a very different process of transmutation whereby those convicted of criminal offences have gradually undergone a metamorphosis from 'clients' into 'offenders' or, at best, into 'cases' in a case management system. Within the context of reductionist and impersonal nomenclature of this kind, it is arguably more important, if more difficult, than ever for the authors of Pre-Sentence Reports (PSR) to aspire towards the kind of narrative makeover described by Wootton. Indeed, the challenge is all the more daunting given the proposed national introduction of PSR templates and standardized, short-format reports (Cabinet Office 2004; Home Office 2004a), designed to be closely linked to and 'pre-populated' from the electronic Offender Assessment System (e-OASys). These initiatives suggest that we may already be uncomfortably close to realizing Ann Worrall's nightmare vision of court reports so severely constrained by policy requirements and National Standards as to be capable in many instances of being produced by computer software (Worrall 1997). If so, report writers will have their work cut out if they are to ensure that unique, complex individuals rather than nondescript offender-types emerge from the heavily regulated pages of their pre-sentence assessments.

Nevertheless, even within the rigid limitations increasingly imposed on report writers it may still be possible to go beyond simplistic, formulaic and dehumanizing accounts of offence circumstances, criminogenic needs, risk factors, and sentencing options. After all, prototypes and regional variants of the forthcoming standardized short-format report point towards the eventual adoption of a design which, whilst heavily reliant upon tick-boxes, pull-down menus, stock phrases and mandatory (sub-) headings, is almost certain also to incorporate expandable sections allowing for the inclusion of some detail and affording the PSR author real, albeit fragmented, opportunities 'for a clear exposition of complex reality...in stories which engage the heart as well as the head...' (Harris 1996, p.133).

Report writers willing and able to seize these limited narrative opportunities are likely to derive considerable job satisfaction from continuing to produce pre-sentence assessments sufficiently customized, rich in human interest and attentive not only to individual deficits and dangers but also to strengths and potential, as to make a real contribution to the re-authoring of offenders' lives and to exert genuine influence on sentencers. They will probably take additional professional pride in the greater utility of such reports to, on the one hand, prison and probation colleagues responsible for subsequent sentence planning and supervision planning and, on the other, an expanding range of staff in associated statutory and non-statutory agencies for whom, with the introduction of the National Offender Management Service (Carter 2003; Home Office 2004b), the PSR seems destined to become a progressively crucial indicator of required intervention and services. In this context, those who successfully mould their storytelling expertise to the ever more prescriptive PSR requirements of National Standards (Home Office 2000, revised 2002) will contribute to the longstanding, chameleon-like tradition of the Probation Service, in which they are predominantly still employed, of adapting its report writing and other skills to ideological, legislative and policy changes and to the shifting, sometimes self-contradictory, expectations of politicians, academic commentators and the general public.

A brief history of the Pre-Sentence Report

Detailed consideration will follow as to how the report writer might yet aspire to the role of 'the understanding poet' (Moore 1984, p.20), who co-constructs meaningful, persuasive stories even within the straitjackets of National Standards and OASys. Beforehand, however, it is worth briefly recalling the development of the PSR from its origins in the 1991 Criminal Justice Act. This piece of legislation was the hybrid offspring of penal reformers and government auditors which, by formalizing the principles of bifurcation and proportionality, or 'just deserts', and by re-naming the 'Social Enquiry Report' the 'Pre-Sentence Report', accelerated the transformation of the Probation Service from a social work agency concerned with *offenders* into a criminal justice agency concerned with *offending*. Essentially the Act required two new skills of report writers:

1. the explicit assessment of seriousness, which hitherto had been only an implicit, 'second guessing' aspect of the task

2. the assessment of risk, which was now to extend beyond the existing focus upon potential re-offending to a consideration of any future harm to the public posed by the perpetrators of violent or sexual offences, for whom the new legislation authorized non-commensurate, preventative sentencing (Kemshall 1998; Worrall 1997).

In the event, the expectation that report writers directly address offence seriousness in their PSRs turned out to be something of a nine-day wonder. This happened partly because of disquiet about probation officers encroaching upon judicial territory, but partly also because of a significant dilution of the principle of proportionality in the 1993 Criminal Justice Act which, in response to an arguably small but vociferous element among the magistracy, abolished both the recently introduced system of unit fines and, even more importantly, restrictions on the extent to which courts could take into account associated or previous offences. Risk assessment, by contrast, proved to be a more enduring and complex facet of report writing, reflecting a growing emphasis upon public protection and the minimization of risk as core elements of the broader Probation Service remit and penal policy (Kemshall *et al.* 1997).

The prioritization of public protection and harm reduction in the 1991 Criminal Justice Act was reinforced in a raft of subsequent legislation and Home Office publications. Sadly, however, this almost frenetic activity was not always accompanied by a commensurate degree of clarity. On the contrary, the Association of Chief Officers of Probation's document *Guidance on the Management of Risk and Public Protection* (ACOP 1994) was rightly criticized for its 'somewhat embryonic understanding' of risk prediction and predictive instruments, for presenting exemplars 'as if prediction were not plagued by unreliability' and for combining actuarial and clinical methods in 'an haphazard fashion' (Kemshall 1996b, p.138).

Similarly, the first revision of National Standards (Home Office 1995) unhelpfully merged the distinct concepts of risk of recidivism and risk of harm in a new section to be included in all Pre-Sentence Reports and entitled 'Risk to the Public of Re-offending' (Home Office 1995, p.11). Small wonder if, in the face of such confused leadership, probation officers sometimes struggled to separate risk of custody, risk of re-offending and risk of harm (Worrall 1997), as they sought to adapt their report-writing practice to a criminal justice context which has been labelled 'the new penology' (Feeley and Simon 1992) and which is typified by actuarial calculations of risk and probability, a systems management approach, and the aggregation of offenders (Kemshall *et al.* 1997). Small wonder, either, that with the increasing and continuing expectation that probation officers make use of assessment tools such as the Offender Group Reconviction Scale (OGRS; Copas, Ditchfield and Marshall 1994), the Level of Service Inventory – Revised (LSI-R; Andrews and Bonta 1995), the Assessment, Case-recording and Evaluation system (ACE; Roberts *et al.* 1996), and, more recently, the Offender Assessment System (OASys; Home Office 2002), the processes of assessment and, especially, report writing assumed the *appearance*, if not necessarily the appliance, of science.

Sacrificing storytelling on the altars of 'relevance' and regulation

The 'fuzzy thinking' (Kemshall 1995, 1996a; Webb 1996) and semblance of rigour which have characterized this pendulum swing from quasi-clinical to quasi-actuarial assessments of risk have also bedevilled another aspect of the Pre-Sentence Report during its short history to date. In the immediate aftermath of the 1991 Criminal Justice Act, considerable debate took place among probation practitioners and managers about a potentially over-enthusiastic application of the relevance test when considering what to include in, or more precisely what to exclude from, the designated section of the PSR comprising 'relevant information about the offender' (Home Office 1992, p.19). Interestingly, these original National Standards explicitly affirmed the professionalism, skill and expertise of the report writer and located squarely with him/her the task of maintaining an appropriate balance between the extremes of report content which would be either unnecessarily detailed or insufficiently informative for sentencers. They also incorporated a generous, but by no means exhaustive, list of issues which the report writer might deem to be of possible relevance to the offence, the likelihood of re-offending and the sentence of the court, including:

the offender's explanation for the offence, acceptance of responsibility and feelings of guilt or remorse, attitudes, motivation, criminal history, relationships (e.g. family, friends and associates), strengths and skills, and personal problems, such as drug or alcohol misuse, or financial, housing, employment, medical or psychiatric problems. (Home Office 1992, p.15)

However, it was not long before PSR authors with a natural instinct for survival developed a highly circumspect and selective approach to the determination of relevance, despite this early explicit Home Office permission for them to exercise professional judgement in calculating the extent to which information from these or other avenues of enquiry should be included in the final report to court. A disproportionately influential role in the initial stages of their shift towards caution was played by highly exaggerated, if occasionally entertaining, caricatures of the supposedly rambling, unfocused Social Enquiry Reports which PSRs were intended to replace, some anecdotal, others pseudo-academic (Raynor, Smith and Vanstone 1994). In their eagerness to avoid censure, ridicule or any association with outmoded, albeit largely mythical report-writing practices, practitioners often unwittingly and ironically contributed towards the erosion of their own professional autonomy and narrative freedom by choosing to interpret relevance so conservatively as to impose upon themselves a directive to 'when in doubt, leave it out'.

This tendency was further reinforced by the subsequent introduction of more prescriptive National Standards (Home Office 1995), which contained significantly more detailed requirements and considerably less wriggle room with regard to the form and content of PSRs. Although there was still an expectation that the section on relevant information about the offender should set out the strengths as well as the weaknesses of a particular individual, the relatively limited scope for bringing to life a person more multifaceted than his/her criminal profile was evident from:

1. repeated use of the word 'relevant'

2. a failure to articulate any of the personal and social circumstances to be assessed and recorded in a 'concise' and 'selective' manner

3. a strong focus on previous convictions, patterns of offending, response to earlier court sentences, and the suitability of sentencing options (Home Office 1995, p.10).

Add to this the understandable aversion of report writers to falling foul either of mechanistic local 'gatekeeping' procedures, whereby reports are scrutinized by colleagues (often specialist court staff), or of regular regional and national auditing of Pre-Sentence Reports against a strictly enforced checklist devised by H.M. Inspectorate of Probation, and it is unsurprising that interesting, complicated individuals only rarely emerged from reports more commonly and more accurately characterized as 'bland' (Worrall 1997). These reports were often so minimalist in their operationalization of 'recording relevant personal or social information' (Home Office 1995, p.10) as to make it virtually impossible for the reader either to differentiate one particular offender from any other or to be sufficiently curious about, engaged with, or interested in their anodyne, one-dimensional stories to care what may have happened, or might happen, to them.

The narrative appeal of PSRs was hardly enhanced by the advent of even more directive National Standards just after the turn of the century (Home Office 2000, revised 2002). These new practice requirements followed the precedent of their immediate predecessors in closely specifying, albeit modifying, the necessary layout and headings of the PSR. However, they also went considerably further in terms of circumscribing the content of each section, especially the section previously entitled 'Relevant Information about the Offender' and now headed 'Offender Assessment'. Here, whilst a number of areas for possible attention (e.g. family crisis, substance abuse, mental illness, racism, personal background) were qualified by the word 'relevant' or phrases such as 'where directly relevant to the offence' (B8), no such qualifications were attached to consideration of the offender's status in relation to literacy and numeracy, accommodation and employment. As a consequence, PSR authors were henceforth obliged to address these particular issues in *all* of their reports, even where there was manifestly no connection whatsoever between the offence(s) committed and the offender's living arrangements, job status and competency or otherwise in reading, writing and arithmetic. Paradoxically, this meant that pre-sentence assessments for the court were now expressly required to include irrelevant material, and, should they fail to do, were likely to be adjudged 'Not Satisfactory' or 'Very Poor' during Performance Inspection Programmes, despite having been previously lampooned for containing 'material whose relevance to the offence was obscure to say the least' (Raynor *et al.* 1994, p.40).

It would be simplistic, of course, to suggest that these self-contradictory messages about relevance were primarily intended to undermine the autonomy or status of report writers. It would be equally naïve to imagine that inconsistency of this kind made only a coincidental contribution to what has been depicted by Mike Nash as a systematic attempt 'at controlling professional discretion using guidance and rules emanating from the Home Office' (Nash 2003, p.104). Nevertheless, the mandate for PSR authors to routinely address an offender's basic skills, living arrangements and job status was perfectly compatible not only with existing evidence about a correlation between difficulties in these areas and offending (Chapman and Hough 1998; Farrington 1997; Underdown 1998), but also with emerging evidence about the importance of such issues in terms of social exclusion (Social Exclusion Unit 2002) and desistance from crime (Farrall 2002). Unfortunately, the selective exemption of these indicators of structural disadvantage from the usual relevance test was clearly at odds with the principles of National Standards and ran counter to the heavy weighting still attached by the Home Office to other criminogenic factors of a more psychological nature, namely thinking skills deficits, minimization/denial of responsibility and lack of victim empathy.

It was perhaps inevitable, therefore, that report writers faced with increasingly restrictive and illogical regulations of this kind, and under pressure to help meet the often unrealistic referral/completion targets of a range of cognitive-behavioural pathfinder and accredited programmes (see Chapter 1 for more detail), would struggle to maintain their storytelling artistry and any aspirations towards the 'postmodern narratives' advocated by Harris (1996, p.133). It was perhaps similarly inevitable that they would become ever more prone to employing stock phrases of their own devising or borrowed from largely optional, but sometimes compulsory, PSR templates, in order to compile reports more geared towards echoing the language of National Standards and satisfying the requirements of Performance Inspection Programmes than towards assisting sentencers or professional colleagues. At their worst such reports were, and still are, inferior to the often well-crafted, focused Specific Sentence Reports compiled at court and explored in detail in Chapter 5. Certainly, a habitual reader of PSRs prepared during this period would encounter with monotonous regularity almost interchangeable 'identikit' pictures of offenders, whose social circumstances were rarely explained beyond a formulaic account of their problems (or, more bizarrely, their lack of problems) with literacy/numeracy, accommodation and employment. Instead, they were frequently portrayed not so much in terms of their uniqueness and humanity but rather in terms of a predetermined list of characteristics and attributes: 'culpability', 'level of premeditation', consequential/victim awareness, 'positive action', 'patterns of offending', 'response to previous supervision', 'likelihood of re-offending', 'risk of causing serious harm to the public', 'risk of self-harm', 'motivation to change', suitability or otherwise for a community sentence (Home Office 2000, revised 2002, B7–B10).

This process of depersonalization, which saw first the removal of the 'social' from pre-sentence enquiries (Worrall 1997) and, more recently, the shrinkage, if not the disappearance, of the individual, continues to be exacerbated by the Offender Assessment System (OASys; Home Office 2002). Developed jointly by the Prison and Probation Services, OASys is a national system for assessing the risks and needs of offenders, closely associated with the Effective Practice Initiative (Home Office 1998), and designed to inform not only the planning and evaluation of community-based and custodial interventions but also further specialist risk assessments and risk-management procedures. The latest National Standards stipulate that 'a PSR shall…be based on the use of the Offender Assessment System (OASys), when implemented' (Home Office 2000, revised 2002, B5), and it is currently standard practice for report writers to complete the relevant sections of OASys during the course of their enquiries. Much of the task involves entering codes and numbers for subsequent, sometimes automatic, scoring, especially in the embedded Offender Group Reconviction Scale (OGRS; Copas *et al.* 1994) and in a series of sections covering factors identified by a variety of researchers (Home Office 2002, pp.15–18) as being related to offending: accommodation; education, training and employability; financial management and income; relationships; lifestyle and associates; drug misuse; alcohol misuse; emotional well-being; thinking and behaviour; attitudes; health and other considerations. There is a requirement to provide evidence in each of these latter sections in support of the ratings entered against statements about a particular offending-related issue (0 = 'no problems' in that area; 1 = 'some problems'; 2 = 'significant problems'), and to identify corresponding risks and strengths. Whilst this might arguably be seen as a sequence of invitations to eloquent, detailed storytelling and, hence, as a narrative opening, it is more usually considered by report writers to be yet another chore given that these sections, and the other sizeable elements of OASys, do not currently map onto the PSR format and are often, therefore, perceived as generating extra and/or repetitive work.

It would appear from two separate, recent initiatives that the government is not unsympathetic to this perception. For example, in September 2004, a Probation Circular entitled *Pre-Sentence Reports and OASys* acknowledged the frustration of many practitioners, wrestling with the incompatibility of purportedly complementary activities, by announcing the introduction of a revised version of an earlier PSR template which had been issued alongside Version 2 of the electronic Offender Assessment System (e-OASys) and which

> will allow information from OASys to be automatically pulled through into a Word document which can then be edited as necessary. This will

avoid double keying of data and significantly reduce the overall time needed to complete assessments and prepare reports. (Home Office 2004a, p.3)

A few months earlier, in July 2004, the Regulatory Impact Unit of the Cabinet Office had offered similar reassurance when it declared that: 'The introduction of e-OASys will reduce the manual collection of data for pre-sentence reports, removing the need for staff to complete additional forms' (Cabinet Office 2004, p.5). However, a rather worrying adjunct to this earlier announcement was the news that, together with the Probation Service, the Cabinet Office would be brokering an agreement across all courts to adopt a national short-format report intended to be 'pre-populated from OASys' and to ensure 'a shorter and more standardised approach to pre-sentence reports' (Cabinet Office 2004, p.5). A robust challenge to the wisdom of this idea was quickly forthcoming from the National Association of Probation Officers, which in November 2004 called for the immediate cessation of short-format PSRs 'primarily on the basis that their use is incompatible with the new sentencing requirements of the Criminal Justice Act 2003' (Napo News 2004, p.8).

Although stopping short of explicitly acknowledging this potential contradiction between short-format reports and the sentencing implications of recent legislation, the Home Office had hinted, perhaps unintentionally, at a possible clash by recognizing that 'given the complexity of the Community Order (with its 12 possible requirements) and Custody Minus the need for good quality offender assessment at pre-sentence stage will not diminish' (Home Office 2004a, p.3).

It remains uncertain and contentious as to whether this 'need for good quality offender assessment at pre-sentence stage' can be met by short-format reports, even if such reports and e-OASys should, indeed, prove to be as labour-saving and as synchronized as promised. It is also unclear as to precisely when ongoing Home Office modifications to a national PSR template electronically linked to e-OASys will be completed, exactly what the template will look like and when permission will be withdrawn for probation areas to continue using shorter reports of their own design. However, from early versions and local variants of the template, it seems probable that a format which seeks, on the one hand, to mirror the many sections and sub-sections of OASys and, on the other, to satisfy the requirements of National Standards will struggle to facilitate the preparation of genuinely short reports. For example, one local and typical PSR template, which has a standard front-sheet designed to provide details about the offender, the offence(s), the court, the report writer and the sources of information, also contains six major headings and no less than 27 sub-headings, and regularly results in reports running to nine pages or more. In the context of such volume, prescription and fragmentation, further aggravated by the incorporation of 'Yes/No' boxes, a mandatory menu of sentencing options and a readily accessible repertoire of optional stock phrases, the creation of persuasive, bespoke and lucid stories is without doubt exceptionally challenging, albeit not yet entirely impossible.

Reclaiming Pre-Sentence Reports

How then might PSR authors re-appropriate their title of 'storytellers *par excellence*' (Harris 1996, p.118)? Why, indeed, should they even bother trying to do so when the ostensibly easier option is to yield to the seeming inevitability of their literary tradition giving way to the equivalent of 'painting by numbers'? The answer to these questions perhaps lies in the potential of the PSR, even within increasingly stringent constraints, to be a pivotal medium through which the report writer and the offender can *collaboratively* construct and reconstruct a coherent, personal story which endeavours to make sense of past mistakes/misdeeds; integrate present strengths, difficulties and contradictions; and envision a crime-free future. To a limited degree, of course, report writers are already obliged, if variably inclined, to compile reports *with* offenders rather than *on* or *about* them: National Standards (Home Office 2000, revised 2002) require that a PSR should contain 'an outline supervision plan' (B10) and that offenders 'must be aware of the aims of the supervision plan and involved in its formulation' (C11). However, if an offender is to be an active, resourceful agent in a dynamic process of recovery rather than a passive recipient of 'expert' diagnosis, treatment or punishment, s/he needs to be more generally and more authentically included in the preparation of the PSR and, in effect, in the co-authoring of a narrative which seeks 'to reconcile the person he or she was with the one he or she claims to have become' (Toch 2001, p.xvii).

Understandably, neither the viability nor the merits of a more collaborative storytelling approach may be immediately obvious to busy report writers grappling with high workloads, tight deadlines and frequent legislative/policy changes. It is worth, therefore, exploring some of the practice implications of such an approach for each of the four main sections of the PSR as articulated in current National Standards (Home Office 2000, revised 2002, B7–B10), in the hope of demonstrating its potential benefits and of showing how, beyond an initial mental adjustment on the part of report writers, it need not make PSR-writing significantly more complicated or time-consuming a task than is already the case.

Offence Analysis (B7)

An earlier version of National Standards (Home Office 1995) indicated that a primary aim of the 'Offence Analysis' section of the PSR was to explain 'why the offender committed this offence at this time' (p.9). Although this phrase neatly encapsulated an expectation that report writers consider three key aspects of a particular incident – namely the specific offender, the specific offence and the specific timing – its emphasis on causal explanations further encouraged an established approach to report writing inconsistent with the participatory, constructive model proposed here. The disappearance of the phrase from more recent National Standards is, therefore, useful in liberating report writers from any explicit obligation to ask 'why'-oriented questions likely to pathologize offenders in terms of perceived underlying problems and to reinforce dominant narratives about what it means to be a person of validity and worth (Milner 2001; White 1989, 1995). Instead, report writers now have implicit permission to analyse the offence(s) before the court from a perspective which draws a clear distinction between the offender and his/her offending and which does not presuppose that the recurrence of criminal behaviour, or for that matter any other problem, can only be avoided through an interpretation of what caused it to happen in the first place.

This perspective, explicated very persuasively by Judith Milner and Patrick O'Byrne (2002) and developed from solution-focused and narrative approaches pioneered mainly in North America and Australia (see, for example, de Shazer 1988; Jenkins 1990; O'Hanlon and Weiner-Davis 1989; White 1989, 1995), still necessitates a detailed interrogation of the circumstances of the offence. Consequently, it remains as important as ever that report writers should have sophisticated interviewing and communication skills, particularly in terms of questioning, listening and empathy (Egan 1998; Kadushin 1972; Rogers 1965). However, their frame of reference needs to be very different to that of more traditional PSR practitioners, who tend to ask questions based on assumptions about causal links between a person's offending and his/her cognitive or other deficits, and to listen, accordingly, for evidence of those links and deficits. By contrast, a report writer using a constructive approach will be asking questions designed to identify the traditions, beliefs and habits which sometimes restrain a particular offender from behaving as the basically capable and decent citizen s/he is assumed to be, and will be listening for evidence of competence and resistance to those restraints.

The challenge here is for the report writer to frame questions which at once acknowledge an offender's better self and at the same time hold him/her to account for allowing that better self to be silenced. Thus, an assessment of the offender's level of premeditation and culpability might be partly informed by the answers to questions such as 'What legal alternatives to the offence did you consider, however briefly?', 'Who or what dissuaded you from each of these legal alternatives?' and 'How did you try to justify your decision to ignore these legal alternatives (a) at the time? (b) afterwards?' Similarly, an exploration of the extent, if any, to which victims and consequences were considered might be facilitated by questions along the lines of: 'How did you manage to override the victim's wishes/feelings?', 'How did you try to keep the victim out of your mind?' and 'How did you overcome your awareness of what your offending might result in for you/others?' Fundamental to the framing of questions in this way are two presumptions: first, that the majority of offenders have the capacity for law-abiding and non-abusive behaviour, pro-social decision-making, forward thinking and sensitivity to others; second, that they are answerable for allowing whatever it may be that from time to time impairs or neutralizes this capacity (e.g. drink, drugs, peer pressure, rationalization, anger) to triumph over their more responsible selves.

The final requirement in the 'Offence Analysis' section of the PSR to 'indicate whether any positive action has been taken by the offender' (Home Office 2000, revised 2002, B7) is one which is often only perfunctorily addressed by report writers. This is a pity, as it provides an early and welcome invitation to present a more hopeful picture of an individual, hitherto portrayed largely in terms of his/her offending. As such it is potentially the first chapter in a re-storying process, and a strategic opportunity for the report writer to begin 'searching for seeds of solutions in the client's own repertoire while avoiding a search for explanation or cause' (Milner and O'Byrne 2002, p.2).

Offender Assessment (B8)

Given that compatibility with e-OASys is central to the standardized, national PSR template currently being designed, report writers will, as a matter of routine, be expected in the 'Offender Assessment' section of any report to consider each of the factors listed earlier for which, according to research, there is a correlation with offending (Home Office 2002, pp.15–18). However, an increasing tendency for these factors to be described by researchers and policy-makers as 'offending related' rather than 'criminogenic' (i.e. causing, or likely to cause, criminal behaviour) means that PSR authors are not obliged to write about issues such as accommodation, education, etc. in terms of *causality*, but are free, should they see fit, to address them as issues which serve as *obstacles to desistance* from crime.

This is much more than a semantic distinction, not least of all because of the way in which it relocates the offender from a problem-saturated story to a comparatively optimistic narrative, in which s/he is assumed to be capable of and motivated towards desisting from crime, even though s/he may need some support or help in overcoming barriers to doing so. Furthermore, it is a distinction underpinned by the findings of important, recent research (Farrall 2002), which demonstrates a strong association between offenders' desistance from crime and their progress in terms of employment and personal relationships. Obviously, it would be indefensible for report writers to substitute a mechanistic classification of offenders according to disaggregated desistance-related factors for a mechanistic classification of them according to disaggregated criminogenic factors. It remains crucial, therefore, that PSR authors continue to carefully investigate an offender's unique circumstances and personal background in determining the relevance or otherwise of particular data. However, the research provides an evidence-based legitimacy for report writers to prioritize employability and relationships over other factors on the e-OASys inventory, and perhaps especially over thinking skills given that Farrall reports encountering 'very few examples of cognitive behavioural obstacles to desistance' (2004, p.202).

It is equally legitimate for report writers to infer that the obligation 'to evaluate patterns of offending' (Home Office 2000, revised 2002, B8) subsumes the more detailed instructions of earlier National Standards to examine any 'lengthening or shortening of time between convictions' (Home Office 1995, p.10). Close attention to the gaps between previous court appearances is, in effect, a quest for 'exceptions' to the offending behaviour (de Shazer 1988). PSR authors who choose to forensically investigate these exceptions, including in particular any 'near misses', and to question precisely *how* the offender managed to steer clear of trouble during these periods, might appear to be unduly preoccupied with the past. Paradoxically, however, their focus is future-oriented in that meticulous scrutiny of ostensibly crime-free interludes and how they were achieved provides not only invaluable indicators of the offender's proven, if episodic, aptitude for 'going straight', but also vital clues as to how behaviours and strategies which have contributed to these interludes might be repeated, augmented and incorporated into a more enduring success story.

Assessment of the risk of harm to the public and the likelihood of re-offending (B9)

A collaborative, constructive approach to the short but critical risk section of the PSR is highly contingent upon the report writer making a fundamental philosophical shift away from notions of assessing and managing risks towards the discourse of co-constructing safety. This discourse is fully considered elsewhere in the present volume (see Chapter 4), and it will not, therefore, be addressed in detail here. Suffice it to say that for the report writer, two significant corollaries of the necessary philosophical shift are that s/he should include the offender in an assessment of risks and the proposed management thereof (Strachan and Tallant 1997), and that offenders should be held 'accountable for safety rather than for harm...be it for their own safety or for that of others...' (Milner and O'Byrne 2002, pp.141–2).

Once again, there are implicit assumptions here about competency and exceptions to criminality, in this instance in the form of presuppositions that most offenders are capable of understanding the risks which they pose in terms of re-offending, harm to others and self-harm, and that they will have managed those risks more effectively, and more responsibly, on other occasions. In this context the expertise of the PSR author lies not so much in the technically proficient, and often solitary, completion of OGRS, OASys and other specialist risk assessments as in the twofold ability to:

1. involve the offender in collating, scoring and making sense of data required by these instruments

2. ask questions which usefully highlight resources, people and strategies which have facilitated, or might facilitate, alternative, safer behaviours to the offending, violence or self-harm under consideration.

Conclusion (B10)

The concluding section of the PSR, and the specific issues which have to be addressed therein in order to satisfy the requirements of National Standards (Home Office 2000, revised 2002, B10), provide a number of opportunities for narrative partnership and constructive work. Express stipulations to indicate the suitability or otherwise of the offender for a community sentence and to identify the potential impact of a custodial sentence on his/her family circumstances, current employment or education amount to an open invitation to the report writer to confront the court, like a Hollywood preview audience, with alternative endings to a particular story. In responding to the invitation and formulating a proposal, the PSR author has a dramatic opportunity to outline the anticipated implications of competing custodial and non-custodial sentencing disposals, whilst summarizing, sometimes in the offender's own words, a complicated, often contradictory tale in which exceptional instances of valiant resistance to offending vie for ascendancy with examples of weakness and feeble surrender to temptation.

In addition, the obligation for report writers to evaluate the offender's motivation and ability to change includes a codicil to the effect that, 'where relevant', action intended to improve motivation should be identified. This explicit, if somewhat begrudging, acknowledgement of a shared responsibility for motivation resonates with the collaborative ethos of motivational interviewing literature (Miller and Rollnick 2002), and suggests that there is scope for PSR authors to include offenders in the assessment of their own motivation and its possible enhancement, rather than arbitrarily placing them on the Cycle of Change (Prochaska and DiClemente 1994). Similarly, the requirement for report writers to draft an outline supervision plan in cases where either a Community Rehabilitation Order or a Community Punishment and Rehabilitation Order is being proposed encompasses another condition of National Standards (C11), which, in its emphasis on the importance of offenders being aware of the aims of the supervision plan and involved in its formulation, assumes a degree of negotiation and joint ownership of goals perfectly consistent with the principles of best practice. It is crucial that in the mutual drafting of such goals, report writers and offenders work together towards avoiding negatively expressed outcomes (e.g. 'I will not be using drugs' or 'I will avoid being violent'), and towards articulating what will be happening instead, given that stories framed in the language of problematical behaviour 'actually direct clients' attention to that which they are supposed to avoid' (Miller 1997, p.75).

Concluding remarks

The PSR is the culmination of developments in pre-sentence assessments for the courts spanning slightly more than a hundred years, during which time the focus has shifted from salvation via treatment/non-treatment to control, from needs assessment to risk assessment, from the clinical to the actuarial and from individual offenders to aggregated offences. It currently enjoys a centre-stage role as a strategic mechanism for classifying offenders in terms of offence type and risks in a cash-limited, angst-ridden and uncomfortably exposed National Probation Service edging uncertainly into a new millennium and battling for survival. The challenge of routinely constructing collaborative, sophisticated narratives in such a highly pressurized context and within a framework of excessive workloads, strict time limits and increasing standardization, regulation and automation is not underestimated. However, the most adept and most committed PSR authors may yet continue, against all the odds, to produce reports which engage and persuade the reader whilst remaining 'incomplete' and even 'disturbing' (Harris 1996, p.133). The prospects of this seemingly improbable outcome may ultimately hinge upon whether report writers are able to complete the philosophical shift from a problem-orientation to solution talk, to develop a working familiarity with emerging desistance research and, above all, to adapt their existing narrative skills to the ever-tightening constraints of National Standards and the burgeoning, but expandable, compartments of the PSR template.

References

ACOP (Association of Chief Officers of Probation) (1994) *Guidance on the Management of Risk and Public Protection.* Wakefield: Association of Chief Officers of Probation.

Andrews, D.A. and Bonta, J.L. (1995) *Level of Service Inventory – Revised Manual.* Toronto: Multi-Health Systems Inc.

Cabinet Office (2004) *Making a Difference: Reducing Post Sentencing Burdens on Front Line Staff.* London: Regulatory Impact Unit – Public Sector Team, Cabinet Office.

Carter, P. (2003) *Managing Offenders, Reducing Crime: A New Approach.* London: Home Office.

Chapman, D. and Hough, M. (1998) *Evidence Based Practice: A Guide to Effective Practice.* London: Home Office.

Copas, J., Ditchfield, J. and Marshall, P. (1994) *Development of a New Risk Predictor Score.* Research Bulletin 36. London: Home Office RSD.

de Shazer, S. (1988) *Clues: Investigating Solutions in Brief Therapy.* New York: Norton.

Egan, G. (1998) *The Skilled Helper* (6th edition). Pacific Grove, CA: Brooks/Cole.

Farrall, S. (2002) *Rethinking What Works with Offenders: Probation, Social Context and Desistance from Crime.* Cullompton: Willan Publishing.

Farrall, S. (2004) 'Supervision, motivation and social context: What matters most when probationers desist?' In G. Mair (ed.) *What Matters in Probation.* Cullompton: Willan Publishing.

Farrington, D.P. (1997) 'Human development and criminal careers.' In M. Maguire, R. Morgan and R. Reiner (eds) *The Oxford Handbook of Criminology* (2nd edition). Oxford: Clarendon Press.

Feeley, M. and Simon, J. (1992) 'The new penology: Notes on the emerging strategy of corrections.' *Criminology* 30, 4, 449–75.

Harris, R. (1992) *Crime, Criminal Justice and the Probation Service.* London: Routledge.

Harris, R. (1996) 'Telling tales: Probation in the contemporary social formation.' In N. Parton (ed.) *Social Theory, Social Change and Social Work.* London: Routledge.

Home Office (1992) *National Standards for the Supervision of Offenders in the Community.* London: HMSO.

Home Office (1995) *National Standards for the Supervision of Offenders in the Community.* London: Home Office.

Home Office (1998) *Effective Practice Initiative: National Implementation Plan for the Supervision of Offenders.* Probation Circular 35/1998. London: Home Office.

Home Office (2000, revised 2002) *National Standards for the Supervision of Offenders in the Community.* London: Home Office.

Home Office (2002) *Offender Assessment System, User Manual.* London: Home Office.
Home Office (2004a) *Pre-Sentence Reports and OASys.* Probation Circular 53/2004. London: Home Office.
Home Office (2004b) *Reducing Crime – Changing Lives. The Government's Plans for Transforming the Management of Offenders.* London: Home Office.
Jenkins, A. (1990) *Invitations to Responsibility: The Therapeutic Engagement of Men who are Violent and Abusive.* Adelaide: Dulwich Centre Publications.
Kadushin, A. (1972) *The Social Work Interview.* Columbia: Columbia University.
Kemshall, H. (1995) 'Risk in probation practice.' *Probation Journal* 42, 2, 67–72.
Kemshall, H. (1996a) 'Risk assessment: Fuzzy thinking or decisions in action?' *Probation Journal* 43, 1, 2–7.
Kemshall, H. (1996b) 'Offender risk and probation practice.' In H. Kemshall and J. Pritchard (eds) *Good Practice in Risk Assessment and Risk Management, Volume 1.* London: Jessica Kingsley Publishers.
Kemshall, H. (1998) *Risk in Probation Practice.* Aldershot: Ashgate.
Kemshall, H., Parton, N., Walsh, M. and Waterson, J. (1997) 'Concepts of risk in relation to organizational structure and functioning within the personal social services and probation.' *Social Policy and Administration* 31, 3, 213–32.
Miller, G. (1997) *Becoming Miracle Workers: Language and Meaning in Brief Therapy.* New York: Aldine de Gruyter.
Miller, W.R. and Rollnick, S. (2002) *Motivational Interviewing: Preparing People for Change* (2nd edition). New York: The Guilford Press.
Milner, J. (2001) *Women and Social Work: Narrative Approaches.* Basingstoke: Palgrave.
Milner, J. and O'Byrne, P. (2002) *Brief Counselling: Narratives and Solutions.* Basingstoke: Palgrave.
Moore, G. (1984) *The Practice of Social Inquiry.* Aberdeen: Aberdeen University Press.
Napo News (2004) *Important PSR Developments.* Issue 164 (November 2004). London: National Association of Probation Officers.
Nash, M. (2003) 'Pre-trial investigation.' In W.H. Chui and M. Nellis (eds) *Moving Probation Forward.* Harlow: Pearson Education Limited.
O'Hanlon, W.H. and Weiner-Davis, M. (1989) *In Search of Solutions.* New York: Norton.
Prochaska, J.O. and DiClimente, C.C. (1994) *The Transtheoretical Approach: Crossing Traditional Boundaries of Therapy.* Malabar, FL: Krieger.
Raynor, P., Smith, D. and Vanstone, M. (1994) *Effective Probation Practice.* Basingstoke: Macmillan.
Roberts, C., Burnett, R., Kirby, A. and Hamill, H. (1996) *A System for Evaluating Probation Practice.* Oxford: Probation Studies Unit.
Rogers, C. (1965) *Client-centred Therapy: Its Current Practice, Implications and Theory.* Boston: Houghton Mifflin.
Social Exclusion Unit (2002) *Reducing Re-offending by Ex-prisoners.* Wetherby: ODPM Publications.
Strachan, R. and Tallant, C. (1997) 'Improving judgement and appreciating biases within the risk assessment process.' In H. Kemshall and J. Pritchard (eds) *Good Practice in Risk Assessment and Risk Management, Volume 2.* London: Jessica Kingsley Publishers.
Toch, H. (2001) 'Foreword.' In S. Maruna, *Making Good: How Ex-convicts Reform and Rebuild their Lives.* Washington, DC: American Psychological Services.
Underdown, A. (1998) *Strategies for Effective Offender Supervision: Report of the HMIP What Works Project.* London: Home Office.
Webb, T. (1996) 'Reconviction prediction for offenders.' *Probation Journal* 43, 1, 8–12.
White, M. (1989) *Selected Papers.* Adelaide: Dulwich Centre Publications.
White, M. (1995) *Re-Authoring Lives: Interviews and Essays.* Adelaide: Dulwich Centre Publications.
Worrall, A. (1997) *Punishment in the Community: The Future of Criminal Justice.* London: Longman.

Chapter 7

Dangerous Constructions
Black Offenders in the Criminal Justice System

Lena Dominelli

Introduction

'Had Zahid been white, he would not have died'

Trevor Phillips, Chair of the CRE (CRE 2003, p.1)

'Black' offenders[1] are overrepresented in the punitive aspects of the British Criminal Justice System (CJS). Black people of African and Asian descent constitute 6 per cent of the British population (ONS 2002), but form 25 per cent of prison inmates (CRE 2003). Yet they are under represented as employees within the CJS. For example, only 3 per cent of probation officers are 'black' (NACRO 1994; NAPO 1999). Few black lawyers and judges are found within the CJS. The same picture of being absent in positions of authority emerges with respect of senior managers in either the probation or prison service. We have yet to see significant numbers of 'black' people appointed as chief police constables or chief probation officers.[2]

Amidst this depressing picture is a more alarming statistic: the proportion of black offenders in prison is rising faster than that of white offenders as harsher sentences are passed on them (NACRO 1994). And they are harassed more while serving these. The Commission for Racial Equality's (CRE's) report on Zahid Mubarek, a young man of Asian origins murdered in Feltham Young Offenders Institution (Feltham) by a self-proclaimed white racist youth, Robert Stewart, revealed that, while the overall prison population grew by 12 per cent between December 1999 and December 2002, that of the black prison population grew by over 51 per cent during that period (CRE 2003). How do we explain these developments, including the failure of the Prison Service (PS) – now restructured alongside Probation to be part of the National Offender Management Service (NOMS) – to protect those in its care while they serve their custodial sentences?

In this chapter, I use the case of Zahid Mubarek to focus on 'black' offenders in the prison system to explore the construction of the 'black' offender as 'dangerous' and therefore in need of control rather than care. This perception is part of the institutional culture of the Prison Service and permeates relationships between 'black' offenders and 'white' offenders, 'black' offenders and other 'black' offenders, 'black' offenders and 'white' prison officers and probation officers, 'white' offenders and 'white' prison officers and probation officers, and 'black' offenders and 'black' prison officers and probation officers. Additionally, the 'black' offender is created in a process of 'othering' that links the 'black' offender with the 'white' offender and involves both in the creation of the stereotypes that are applied to each. In other words, racialized dynamics become embedded within the institutional culture and influence all those living in that environment, whether they are members of staff or inmates. Moreover, I argue that this institutional culture is constantly being created and recreated to take account of factors that emerge both within the institution and outwith it and is crucial in promoting racial discrimination in the Prison Service at the personal, institutional and cultural levels.

Racial discrimination

Zahid Mubarek was a 19-year-old offender serving a three-month prison sentence at Feltham for stealing razors worth £6, interfering with a motor vehicle and failing to deal with his drug problems. He was battered to death a few hours before his release on 21 March 2000, while he was asleep, by his white cellmate, 19-year-old Robert Stewart, who was a self-confessed racist. Initially, Mubarek's parents were refused a public inquiry into his death. But in November 2004, the Law Lords ordered David Blunkett, the then Home Secretary, to hold a public inquiry into this murder. He agreed to it, and the inquiry, chaired by Mr Justice Keith, is due to report in early 2006. Meanwhile, several other inquiries into the murder have been undertaken. One of these, held under the aegis of the CRE, reported in July 2003 with a formal finding of unlawful discrimination. It confirmed Stewart's violent history, much of it evidenced in the 200 letters he wrote from prison. The CRE also found over 20 system failures within the Prison Service, each of which, if acted upon, offered opportunities for dealing with Stewart and thus could have prevented the murder. An inquiry a year earlier had found that the Feltham Young Offenders Institution perpetrated institutional racism. The interaction between prison inmates and staff created the racialized identities that lay at the heart of this event.

Identity is formed through social interactions between people in a process whereby each creates the other while being created him/herself. Thus, no one person is created in and of him/herself. This dynamic holds regardless of the particular aspect of identity that is being considered. And since human beings are multidimensional entities with many social divisions that can be applied to them, identity has to be understood as multidimensional and fluid. However, as identity is socially constructed, a person can choose to focus on a particular element of it for a given purpose. Because this chapter is about the racialization of identity, I shall focus on the socially constructed but fraught term 'race' and the racist dynamics that accompany its formation, production and reproduction in the social arena. But while I focus largely on 'race', the reader should not forget that 'race' is gendered and otherwise fractured across a number of social divisions including class, age, disability and sexual orientation. It would be easy to overlook this element given that the discourses about Zahid Mubarek treat 'race' as a homogeneous category, even when acknowledging that Zahid was part of a category of 'black' offenders known as 'Asian'. This term is itself problematic when used to classify people because it includes people whose origins are in the Indian subcontinent, China and other parts of the geographical region known as Asia and with diverse ethnicities, socio-political formations, religious and other cultural attributes.

The racialization of identity in ways that privilege some groups over others is a socially constructed process that is evident in many aspects of British society, not just in the Prison Service, and there is a vast array of literature that attests to this point (Ahmad 1993; Brown 1984; Dominelli 1988; Fernando 1988; Kelaher *et al.* 2003). Although at one level each individual's identity is unique, at other levels it is part of a broader collective grouping or groupings. These other dimensions may or may not emerge in any one social transaction. Whether they do or not depends on what a particular individual is seeking to achieve. So, for example, when a 'black' middle-class woman is talking to a 'black' middle-class man, she may focus on the gendered differences between them while forging connections with him on the basis of 'race'. But in a discussion with a 'white' middle-class woman, she might wish to focus solely on the racialized aspects of her identity, especially if the 'white' woman appears to ignore these when emphasizing similarities in their experiences of gender (Hill Collins 1990; Lorde 1984). In other words, 'race' may be gendered and classed, but references to these particular aspects of their experience will depend on the context in which an interaction takes place and the objectives that those involved in the interaction seek to achieve (Morrison 1984; hooks 1989, 1990).

Postmodernists (Modood, Beishon and Virdee 1994; Nicholson 1990) have cautioned readers against the use of identity attributes to suggest that these are either monolithic, homogeneic or essentialist. However, borrowing from Sandra Harding (1990) and Nancy Hartsock (1987), I would argue that, in social discourses, identity is usually socially constructed from a particular standpoint that might produce these precise forms of identity. Indeed, I intend to show in this chapter that Robert Stewart constructed Zahid Mubarek as an essentialized black man – a stereotypical figure that he could hate and ultimately murder to get himself out of Feltham. In other words, Stewart used the process of 'othering' to subordinate Mubarek's unique personality to his own ends and deny its existence in a setting that allowed him to do so unchecked.

I define racism as the abuse of people on the basis of 'race'. It becomes a form of social interaction that racializes identities to create a binary dyad of superiority and inferiority in which those subscribing to a racist view of the world configure some people's physical and social characteristics as superior and others as inferior. This casting of relationships is normalized to accord those deemed 'superior' with greater power and privileges than those categorized as 'inferior' and supports racialized relations of domination. It is integrated into everyday routines so that an individual from an allegedly superior grouping does not have to consciously designate a particular interaction as one that draws upon racist dynamics. A person holding a racist world-view allocates all people into this binary schema and reserves the privileged one for him/herself. In doing so, he/she produces the phenomenon of *othering* whereby an 'in-group' and an 'out-group' are formed. Consequently, racism creates forms of social inclusion and exclusion, with those encompassed by the former benefiting from racial supremacy, while the latter respond to racial oppression in a variety of ways (Dominelli 2002, 2004).

'Othering' I define as an active process of interaction that creates and re-creates dyadic social relations in which one group is socially dominant and others are socially subordinate. This occurs when an encounter with another is used to organize social relations to establish a superior–inferior dyadic relationship as the context in and through which the domination of one group by another is perpetuated. In 'othering' dynamics, physical or cultural attributes are used as signifiers of inferiority or superiority and create spaces whereby the one cast as 'superior' distances him/herself from those classified as 'inferior'. During this interaction, the dominant group is constructed as 'subject' and the oppressed group as 'object' (Dominelli 2002, 2004).

'Othering' also contains elements of normalization within its dynamics. The 'Other' is different from the norm, and is usually judged negatively as a result. As racist dynamics assume that 'whiteness' is the norm, an individual who is 'white' does not need to identify him/herself as a 'white' person. This is part of the privileging of 'whiteness' (Dominelli 1988; Frankenberg 1997; Lorde 1984) and can be taken for granted. Stewart perceives of himself simply as a person and usually refers to himself in the first person. He never refers to himself as a 'white' person, although he talks about his friends in the north west as '*white* friends' (my emphasis) and the people there as '*white* people' (my emphasis), and bleaching his sheets 'white' to 'make a Klu Klux Klan outfit'. He does not refer to people as 'white' when he is juxtaposing them to 'black' people, as, for example, the skinheads in the *Romper Stomper* film and those who killed Stephen Lawrence. He associates these people with his views of himself and, like him, they do not need to have their racialized identities spelt out.

Moreover, racist discourses position people as those who have *agency* and those who do not. In this, the privileged 'race' is accorded *subject* status and the power to act, while the subordinate one is given *object* status and denied the power to order the world in its own interests. Such interactions create the subject to object relationships that are crucial to a racist configuration of social reality. Stewart is constantly configuring himself as in control, or the subject of social interactions involving him, and when this is not verified in reality, he reacts with violence to resume the upper hand, as he does when slamming his bat on the table when he loses at table tennis.

However, racialized relationships of domination can only be enacted in this way if the person at the receiving end accepts that this is how social relationships should be conducted. In reality, the persons involved in these interactions may accept, accommodate or reject such framings of their relationship and re-story them in other ways. Mubarek did try to resist Stewart's ordering of the world by requesting transfers to other cells, but these were ignored. A prison officer using a constructive approach could have intervened at this point to affirm Mubarek's agency and support him in this trajectory; that is, to become more self-assertive. At the same time, another prison officer could have worked with Stewart to acknowledge the agency of others and decentre him as the centre of the world. By helping him to see the significance that abusing power has in sustaining a fragile sense of self, Stewart could have been helped to become less controlling and more able to engage more appropriately with others. Ultimately, these prison officers could have worked together to facilitate Mubarek's and Stewart's interaction with each other as subjects – that is, people who are both in charge of their environment – and to help propel them into more egalitarian and life-affirming relationships. In egalitarian relationships, both groups of participants act as subjects; that is, they form *subject-to-subject relationships* in which each person exercises agency and negotiates a position that both find satisfying (Dominelli 2002, 2004).

Racist dynamics highlight the racialization of both subject and object identities. Thus, understanding racist constructions of 'whiteness' (Frankenberg 1997) is as important as understanding the racist construction of 'blackness' (Fanon 1963, 1968) and the opposition to it mounted by 'black' people like those participating in the 'negritude movement', for example Aimé Césaire, Leopold Senghor, Léon Gontran Damas and Sekou Toure (Diawara 1998), or Africentric movement (Asante 1987). As evidenced in his letters, Robert Stewart was aware of racist constructions of reality. The film *Romper Stomper*, about ('white', unstated) Australian skinheads assaulting Vietnamese refugees, was symbolic for him. He used it to juxtapose 'whiteness' and 'blackness' and portray 'black' people as losers at the hands of 'white' supremacists. Important parts of his repertoire in achieving this objective within his own epistemological framework included that of dehumanizing 'black' people by referring to them in derogatory terms and distancing himself from them. Such statements, made in the letters he wrote to his friends, reveal his 'othering' of Zahid Mubarek[3] and his use of racist stereotypes to disparage and deny Mubarek's personhood.

Mubarek, as his cellmate, was aware of the danger Stewart posed and, according to his father, had asked to be moved from the cell that they were required to share on several occasions. But his requests were ignored by prison staff and so they became implicated in the untenable situation that Mubarek remained within. He had also told other inmates that he was frightened that Stewart was a member of the National Front. That none seemed able to support his requests show how an institutional culture can absorb individual resistance to being treated in a particular manner. It also evidences Goffman's (1961) findings that in a total institution, the needs of those residing within it are seldom met.

Stewart was self-centred, and portrayed all situations in terms of what he wanted or thought he needed. He was the subject; the others were objects of his will. Stewart's desire to control others and define them in his terms was apparent in his attitudes not only to 'black' people but also to women, as indicated in his letters. He writes to one of his 'friends':

> Dat Denton bird aint faxed back. Tell her to buck up her ideas. I don't want
> to fax her again. Become a 'stalker'. Just tell her the fex [facts] and if you

find any!!! horrible slapper's wiv no friends, I'll be there friend. It's how I like em.

Thus, Stewart was capable of oppressing on both racial and gender dimensions with equanimity.

Creating the 'Other' within the prison setting

Unlike Zahid Mubarek, who was experiencing his first spell in prison, Robert Stewart, as a young person who had been convicted 19 times for 73 offences, including assault, was a seasoned traveller in the corridors of HMS prisons and understood prison politics. His letters indicate that he was also familiar with 'white' supremacist discourses and icons and used them regularly to validate his beliefs, legitimate his behaviour and rationalize his motives. These are evidenced by his references to Hitler and other murderers as role models, and to films in which 'black' people are attacked by 'white' supremacists. That he draws on icons from countries other than Britain is irrelevant. His identity is tied into 'whiteness' and transcends borders except for his desire to remain attached to the north west or the Manchester area where he was born and which he associates with 'white' people, thereby metaphorically obliterating any 'black' people who live and/or were born there. He also verbalizes these feelings when he threatens to 'nail bomb Bradford, Moss Side [part of Manchester] – all those non-white areas'. Drawing on images of 'whiteness' to build and validate his own self-image required him to contrast himself to Mubarek and construct himself in opposition to him. So Stewart creates himself by creating Mubarek as the 'Other'. Understanding these dynamics might have enabled a prison officer to intervene with alternative constructs in working towards changing Stewart's sense of himself as someone who can only survive on racist constructs of himself and others.

Stewart's cool calculations and rationality are also evident in his letters. He hates both his location and the racialized identity that he associates with the place; that is, one dominated by black inmates. He is determined to leave Feltham where he describes the conditions as 'shite'. He cannot see himself 'stickin in ere' and is prepared to 'take extreme measures' and 'kill me fuckin padmate if I have to'. In this construction of events, Stewart reduces Mubarek as a means for reaching his ends. Additionally, his racism allows him to dehumanize Mubarek and, in denying him personhood, affirms his right to control him and commit violent acts against him when the time comes. Prison officers could have intervened to re-configure Mubarek as a human being. However, the evidence given at the Keith Inquiry shows that the prison officers would be unlikely to do this because they themselves subscribed to derogatory constructs of black inmates whom they humiliated, disparaged and sent into the segregation unit in disproportionate numbers.

Stewart also demonstrates that he has analysed his situation and knows how to play the system because the prison officers at Feltham 'don't know me like those at Hindley [where he was in custody earlier]'. He also knows his rights and is willing to 'admit to some shit' or minor crimes he has committed to get out of gaol and have a 'nice spell up [in the] North West [where he originates from]'. This area he identifies with 'whiteness', which he associates with 'Granada TV, hear[ing] some real accents, see[ing] some white people'. And even at the end, he is rational enough to take advantage of the disarray caused by the discovery of the fatally wounded Mubarek for, when transferred to a nearby cell, he washes his blood-stained hands and clothes before a forensic team can collect incriminating evidence and leaves a message about 'white' supremacists achieving their ends by murdering 'black' people.

This formulation of his reality is in contrast with the non-real accents and 'black' people that he claims make up '3 quarters of the jail'. So, having been placed in an environment where he feels he is a minority, Stewart casts 'black' people as a threat to him. In other words, they are 'dangerous' because they threaten his 'white' identity, symbolized also by his repeated references to the film *Planet of the Apes*. That this view of the world is not reflected in objective reality is immaterial: as the transcripts of the inquiry conducted under Mr Justice Keith indicate, 'black' inmates made up no more than 8 per cent of the population at the time he was in Feltham. His perceptions would have been strengthened by virtue of the fact that he, but not other ('white') offenders, was sharing a cell with a 'black' person. So Zahid Mubarek became a signifier of a situation that Stewart found intolerable. That none of the prison staff picked up either on Stewart's failure to adjust to this aspect of the reality he was living within at Feltham or to protect Mubarek from his murderous intentions led to an innocent bystander copping it for a racist system (CRE 2003).

Besides his internal world and the rationalizations that he created for himself through his environment, Stewart was also able to draw upon a prison culture that endorsed racist behaviour and the degradation and humiliation of 'black' prisoners. According to the transcripts released as part of the ongoing inquiry into Mubarek's death, the prison officers had designated 'Osprey' wing in Feltham for 'bad' prisoners and used it to house primarily 'black' inmates as a form of punishment, thus indicating that they were 'dangerous' and to be guarded against. Their having such an outlet was crucial to their strategy of controlling 'black' prisoners and keeping them in their place and was known amongst both officers and inmates in Feltham. While the labelling of prisoners as 'bad', 'mad' or 'sad' is typical of many prisons including those housing women (Worrall 1990), the epithet 'dangerous' is applied largely to 'black' offenders (Dominelli 1983) and is multilayered. The use of labels associated with women offenders, 'black' and 'white', in institutions housing men also reflects the changing nature of gendered and racialized social relations, as research and lived experience reflect shifting realities in the social world. 'Black' men who stepped out of line have been considered 'dangerous' to the status quo for some time and, as Hall *et al.* (1978) demonstrated in their study, the 'black' man as a potential criminal was always 'dangerous'.

Osprey wing was particularly important in Feltham's regime of institutionalized racism. As the transcripts depict it, Osprey wing was the 'bad' boys' wing and used to punish those who misbehaved. The unit was considered a 'basic unit'; that is, one without TV or other facilities, and one that had a disproportionately high percentage of 'black' prisoners. As one of the officers testifying to the inquiry put it: 'My line manager perceived Osprey as the wing to put more difficult prisoners…for sustained periods.'

'Difficult' in this instance becomes a code word for 'black' because the questioner was probing the differentiated treatment of 'black' prisoners. And so, who the people were rather than the offences they had committed became a crucial determinant of how prison officers and inmates responded to one another. The message that 'black' offenders needed more controls to contain their 'dangerousness' than 'white' ones became part of the cultural norms within the institution. It did not need to be spelt out in so many words, but everyone knew it. And so, Osprey became part of the cultural mythology that legitimated racist practices at both institutional and personal levels. It also demonstrates how the three dimensions of racism – personal, institutional and cultural – interact with and feed off each other.

Personal racism refers to the attitudes or beliefs that individuals hold and use to guide their actions and behaviour. Institutional racism is about the policies and practices that make up daily routines in a given organization. Cultural racism relates to the values and norms that typify a particular society and cement individual relationships into a recognizable whole (Dominelli 1988). In his behaviour, Stewart displays the interlinkages between personal, institutional and cultural racism and how they intersect and interact with each other in specific situations and contexts. Stewart's personal racism is evident in his ontological view of the world and how he portrays himself and others as racialized beings, even though his personal construct of himself as 'white' is by association with 'white' supremacist culture and icons.

The institutional racism permeating prison life comes across in the various inquiries into the murder of Zahid Mubarek. The transcripts to the inquiry and the CRE's (2003) report on the matter indicate that prison officers discriminated against 'black' prisoners in a variety of ways – a fact that was picked up by offenders, 'black' and 'white'. One can add that the passing of a custodial sentence on Mubarek for fairly minor offences, even if it was because he failed to tackle his drug problem as claimed in the transcripts of the inquiry, was another instance of institutional racism and one which brings the broader criminal justice system into the picture. It is unlikely that a 'white' male offender would have been subjected to such a sentence. Moreover, institutional racism draws upon more generalized racist discourses in society. These are evident in the media, social policy and everyday life. For example, one only has to pick up the newspapers to find negative depictions of refugees and asylum seekers portrayed in these outlets to get a sense of how pervasive racist stereotypes are in contemporary Britain.

Whilst some of the institutional racism prevailing in this facility constituted of indirect discrimination in the eyes of the CRE, it served to keep 'black' prisoners in their place. Other failings suggestive of institutional racism include prison officers' failure to read Stewart's files when he was transferred from Hindley, placing a self-proclaimed racist with a 'black' prisoner when apparently there were other options available at Feltham and the delay in reporting the attack and getting medical treatment to Mubarek. The CRE (2003) report catalogued over 20 such failings. One, admitted by the then Director General of the Prison Service, Martin Narey, concerned the failure of prison procedures to be observed and the failure to 'unearth the racism in his [Stewart's] correspondence', although a prison officer had noted this problem in one of Stewart's earlier spells in Feltham. Additionally, the Mubarek family felt this institutionalized racism when they visited their son in prison. His father claimed that they were treated differently to 'white' visitors. It was evident in the officers' attitudes and the way they looked at them. The officers were 'harsh' towards them and 'pushed them around' as if they were prisoners too.

A report into racist practices at Feltham compiled by Satvinder Buttar (2004) for the Hounslow Racial Equality Council found evidence of widespread racial abuse from some 'white' prison officers. They were given examples of where fights involving a 'black' and a 'white' offender resulted in the 'white' prisoner being left on the unit, while the 'black' one would be taken to the segregation unit. Moreover, 'black' prisoners were twice as likely to be restrained as 'white' ones. Additionally, the report evidenced how some 'black' prison officers would ignore reports of racial abuse so as not to antagonize their 'white' colleagues, thus colluding with the perpetuation of racist dynamics at Feltham.

Intimidation is a powerful force in securing compliance amongst groups that are being oppressed. That it can be subtle and covert does not detract from its capacity to shape human behaviour in particular ways. This structuring of social relations within the prison environment also indicates that both 'black' and 'white' staff have been drawn into the reproduction of racist dynamics. Furthermore, these practices would have added to a culture of disparaging 'black' inmates, legitimating racist behaviour and showing how both 'black' and 'white' prison officers and inmates become enmeshed in racist dynamics at the personal, institutional and cultural levels.

Care or control?

The issue of providing 'care' and 'control' for offenders whilst in custody is a contested one. Politicians vary their approach to the Prison Service between focusing on caring for the offender to ensure his (most offenders are men) welfare, rehabilitation and subsequent return to the community (at least in theory) and punishing them by controlling every aspect of their lives. Modern prisons, according to Bauman (2000), have become warehouses for offenders and there is little concern for their longer-term well-being or what will happen to them once they leave these institutions. The more welfare-oriented approach to offenders signalled by the 1991 Criminal Justice Act was jettisoned when Michael Howard became British Home Secretary and promoted the 'what works' approach to imprisonment. His view was that someone who was in prison could not commit other crimes, and so the prison system was effective in meeting its objectives. This approach has been affirmed by subsequent Home Secretaries. But, as the murder of Zahid Mubarek shows, horrendous crimes can and do happen within its borders. As the Mubarek family have insisted, the Prison Service had a duty to care for their son. Because it did not do so, they continue to challenge his treatment through the courts, using the Human Rights Act to pursue their concerns.

Racist dynamics are produced when a racially dominant person or group exercises *power over* relations to control people they deem racially inferior. These are heavily implicated in a denial of the duty to care for people who are 'black', regardless of whether they are prison inmates, staff, or the lay man or woman on the street or in their home. Figure 7.1 indicates the complex variety of mechanisms through which this racialized control occurs.

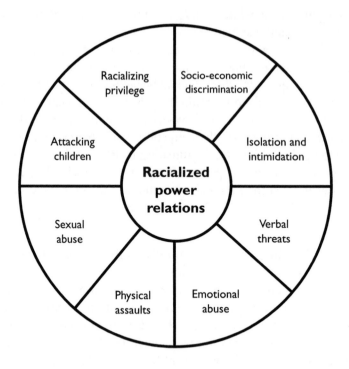

Figure 7.1: Controlling racialized relations. Compiled from Dominelli, L. (2002) Anti-Oppressive Social Work Theory and Practice, *London, Palgrave.*

We see that many of these mechanisms had been utilized in Feltham and that they were employed not only by Robert Stewart, but also by both inmates and prison officers within the custodial facility. Their enactment takes place within the generalized context of the racialized privileging of 'white' prison officers and inmates. The isolation of Mubarek as an 'Asian' prisoner was evident in his being placed with Stewart rather than with another 'Asian' prisoner. Stewart was able to use this to his advantage to intimidate Mubarek by fixing him with his 'stare' – all day long, as Mubarek told his father. This, alongside the derogatory language that Stewart used in referring to 'black' people, can also be construed as part of a sustained attempt at emotional abuse. Stewart also had 'RIP' and a cross tattooed onto his forehead which could also be considered intimidating, especially when placed within the context of his racist taunts. Some allegations placed before the inquiry suggest that prison officers provoked fights between 'black' and 'white' inmates and placed 'bets' on them. These constitute physical attacks on 'black' offenders, even if they fall far short of the murderous one that killed Mubarek. So, in that respect, Stewart was merely taking a particular approach to 'black' inmates to its logical conclusion.

There are many examples of Stewart being depicted as the racially privileged one when he is counterposed to 'black' offenders. However, Stewart is himself low on the pecking order of 'superior' beings within the prison system. He is reported not to have had any friends amongst the other inmates at Feltham and, according to those testifying at the inquiry, was commonly referred to as 'Madman', 'Sicko' or 'weird'. This, plus the bravado in his letters to his friends, suggests a troubled as well as troubling personality.

Whilst this in no way detracts from holding him responsible and accountable for his behaviour (long before he murdered Mubarek), the reader is entitled to ask a question about what Stewart was trying to cover up by his attitudes and lifestyle. Did his own feelings of inadequacy, as indicated by his aggression at losing games of table tennis, loneliness and worthlessness get transposed onto Mubarek? Was he trying to kill what he hated most in himself when he murdered his cellmate? These questions may never receive answers other than those of crude psychology. But they do highlight how children whose childhood traumas are not addressed can go on to become tyrants and bullies who abuse others, including causing their deaths (Miller 1981, 1983).

Stewart had a 'troubled childhood' and got into trouble with the authorities for arson on several occasions in his early teens. Why did he not get the help he deserved then? This question could have been answered differently if someone had worked with Stewart to validate his hurts and set him on a healing path that could have eventually affirmed him as a valued person with rights to a healthy lifestyle. Or even after he was convicted, when psychiatrists, mental health nurses and prison officers at different stages in his criminal career identified disturbing behavioural problems, or labelled him as a 'very dangerous young man', why was he not given the personal support he needed to change his behaviour and turn his life around? Stewart was only 19 years old when he killed the 19-year-old Mubarek and he had been inside the young offenders' custodial system since the age of 13. On this basis, the Prison Service has to be held accountable for letting both Mubarek and Stewart down. This criticism holds even if the Prison Service had concluded, as did a mental health nurse who examined Stewart in 1999, that he was 'untreatable'. Why was no one else consulted, even at this point? And if Stewart was 'untreatable', what other mechanisms or systems could have been used to control his 'dangerousness' to himself (he had attempted self-harm on several occasions) and others?

A prison officer or probation officer attempting to intervene might think that Stewart is beyond the assistance that could be provided through constructive social work. This outcome has to be considered a very real possibility. Work undertaken with young skinheads in London by Phil Cohen (1989) indicated that it might not be possible to fundamentally alter the attitudes of young racists. Additionally, the demonizing of young offenders and the 'trashing' of both 'black' and 'white' inmates by society in general and prison officers in particular contribute to the presumption of their being unworthy of treatment and perpetuate the belief in the impossibility of working in ways that are consistent with constructive theory. Moreover, the culture of the prison itself mitigates against it.

Prisoners' views of other inmates and their assessments of them are usually circulated fairly quickly around a closed institution and they soon reach the ears of the prison officers and other staff. So, why were their concerns about Stewart's instability and aggression not picked up by any of the staff until after Mubarek's murder? Even Malcolm Nicholson, who responded to the alarm that Stewart set off while attacking Mubarek, failed to respond appropriately to the situation by radioing for help, getting prompt medical attention to the injured man, taking steps to restrain the attacker even if only to tell him to 'drop the stick' (as his senior colleague did a few minutes later, but after Stewart had struck the dying Mubarek with further blows) or following procedure, despite seeing that Mubarek was 'injured around the head and covered in blood'. Although he justifies his action as 'I must have realised at this stage that the injury to Mr Mubarek was serious but I was shocked and it had not really sunk in that his injuries could be life-threatening', the reader is entitled to ask, would he have reacted in a like manner if the man lying in a pool of blood had been Stewart? By asking such questions, the assumptions about people's behaviour can be exposed. In an institution threaded with racist dynamics, an officer's expectation, albeit unstated, that violent or *dangerous* 'black' offenders would behave in this manner might have prompted him to radio for help and not leave the injured 'white' man's side until others came to his assistance, thereby ensuring that no further beating took place. Within Feltham's racist culture which legitimated a certain amount of 'white' on 'black' violence, one framing of the situation could be that the greater acceptability of seeing a supposedly superior 'white' individual assault a sleeping 'black' man could have produced the shock that dulled the procedural requirement that should have been enacted as second nature in a well-trained prison officer: of taking immediate action to prevent further harm being done to the person being assaulted.

Sadly neither these issues nor these questions are new. The Prison Service has been condemned before for not addressing adequately its 'race relations' problems (Genders and Player 1989). Despite several revisions to its policies, the creation of a Prison Service Race Relations Group (PSRRG) in 1998 to enhance race relations in the service, and the formation of projects such as RESPOND and RESPECT, little appears to have changed in the intervening period. Clements (2002) conducted a review of the literature that echoed findings similar to those uncovered by Genders and Player (1989) and Burnett and Farrell (1994) earlier. These found verbal abuse, threats and other forms of racial discrimination and a differentiated use of discretion that favoured 'white' inmates, especially in receiving scarce resources such as jobs, as well as inadequate attention paid to religious and other dietary requirements.

These considerations raise broader questions which are also shaped by the appalling state of Feltham itself: staff supervision was negligible, staff illness was high, recruitment of new staff was low, prisoners were 'demoralized' and treated like 'animals'. Evidence given to the inquiry suggests that there appeared to be no one in charge of the administration and good governance of the facility. As one prison officer commenting on this state of affairs put it, 'there was no structure there at all'. In such circumstances, the unexpected can easily become the reality. This context could have been altered through interventions aimed at creating alternative stories of life within the prison setting and thus initiating movement in the organizational culture that could have produced behavioural changes amongst both inmates and staff in the prison, 'black' and 'white'. Re-storying the possibilities of place can become important in transforming policies and practices in a total institution like the prison setting. Management can play a key role in this by facilitating organizational change and supporting officers engaging in innovative forms of practice.

What happened to the management of Feltham? A number of earlier inquiries into the establishment, including one conducted by Sir David Ramsbotham, when Chief Inspector of Prisons, had found it seriously deficient. But it seems that not much had changed by the time that Mubarek was murdered. Both the CRE's (2003) report and that published by Buttar (2004) are optimistic that Feltham can be turned around. Earlier, a report compiled by the Chief Inspector of Prisons after a team examined Feltham in 2002 concluded that it was 'off the critical list' because its 'culture, regime and vision were fundamentally changed'.

However, my analysis of the situation prevailing at the time of Mubarek's death shows that the matter is much more complex and profound than had been anticipated, and so I am not convinced that the changes of personnel and structures introduced thus far will produce a less oppressive prison environment for either inmates or staff. An institution that takes juveniles aged 15 to 17 and young offenders aged 17 to 21 from a large catchment area that covers 120 courts is a complex organization that requires skilled expertise in complicated human relations, crowd control, governance and resource management. This is difficult to find and therefore acts as a major barrier to reform.

Also central to my critique of the current initiatives being taken is my scepticism about the increasing attraction of running the Prison Service through poorly trained staff, checklists, decontextualized skills, 'scientific' risk management training and budget reductions in crucial areas of work including the rehabilitation of offenders. In the absence of a strategy that focuses on undoing the bad habits an inmate has learnt prior to arrival at a custodial facility, invests considerable human and financial resources in rehabilitating offenders by making them capable of returning to live in communities as productive members of those communities who are tolerant of diversity, and works with people in those communities to help support and befriend the returning convict I continue to think that the path to change currently adopted will prove barren.

Conclusion

Feltham has served its inmates and staff, 'black' and 'white', badly. But only a young man of 'Asian' descent lost his life over its failures. The situation of 'black' offenders being constructed as lesser people because they are 'black' and therefore discriminated against on the basis of 'race' is not acceptable. Fundamental changes are necessary to ensure that 'black' offenders are not cast as 'objects' who should be satisfied with what they get, however appalling this may be. Also, 'black' people should not be configured as 'dangerous' offenders who have to be subjected to more mechanisms of control than are used in handling their 'white' counterparts. Dealing with these problems requires the Home Office to rethink its approach to prisons and its treatment of offenders, 'black' and 'white', in its entirety. It also has to find ways of working differently with its 'black' and 'white' staff in these institutions, especially if they are expected to uphold the human rights of offenders entitling them to 'care' as a key part of their remit alongside their concern to 'control' unacceptable behaviour.

Notes

1. I use the term 'black' within a context of racialized identities. 'Black' simply refers to those at the receiving end of racist dynamics in British society. It is not intended as a descriptor for a person's or group's identity. Similarly, the term 'white' refers to those who see themselves as those who define which 'race' becomes accepted as the norm and therefore 'superior'.

2. Since writing this article, a couple of appointments have made a small dent in this picture. In December 2004, Carol Bernard was appointed Regional Offender Manager of Wales, having earlier served as Chief Officer for Northamptonshire as the first 'black' woman (or man) in such positions. Anne Scott, after lobbying for the promotion of 'black' officers into the senior ranks of the police service, was seconded for two years as the General Secretary for the National Black Police Officers Association at the end of December 2004.

3. I have not reproduced the terms that Stewart used. This is because I do not wish to give them additional circulation and currency. They are available to anyone who wishes to read them in the transcripts of the official inquiry into Zahid Mubarek's murder. These are available via the CRE website www.cre.gov.uk and also via www.monitoring-group.co.uk.

References

Ahmad, W. (ed.) (1993) *'Race' and Health in Contemporary Britain*. Buckingham: Open University Press.

Asante, M. (1987) *The Africentric Idea*. Philadelphia: Temple University Press.

Bauman, Z. (2000) 'Issues of law and order.' *British Journal of Criminology* 40, 205–21.

Brown, C. (1984) *Black and White Britain: The Third Policy Studies Institute Survey*. London: Heinemann.

Burnett, R. and Farrell, G. (1994) *Reported and Unreported Racial Incidents in Prisons*. Oxford: The University of Oxford, Centre for Criminological Research, Occasional Paper No. 14.

Buttar, S. (2004) *Racial Abuse at Feltham Youth Prison*. London: Hounslow Council for Racial Equality.

Clements, J. (2002) 'Diversity and equality: Making a new future around racial equality.' *Prison Service News*, July/August.

Cohen, P. (1989) *Tackling Common Sense Racism: Cultural Studies Perspectives Annual Report*. London: Cultural Studies.

CRE (Commission for Racial Equality) (2003) *Report on Zahid Mubarek*. London: CRE.

Diawara, M. (1998) *In Search of Africa*. Cambridge, MA: Harvard University Press.

Dominelli, L. (1983) *Women in Focus: Report on Women Offenders and Community Service Orders*. Warwick: Department of Applied Social Studies.

Dominelli, L. (1988) *Anti-Racist Social Work*. London: Macmillan/Palgrave. Second edition published in 1997; third edition forthcoming.

Dominelli, L. (2002) *Anti-Oppressive Social Work Theory and Practice*. London: Palgrave.

Dominelli, L. (2004) *Social Work: Theory and Practice for a Changing Profession*. Cambridge: Polity Press.

Fanon, F. (1963) *Wretched of the Earth*. London: Penguin.

Fanon, F. (1968) *Black Skins, White Masks*. London: MacGibbon and Kee.

Fernando, S. (1988) *Mental Health, Race and Culture*. London: Macmillan.

Frankenberg, R. (1997) *Displacing Whiteness: Essays in Social and Cultural Criticism.* London: Duke University Press.

Genders, E. and Player, E. (1989) *Race Relations in Prison.* Oxford: Clarendon Press.

Goffman, E. (1961) *Asylums.* London: Penguin.

Hall, S., Critchen, C., Jefferson, T., Clarke, J. and Roberts, B. (1978) *Policing the Crisis: Mugging, the State and Law and Order.* London: Macmillan.

Harding, S. (1990) 'Feminism, science and the anti-Enlightenment critique.' In L. Nicholson (ed.) *Feminism/Postmodernism.* London: Routledge.

Hartsock, N. (1987) 'The feminist standpoint: Laying the ground for a specifically feminist historical materialism.' In S. Harding (ed.) *Feminism and Methodology.* Bloomington, IN: Indiana University Press.

Hill Collins, P. (1990) *Black Feminist Thought: Knowledge, Consciousness and the Politics of Empowerment.* London: Routledge.

hooks, b. (1989) *Talking Back: Thinking Feminist; Thinking Black.* Boston, MA: South End Press.

hooks, b. (1990) *Yearning: Race, Gender and Cultural Politics.* Boston, MA: South End Press.

Kelaher, M., Paul, S., Lambert, H., Ahmad, W., Fenton, S. and Davey Smith, G. (2003) 'Ethnicity, health and health services utilization in a British study.' *Critical Public Health* 13, 3, 231–49.

Lorde, A. (1984) *Sister Outsider.* New York: The Crossing Press.

Miller, A. (1981) *Prisoners of Childhood.* New York: Basic Books.

Miller, A. (1983) *For Your Own Good: Hidden Cruelty in Child-Rearing and the Roots of Violence.* New York: Farrar, Straus and Giroux.

Modood, T., Beishon, S. and Virdee, S. (1994) *Changing Ethnic Identities.* London: Policy Studies Institute.

Morrison, T. (1984) *Race-ing Justice, En-Gendering Power: Essays on Anita Hill, Clarence Thomas and the Construction of Social Reality.* New York: Random Books.

NACRO (1994) *Statistics on Black People within the Criminal Justice System.* London: NACRO.

NAPO (National Association of Probation Officers) (1999) *Caseloads, Budgets and Staffing: Probation's Crisis.* NAPO Briefing Paper, May. London: NAPO.

Nicholson, L. (ed.) (1990) *Postmodernism/Feminism.* London: Routledge.

ONS (Office for National Statistics) (2002) Census 2001. Data available from the website www.statistics.gov.uk/census last accessed 16 October 2004.

Worrall, A. (1990) *Women Offending: Female Lawbreakers and the Criminal Justice System.* London: Routledge and Kegan Paul.

Chapter 8

Constructive Work
with Women Offenders
A Probation in Prison Perspective

Sue Carless

On 31 December 2004 there were 73,208 people in prison in England and Wales; this population consisted of 69,085 males and 4123 females (Home Office Research Development Statistics 2005), women in prison representing 5.6 per cent of the prison population and serving sentences varying between a few days and life imprisonment. However, this figure disguises the reality that, for example, in one women's prison in 2003–2004 there were approximately 3000 receptions. Many of these prisoners were on remand or serving short sentences under 12 months, some a matter of weeks or days. The intention of this chapter is not to debate the reasons for or rightness of imprisoning women, but to consider the political and historical background, address the reality of day-to-day work for prison and probation staff working in prison and, most importantly, the reality for the women themselves. These issues will be considered within the context of the Probation Service, now part of the National Offender Management Service (NOMS), some of the positive work being undertaken with women in prison, and the potential opportunities for constructive and creative work.

The women's prison context
In the ten years from 1991 to 2001 'the female prison population doubled, whilst the male population increased by about 50%' (Carlen and Worrall

2004, p.35). Despite this increase in the female prison population, women represent only a small proportion of the total prison population. Consequently, policy tends to focus on the needs of male prisoners and the largest proportion of resources is directed towards males.

Historically women's prisons have been modelled on male prisons. However, Carlen and Worrall identify two opposing trends in women's imprisonment:

> On the one hand it can be argued that the fundamental problem with women's prisons is that they are inappropriately modelled on institutions designed for men. On the other, it can be argued that the actual operation of women's establishments has always been infused with both a paternalism and an actual recognition that women *are* different to men. (Carlen and Worrall 2004, p.9)

Together with this realistic assessment, the complexities involved should also be considered, including finance and resources, and budgets predicated on male prisoners' needs. When political imperatives, such as the 2003 Criminal Justice Act (Home Office 2004a), the formation of NOMS and the moves towards contestability are entered into the equation, it is not difficult to see how even the most enlightened and forward-looking prison governor may find it difficult to implement the type of regimes which would facilitate more constructive work with women offenders. Undoubtedly a paternalistic attitude still makes its presence felt, coupled with a focus on security. However, many prison managers and staff working with women in prison do recognize gender differences and seek greater opportunities to use different approaches in their work that would allow women's voices to be heard in a more constructive way.

Sir David Ramsbotham, Chief Inspector of Prisons 1995–2001, referring to the rising numbers of women in prison, stated:

> Simply being tough on crimes committed by women but not being equally tough on the social and economic factors behind the offending…risks making matters worse not better… But they [those he considered responsible for the current crisis] must make it their business to listen to, and not ignore, such advice in the future, so that the damage that imprisonment currently causes to women is eliminated, the public are protected, and no one has to struggle for justice. (Ramsbotham, Foreword in Carlen 2002, p.xi)

Sir David Ramsbotham also referred to the positive development of a Women's Policy Group in 1998 and an operational manager for women's prisons in 2000 (HM Inspectorate of Prisons and Probation 2001, Preface).

However, the Women's Policy Group was disbanded in 2004 and replaced by a much reduced Women's Policy Team. At the same time, the management of women's prisons under a separate Women's Estate was returned to regional management alongside male prisons. Thus the listening Ramsbotham referred to has currently become distant or subsumed in the welter of other criminal justice policy imperatives outlined elsewhere in this chapter. Unless women offenders become a media story, either pejoratively in, say, a piece about women as 'drug mules', or more sympathetically in an item about miscarriages of justice, for example women wrongly convicted of murder in cot deaths, they remain politically invisible, which has serious implications for the resourcing and development of creative regimes in women's prisons.

Sentence planning and women's needs

The sentence planning process for those serving 12 months or more is now informed by the risk/needs assessment system OASys, which is underpinned by the concept of criminogenic need (see Chapter 4 in this book by Michelle Hayles). The Pre-Sentence Report (PSR) will soon be radically changed to encompass a computerized, drop-down, mechanistic system that is drawn through from OASys (see Chapter 6 by Kevin Gorman). Thus the opportunity for experienced professionals to exercise their assessment skills, experience and knowledge of an offender and her circumstances, and for the offender's voice to be heard, is, at the very least, circumscribed.

Nevertheless, assessments made on the OASys system are still judgements. They are judgements of:

1. the risk of harm an offender presents and what intervention may reduce that risk

2. the needs of an offender which require intervention in order to reduce re-offending, for example drug misuse, employment.

They are judgements which follow offenders through the whole of their contact with the criminal justice system, and which are made by a variety of probation and prison staff, many of whom are not qualified professionals. Margaret Shaw and Kelly Hannah-Moffat (2004) make a similar criticism in discussing the Canadian risk/needs Offender Intake Assessment, suggesting that not only are moral judgements required, but 'there are likely to be differences in interpretation and use between those who construct risk assessment scales and practitioners who apply their tools' (Shaw and Hannah-Moffat 2004, p.95).

In relation to women, the same criticisms can be made of OASys and of cognitive-behavioural programmes:

> When policy makers start talking about 'adapting' programmes and risk assessment tools for use by women, they rightly adopt the language of 'need'. However, rather than analysing and seeking to meet those needs through better access to community resources, 'needs talk' may merely replace 'risk talk' and 'high need' women become 'high risk' women who can then be subjected to the same programming as 'high risk' men. (Carlen and Worrall 2004, p.150)

The lack of appropriate, easily accessible services in the community to meet women's needs contributes to an escalation in their offending and leads to assessments being made on the presumption of increasing risks. Women are then often seen as candidates for offending behaviour programmes largely developed on the basis of research into the behaviour of male offenders. As Carlen and Worrall suggest, there is a structural resistance to considering the causation of women's crime as different to that of men (2004). This is despite a wealth of evidence to 'confirm differences between the social circumstances, needs and possible motivations of male and female offenders' (Gelsthorpe 2001, p.155).

Nevertheless, a distinction between male and female offending is perhaps implicit in a statement made by Beverly Hughes in her former role of Prison Minister:

> What is clear…is that women's offending is inextricably linked to their life experiences. Factors such as health, economic stability, level of education, employment and training opportunities, family and community ties and experience of abuse are widely accepted as criminogenic factors for women offenders. (Cited in Lowthian 2002, p.158)

Certainly, the significance of many of these criminogenic factors was emphasized in a subsequent Home Office consultation paper on prostitution: 'High levels of childhood abuse, homelessness, problematic drug use and poverty experienced by those involved strongly suggest survival to be the overriding motivation' (Home Office 2004b, p.12).

Evidence of a more general causal linkage between such issues and female offending was provided by a Supporting People research project across five local authority areas entitled 'Just Surviving' (James, Curteis and Griffiths 2004). This research took place during 2003–2004 and included consultation with 347 potential or actual service users through use of interviews and questionnaires. The majority of respondents were either in prison at the time of the research or had been in the past, had been on probation orders and not been in prison, or had just appeared in court. Of the 347 potential or actual service users consulted, 222 were men and 125 women (James *et al.* 2004, pp.29–32). This research, therefore, involved a much larger female sample than is usual in research on women and the criminal justice system. Some of the findings particularly relevant to understanding the offending-related needs of women and to working constructively with them are summarized as follows:

- 47 per cent of women who had experienced violence or abuse agreed to the statement 'I have self-harmed in the past' (James *et al.* 2004, Appendices p.39)

- 95 per cent of women who had self-harmed had experienced violence or abuse at some point (James *et al.* 2004, Appendices p.47)

- 66 per cent of women said they had a problem with drug or alcohol use (James *et al.* 2004, Appendices p.42)

- 82 per cent of women who had a problem with drug or alcohol use had experienced violence or abuse (James *et al.* 2004, Appendices p.44)

- 77 per cent of women who had experienced violence or abuse had also used drugs or alcohol to blot out problems (James *et al.* 2004, Appendices p.39)

- 55 per cent of women identified a need for counselling (past or present) (James *et al.* 2004, Appendices p.32)

- 85 per cent of the women who had experienced violence or abuse identified a need for counselling (James *et al.* 2004, p.152).

These findings demonstrate that female offenders are often women who have experienced abuse and domestic violence, who have turned to drug/alcohol misuse, self-harm, and/or crime as ways of 'blotting out' or 'coping' with their experience, and who clearly have a high level of need. Frequently, what they need is housing away from abusers; support with child care; drug and alcohol services; counselling and support services; education and training opportunities.

Current policy dictates that the main focus of work with women in prison is undertaken through the medium of cognitive-behavioural programmes. A prison may deliver lengthy programmes such as Enhanced Thinking Skills (ETS) which comprises 21 sessions delivered over about eight weeks to approximately ten women per course. The ETS programme focuses on remedying 'thinking deficits' in areas such as impulsivity, consequential awareness and irrationality. It is important to note that women do not come to the ETS course without any skills. Pre-course assessments show that women bring varying types and levels of cognitive skills to the course. Observation suggests that the majority of women who have undertaken these programmes have gained in knowledge and enhanced their skills. However, this opinion must be qualified, as observation also suggests that a significant proportion of attenders have acquired some skills at a superficial level, but have failed to grasp underlying concepts. Consequently, there is a likelihood that their skills will not be maintained and/or that they will apply their learning inappropriately and become de-motivated when the misapplication does not work. There may be numerous reasons for this, one of which almost certainly relates to education and literacy levels, whilst another explanation may be that the programme, despite being presented as gender-neutral, fails to provide a 'fit' with women's needs.

In addition to generic offending behaviour programmes like ETS, prisons may also deliver shorter courses such as Assertiveness and Decision Making or Anger Management, which run on half days over two weeks, are accredited via the Learning and Skills Council and can be delivered to greater numbers of women. These prison-based treatment programmes are usually staffed by multidisciplinary teams which may include psychologists, prison officers, teachers and probation officers. Because not every prison runs all of the relevant programmes, women often have to move to another prison so that they can fulfil them. These moves take place in an already overcrowded system where women may be moved hundreds of miles from their home area purely due to population pressures. Thus, despite the recognized importance to women of attachment and affiliation to others (see, for example, Miller 1976), women prisoners are not only separated from home, children, partners, family and friends by virtue of their imprisonment, but they are also often living long distances away from their home areas and may move around the country from prison to prison.

None of these programmes focuses on the specific and individual circumstances of a woman in her social context. This provision was traditionally fulfilled by professionals in custodial and non-custodial settings being afforded time to undertake one-to-one work with offenders and by providing flexibility in the method of intervention. However, the skills and experience of Probation and Prison Service practitioners in terms of listening and dialogue, relationship building and helping women to re-story their lives, have taken a back seat to political and organizational priorities reinforced by key performance indicators and the ever-increasing pace of change. The 'What Works' agenda has resulted in a failure to support practitioners in the development and delivery of differing theoretical perspectives and a varied methodology premised on individual work with offenders. The introduction of NOMS with its separation of services offers little hope that one-to-one work and flexibility of methodology will take a high priority.

Interestingly, the value of one-to-one work, differing theoretical perspectives and complementary methods of intervention is exemplified by monitoring and evaluation of a counselling service provided by an outside agency within a particular prison. This indicated that many women who received counselling at the same time as participating in the ETS course shared the view that it was extremely helpful to be undertaking both activities at the same time. Further questioning revealed that they felt the need to deal with 'what's in my head and how it affects everything' (by which they frequently meant relationship difficulties and/or experiences of abuse) and that they considered counselling strategies, together with ETS skills, to have offered various ways of addressing past, present and future situations.

The main tenet of much one-to-one work is building a relationship in which an offender's strengths can be maximized. Jackie Lowthian of the National Association for the Care and Rehabilitation of Offenders (NACRO), referring to women's negative experiences including abuse, poverty and debts, comments, 'many of them had shown incredible resourcefulness, courage and strength in coping with these experiences and surviving' (Lowthian 2002, p.159). If we are to fulfil the aims of reducing re-offending and protecting the public, then surely we should be maximizing the strengths of women offenders, using constructive approaches to build on women's resourcefulness and courage, on their previous experiences of resistance to problems and on what allowed them to desist.

In April 2005 a new programme will be rolled out in the community, entitled 'The Women's Programme', aimed at what is considered to be the largest group of women offenders on probation caseloads, 'those whose offending is motivated by financial gain' (Home Office 2004c). The programme design is said to be different to other offending behaviour programmes: 'The focus is upon building motivation to change, through the initial identification of personal strengths, positive goals and strategies, then learning thinking skills to maintain the change' (Home Office 2004c). It remains to be seen how far the difficulties related to understanding underlying concepts or 'fit' have been overcome, or whether access to appropriate services will be facilitated through this programme, or even available.

Women's voice

If women's prinsons are modelled on male establishments, but if there is a recognition that women are different to men, what differentiates a women's prison from a men's prison? If, for instance, you were to be bindfolded and set down in a prison, how would you know if it were a women's prison? I suggest that you would know through voice, women's voice; through their language, chatter, gossip, repartee, their relationships with others; through all the subtleties and tones of speech and conversation, shouting, crying, admonishing, threatening, laughing, caring, sympathizing. The most striking womanly feature of women's prisons is the level of noise, of voice, communication and relationship, between the prisoners and between prisoners and staff. This is not to suggest that male prisons are silent; they are not. However, voice, communication and relationship in male prisons appear less obvious, more muted, often more hierarchical. It is in this voice, in the narrative of women's voices and their relationships, that the greatest opportunities lie for change in work with women offenders, and for the exercise of professional skills in work with women by both the Probation and Prison Services.

In discussing insights into the relationship between women's psychology and the prevailing social order, Gilligan posits: 'A new psychological theory in which girls and women are seen and heard is an inevitable challenge to a patriarchal order that can remain in place only through the continuing eclipse of women's experience' (Gilligan 1998, p.xxiv). An extension and variation on this theme is discussed by Milner who, in considering narrative approaches and gender specificity, says: 'A womanly way of practicing solution-focused and narrative approaches to social work...involves consensus building, negotiation through give and take, conciliation rather than confrontation, paying attention to personal issues, and the use of tentative language' (Milner 2001, p.66). She also discusses the theme of 'serious gossip', stating that 'serious gossip is a natural discourse of women in which participants use talk to reflect about themselves, examine uncertainties, and provide a source of influence' (Milner 2001, p.66).

'Serious gossip' (Milner 2001) and moral reasoning based upon caring and sharing (Gilligan 1998) are such prevalent features of daily life in a women's prison that it would be impossible to ignore them. Staff do not necessarily have to be familiar with these concepts to recognize, for example, women's support for each other when bad news is received, whether in terms of sentence, relationships or family. Similarly, staff recognize the supportive interaction of women consoling each other, listening to each other, sympathetically hugging or giggling, joking and shouting conversations from one window to another after lock-up and forming friendships.

Due to the nature of a prison, these activities are undertaken in a public arena. Not only are they obvious, they can also be subversive in the sense that others are drawn in, including staff. This relates again to Milner's concept of 'serious gossip' as a 'natural discourse of women in which participants use talk to reflect about themselves, examine uncertainties and provide a source of influence' (Milner 2001, p.66). Prison staff are not only the subjects of disclosure of problems and subsequent support, they are also laughed with (as well as 'at'), and included in repartee. All of these interactions raise issues of boundaries, authority and distance. Not only can they subvert the dominant discourse of 'imprisonment' through an implicit refusal to accept others' pejorative definitions of women as 'offenders', as 'bad women', they can also subvert personal discourses. Laughing together can, of course, be problematical when staff also have to deal with issues of harm, bad behaviour or bullying. More positively, however, laughter is one of a number of shared activities which can contribute to strengthening resistance and increasing the range of solutions (Milner 2001, pp.65–6).

Women are encountered daily in women's prisons talking in pairs and in informal groups, often very briefly. Ongoing dialogues can be overheard reflecting, for example, on offending behaviour, on relationships, on prison regimes, or searching for answers, solutions, norms. Conclusions may sometimes appear faulty or skewed, but quite frequently they may be positive, helpful and motivational. They are undoubtedly influential but, sadly, the influence largely remains within the peer group because there is often no opportunity, system or channel for assisting women to develop these dialogues constructively on an individual or group basis.

Another daily feature of life in a women's prison is the expression of anger by inmates, reflecting perhaps the experience of physical, sexual and emotional abuse common to a large proportion of women offenders and the prevalence of problems related to drug misuse, (mental) health, relationships, sexuality, parenting, child care, alienation, coping behaviours, community support, discrimination, debt, accommodation and employment. This anger can manifest itself in a woman destroying her property or her cell and furnishings, in outbursts of abuse and violence against staff or other inmates and, frequently, in self-harming behaviour. It is particularly noticeable in, although by no means exclusive to, the juvenile population: those inmates who are 17 and who are legally children.

There are frequent occasions when a woman can be seen to be 'spilling over' with the need to 'tell her story'. This may start in a discussion with a staff member she knows and trusts and there may be an initial brief allegation that she was abused. The need to 'tell' is so overwhelming, she may then tell 'bits and pieces' of her story to various other members of staff, often regardless of role or rank, whether she knows that person or not. The anger about her experience is so palpable, it can be seen simmering just below the surface, exploding and manifesting itself in destructive behaviour that is directly harmful to herself or indirectly harmful in terms of behaviour that may provoke sanctions against her.

Women voicing these problems can be referred to the counselling service. They can also be assisted to take legal recourse against their alleged abuser, and Safeguarding Children procedures are invoked in the case of juveniles. However, as Milner suggests, legal proceedings can be a damaging experience (Milner 2001, p.44). Additionally, evidence may be difficult to substantiate and a prosecution may not succeed; there may be the total breakdown and loss of family relationships and there can be the ongoing threat of repercussions to the victim or other family members. Many women perceive the costs of providing sufficient information for any legal, preventative or protective action to be too great and more than they are able to cope with, despite their anger, the need to 'tell their story' and the harm they direct against themselves.

These women are already externalizing the problem and beginning an 'externalising conversation' (Parton and O'Byrne 2000, p.85), but the options available to assist them in constructing different stories are limited. The additional option of one-to-one, solution-focused/narrative work focused on a consensus-building approach would not only provide women with a wider choice, but perhaps go some way towards hearing women's voices and addressing the issue that 'in the different voice of woman lies the truth of an ethic of care, the tie between relationship and responsibility, and the origins of aggression in the failure of connection' (Gilligan 1998, p.173).

Potential sites for constructive work with women in prison

What work is currently undertaken with women whilst in prison? Does any of it correspond or relate to methodologies which empathize, which sympathetically acknowledge distress or disclosure, which do not focus on confrontation? How far do relevant staff genuinely hear the voices of women prisoners, recognize their capacity for consensus building and negotiation, acknowledge their personal feelings or allow them to build on their strengths and the sometimes heroic efforts they have made?

In an attempt to answer these questions, consideration will be given first to some of the existing services for women in prison and to their variable potential as sites for constructive work – and solution-focused practice is still possible within such an environment, despite significant practical, policy and resource constraints. Unless otherwise stated, the services outlined immediately below refer to one particular women's prison, as each individual prison may offer a varying range of services.

The CARATS team (Counselling, Assessment, Referral, Advice/ Information and Throughcare Services) provides assessment, treatment and drug referral services in conjunction with Prison Health Care Specialist Nursing staff. Here there is a more personal focus, although throughput targets (95% of women are admitted to the detox unit following reception), time constraints and insufficient staffing conspire to reduce the scope for a genuinely customized, individual approach. The prison also has a large education department affiliated to a local college; contracts in a variety of staff from outside agencies to work on housing, employment and benefits with individual prisoners; and funds a five-day counselling service staffed by an outside provider. Given the correlation identified by Stephen Farrall (Farrall 2002) between improvements in offenders' social and personal circumstances and their resolution of obstacles to desistance to crime, these initiatives hold considerable promise in terms of enabling women prisoners to begin constructing offence-free storylines for the future.

An enormous amount of 'informal' work, particularly in terms of 'listening', is done by prison officers, personal officers (a designated member of prison staff who takes a key worker role) and staff on the accommodation wings. Unfortunately, the staffing ratio again produces severe constraints on the amount of time available for officers to spend listening to or assisting women, and this is a general problem across the female estate. Whilst not every prison officer is skilled in, suitable for or wishes to undertake this work, a lack of training compounds the problems of insufficient time/staff and prevents a potentially invaluable resource being as appropriately used or as widely available as it might be.

The prison health-care department is responsible for an ever-increasing number of women who seemingly cannot be accommodated in appropriate mental health provision. In addition to providing medical care to approximately 3000 women received into the prison in one year, the department deals with an extremely high rate of suicide and self-harm. A recent check with colleagues in two comparable male prisons in the area indicated that, over the six months October 2003 to March 2004, 0.83 per cent and 6.1 per cent of their populations had suicide and self-harm books open at any one time. The women's prison recorded 15.75 per cent over the same period; a reflection, perhaps, of the traumatic experiences many women prisoners have undergone and the apparent inability of the political agenda to recognize women's particular needs.

There is also an increasing number of women labelled 'personality disorder – untreatable' by outside mental health professionals and, in addition, there are those women suffering from 'depression' which, to a greater or lesser degree, could include almost every woman in the prison at some point during her sentence. The availability of forensic psychiatrists and psychologists is limited, and the numbers of nursing staff or in-reach staff (outside professionals coming in to do specific one-to-one work in the prison) insufficient to undertake any meaningful work with all but a limited number of prioritized cases. Additional consequences of the health-care unit housing increasing numbers of mental health patients are the distress caused to other patients on the unit and the stretching of staff and resources beyond reasonable limits in attempting to deliver services to both.

The small probation team is similarly inundated daily with work relating to the problems women face in their lives, past and present, inside and outside the prison walls. In prioritizing work, it is inevitable that the focus is on the assessment and management of risk, in custody and post-release. Probation staff interview every woman who comes through the gates, and during their sentence women make applications to see probation staff. These interviews cover a variety of matters, but frequently relate to home situations, relationships and children. Probation staff also take referrals from prison staff on wings and workshops when matters which the prison staff are unable to deal with arise, or when women are exhibiting or verbalizing distress, all of which may result in ongoing work.

The Prison Probation Department is frequently asked to provide 'victim awareness' work, helping women to understand the effects of crime on victims and accept their responsibility. Due to the small number of probation officers, this work and other offending behaviour work is normally focused on a limited number of serious offenders, usually serving long sentences for violence. Whilst the work often needs to address issues of denial and displacement, it is inevitably bound up in the wider circumstances of women's lives, children, families and past experiences. Similar issues frequently arise for probation officers involved in work with women whose children are in, or may be taken into, the care of the local authority or freed for adoption; with women who are pregnant or living on the mother and baby unit with their babies; or with women referred through Sentence Planning meetings and suicide and self-harm reviews. All of these activities provide potential opportunities for a constructive approach characterized by active, empathic listening and tentative language, and focusing upon personal issues, consensus building, exceptions and resistance to offending, re-storying, and the future. Women faced with such problems and dilemmas have to find ways of coping with imprisonment, and their desired solutions frequently involve maintaining, re-establishing or breaking relationships with partners and/or parents and with children cared for by others. They can also involve optimism for a better future, free from substance misuse, and an aspiration towards living a 'normal life'.

Possibly the most frequent comment made to probation staff by women in prison is that 'this is the first time I have ever had space to think about myself'. Further questioning usually indicates that, freed from the struggle of surviving in often extremely adverse circumstances in the community, without the responsibilities of children or family and substance-free, they have an opportunity to think about their lives; where they have been and where they are going. However, whilst this 'thinking space' often provides a level of motivation for change, it may also bring to the surface flashbacks of previous abusive experiences, self-blame and guilt. Some of the greatest difficulties in using a constructive approach in the form of a combined solution-focused/narrative approach with women in prison lie in goal setting, and assisting women towards constructing a new story. In an environment where most women feel particularly powerless and lacking in control over their lives, and where they are isolated from the outside world, from significant others, and from what they see as their reality, seeing and doing things differently is clearly very challenging.

Two case examples

Ms X's story

One of the most impressive pieces of work I have seen using a combined solution-focused/narrative approach was undertaken with Ms X, an offender who had been involved in repeated offences of harassment/ minor violence and diagnosed by psychiatrists as 'personality disorder – untreatable', and who was now pregnant. A continuing deterioration in the mental health of this intelligent, articulate woman with a previously successful career was evident to all staff in the prison, despite the diagnosis. She became increasingly unable to focus on anything other than re-telling her story in relation to offending, blaming others and becoming distressed, verbally abusive and on occasion physically violent. Her insistence on telling her story to anyone who would listen tested the patience of all staff who, nevertheless, tried to listen to her as often as possible. Unfortunately her behaviour alienated her from other prisoners, from whom she received no support. It was also obvious to probation staff working with her that she was likely to have her child removed at birth, taken into care and probably freed for adoption.

The probation officer working with her listened to her for ever-increasing periods of time, using a conciliatory approach and paying attention to personal issues, attempting always to build on strengths, on previous resistance. This was not successful. Plans made for doing things differently using the considerable skills Ms X had exercised in the course of her business career were never carried through. The discourse always foundered on Ms X's return to a recital of wrongs against her and increasing distress. Her child was removed at birth, and the work moved on to social services' consideration of Ms X's ability to care for the child and her interaction with the baby. Subsequently, the probation officer helped her prepare for visits from social services with the child and for discussion of Ms X's child care abilities. This proved particularly difficult as her discussion of, and interaction with, the child usually lasted only a matter of a few minutes before Ms X returned to constantly repeating her situation with regard to offending, almost always culminating in her becoming distressed, or abusive, or both.

Eventually, the piece of work that had to be undertaken was to prepare her for the child being freed for adoption and to assist her through the process. This involved preparing her to attend court hearings, where it was intended that she would utilize skills from her business experience to stay calm and to put her case rationally, even though this was, in the event, only partially successful. It then involved negotiation and reaching a consensus that whatever Ms X's views were about her own situation in relation to offending and her own coping skills, her child would be freed for adoption. A final meeting with the child was arranged, the inherent distress of the situation acknowledged and plans made for the goals she wanted to achieve: namely, to get through the meeting with dignity, without becoming abusive, and to cause the least possible distress for the baby.

An enormous amount of work was done by the probation officer in helping Ms X to utilize her strengths including, for example, exploring with her how she had 'done' dignity and control successfully in the past. Although distressed, Ms X was able to get through the final meeting without becoming abusive or distressing her baby, and with a minimum of recitation of her story. In view of her troubled mental health, this was a particularly impressive and heroic achievement for Ms X.

Ms Y's story

A further example of a solution-focused/narrative approach relates to Ms Y, a prisoner who was nearing the end of a sentence of several years for an arson offence. An important aspect of this case was the involvement of the home probation officer, who was involved in and furthered release plans.

Ms Y, a middle-aged woman of average intelligence, had experienced an impoverished environment and had previously displayed poor relationship skills, poor coping skills under stress in the community and a dependence on alcohol. One of the major factors involved in her release plan was accommodation. She had the options of initial accommodation in a hostel in a town or with a family member to whom she related reasonably well, but who lived in the country. Ms Y was adamant for quite some time that she only wanted to get her own tenancy in a town, which was not an option open to her.

The probation officer working with her explored situations when Ms Y had coped, when she had related to others reasonably well, when she had resisted alcohol misuse and, above all, how she had done that. Important clues to emerge were as follows: Ms Y had coped better when she did not live with too many other people around her who might also involve her in social situations involving drinking; she had coped better when her time was occupied, which was one of her reasons for preferring to live in a town where she felt more options might be open to her; she had worked for periods of time in the past, but preferred unskilled work where not too many demands were placed upon her; she liked to have 'quiet times' without others around her. She practised some of these previously successful strategies whilst in prison, becoming more selective, for example, about the women with whom she associated and working as a prison cleaner.

She finally decided that her goal would be to live with her relative in the country for at least six months. Her home probation officer assisted in planning for release with both Ms Y and the family member. She negotiated various tasks relating to the house and garden, in which Ms Y could become involved. She also arranged for Ms Y to have access to alcohol misuse counselling and identified various accessible activities in the area which Ms Y could sample. Regular meetings with her probation officer were agreed, including home visits, and it was agreed that the situation would be reviewed six months after release.

Potential and opportunities

Currently, accredited groupwork programmes are heavily resourced both in prison and in the community, although to date the research on outcomes has not been definitive. Additionally, the customized, desistance-oriented practice proposed by McNeill (2003) indicates that constructive one-to-one work focusing on the individual and the individual in her social context may be more effective for women offenders than any kind of groupwork. However, I would suggest that some women gain considerable benefit from cognitive-behavioural, group-based programmes, others gain greater benefit when these are delivered alongside counselling services and some women are motivated by a less didactic groupwork approach.

A similar level of investment to that made in programmes could be used to support gender-specific work and one-to-one work with women using solution-focused/narrative interventions. Expanding the opportunities for working constructively with women in prison and on release would necessitate some change in policy direction, but might also be seen in terms of maximizing the efficiency and effectiveness of resources which already exist.

Probation staff in prison are very keenly aware of women's voice, and many of them have the skills to undertake solution-focused/narrative work. Wherever possible, they already make use of opportunities to engage in constructive work with women, which may arise from a variety of contacts, most frequently from work initially relating to 'offending behaviour'. Often, perhaps, these interventions are not explicitly 'solution-focused' or 'narrative', despite containing elements of one or both of these approaches. They could, however, be re-channelled into a relatively small number of constructive sessions and be supported by other existing servies in the comminity. Other staff could be trained in solution-focused/narrative work, particularly in gaining understanding of the concepts so they could support the work being undertaken. As stated earlier, I believe there are real opportunities here for appropriate prison officers, who probably spend more time in contact with women in prison than anyone else.

If, however, more planned, constructive one-to-one work is to be undertaken with women in prison, it may be that the notion (heretical to some) of recruiting more prison-based probation staff will need to be addressed. Moreover, there will need to be a recognition that 'joined-up' working, or the 'end to end management of offenders' (Home Office 2004d, p.14), cannot just involve a home probation officer visiting an inmate once or twice during sentence. One of the most frequent complaints from women in prison is 'I don't know my home probation officer'. If we accept that women operate on the basis of attachment and affiliation with others, then it follows that their productive relationships with professionals cannot develop or thrive if there is little contact. Additionally, if work begun by probation officers in prison is to have a better chance of lasting success, then it must be continued in the community.

Extending the range of interventions for women prisoners would not exclude those currently available. Instead, it would broaden opportunities for them to change their behaviour, whilst at the same time supporting the aims of reducing re-offending and protecting the public. Opportunities abound in women's prisons for solution-focused/narrative approaches, and in particular for the harnessing of 'serious gossip' (Milner 2001). If women prisoners' statements about imprisonment, that 'this is the first time I have had space to think about myself', are to become the opening lines of different, more hopeful stories, a crucial first step is the acknowledgement that constructive work with women, undertaken on a one-to-one basis, is a valuable and potentially highly effective use of finite resources.

References

Carlen, P. (ed.) (2002) *Women and Punishment.* Cullompton: Willan Publishing.

Carlen, P. and Worrall, A. (2004) *Analysing Women's Imprisonment.* Cullompton: Willan Publishing.

Farrall, S. (2002) *Rethinking What Works with Offenders: Probation, Social Context and Desistance from Crime.* Cullompton: Willan Publishing.

Gelsthorpe, L. (2001) 'Accountability, difference and diversity in the delivery of community penalties.' In A. Bottoms, L. Gelsthorpe and S. Rex (eds) *Community Penalties: Change and Challenges.* Cullompton: Willan Publishing.

Gilligan, C. (1998) *In a Different Voice.* Cambridge, MA: Harvard University Press.

HM Inspectorate of Prisons and Probation (2001) *Follow-up to Women in Prison: A Thematic Review.* London: Home Office.

Home Office (2004a) *Criminal Justice Act 2003.* London: HMSO.

Home Office (2004b) *Paying the Price: A Consultation Paper on Prostitution.* London: Home Office Communication Directorate.

Home Office (2004c) '19/07 national roll out of the women's programme.' *What Works News,* Issue 19. London: Home Office.

Home Office (2004d) *Reducing Crime, Changing Lives: The Government's Plans for Transforming the Management of Offenders.* London: Home Office.

Home Office Research Development Statistics (2005) 'Population in custody, December 2004, England and Wales', available at www.homeoffice.gov.uk/rds/pdfs05/prisq 404.pdf (accessed 15 May 2005).

James, K., Curteis, S. and Griffiths, S. (2004) *'Just Surviving': The Housing and Support Needs of People on the Fringes of Homelessness and/or the Criminal Justice System in West Yorkshire.* Leeds: West Yorkshire Supporting People Cross Authority Group.

Lowthian, J. (2002) 'Women's prisons in England: Barriers to reform.' In P. Carlen (ed.) *Women and Punishment.* Cullompton: Willan Publishing.

McNeill, F. (2003) 'Desistance-focused probation practice.' In W.H. Chui and M. Nellis (eds) *Moving Probation Forward.* Harlow: Pearson Education Limited.

Miller, J.B. (1976) *Towards a New Psychology of Women.* Boston: Beacon Press.

Milner, J. (2001) *Women and Social Work: Narrative Approaches.* Basingstoke: Palgrave.

Parton, N. and O'Byrne, P. (2000) *Constructive Social Work: Towards a New Practice.* Basingstoke: Palgrave.

Shaw, M. and Hannah-Moffat, K. (2004) 'How cognitive skills forgot about gender and diversity.' In G. Mair (ed.) (2004) *What Matters in Probation.* Cullompton: Willan Publishing.

Chapter 9

Constructive Work
with Male Sex Offenders
Male Forms of Life, Language Games and Change

Malcolm Cowburn

This chapter problematizes the 'scientific' standpoint from which cognitive-behavioural treatment (CBT) programmes for sex offenders are developed. The objective of cognitive-behavioural (CB) programmes is to deconstruct the offender's initial account of his offences and replace it with one that fully recognizes offender responsibility and victim harm. This is generally accomplished in either individual work or, more commonly, groupwork. The therapeutic process is monological insofar as there is no dialogue between the worker(s) and the offender(s). Within the cognitive paradigm the worker(s) is/are unaffected and unchanged by the therapeutic process; the offender (one hopes) is transformed. The worker helps the offender identify his or her cognitive distortions and thereafter change them. This chapter raises questions about CB approaches, offers a dialogical perspective on the processes of working with offenders, considers how masculinities are constructed through language, discusses the use of power in programmes and concludes by suggesting a constructive approach to work with male sex offenders that moves beyond the current CB model. However, I begin with a problem that may be familiar to readers who have worked with sex offenders.

Talking the talk or walking the walk?

A few years ago I evaluated a sex offender treatment programme. Apart from administering psychometric tests, I home-visited all men who had completed the programme. The psychometric data in relation to James (pseudonym) were positive; they indicated that his attitudes (concerning responsibility for his offences, victim harm and his attitude to women) had shifted significantly. I asked James if the programme had changed him in any way. He said that it had, indeed, changed him. Prior to the programme he was an 'MCP' (male chauvinist pig), but his attitudes had changed. As he told me this, he repeatedly interrupted our conversation to instruct his wife to make me tea, iron his clothes and obtain money for their night out which was to begin after I had left the house. This presented me with a problem in interpreting the data: the psychometric questionnaires and James's answer to my question indicated that treatment had had a desired effect, but his behaviour towards his wife contradicted this.

Workers operating within the CB paradigm are sceptical about the effectiveness of their work. The opinion of the offender is treated with suspicion (Salter 1988, p.85). Briggs *et al.* (1998, p.56) note:

> Many workers become concerned when assessing sexual abusers that what their clients say might be different to what their clients think, feel and do. Indeed the phrases 'talk the talk' and 'walk the walk' have entered the vernacular to capture this dilemma.

The response of forensic psychology to this dilemma is to increase methods of evaluation. Beech, Fisher and Beckett (1999, pp.44–51) employed 25 psychometric tests in evaluating the English Prison Service's Sex Offender Treatment Programme. By using a large number of tests, researchers expect to identify, more clearly, patterns of change (Beech *et al.* 1999, p.45) and thus the objective 'truth' concerning the effectiveness of treatment can be discovered.

However, there is a sceptical standpoint in CBT in relation to sex offenders – they deny responsibility for planning and executing their offences, they minimize the harm that their actions cause to victims, they lack empathy towards their victims, and their accounts of their lives and offending behaviours are riddled with 'cognitive distortions' (see Briggs *et al.* 1998; Leberg 1997; Salter 1988). It may be that, because of this orientation, doubts about treatment effectiveness remain. Thus, although the use of psychometric tests has increased, doubts remain about what they reveal (Kendall 2004).

Problematizing cognitive-behavioural programmes

Crowle (1990) raises questions about working with offenders from a perspective that believes that offenders know why they committed offences on every occasion and that they deliberately conceal this information from clinicians and researchers. He uses statistical models, focusing on deviance-inhibiting and deviance-promoting factors (both of which he considers to be in 'our culture') to show the absurdity of positivist attempts to monitor the truth of what offenders say about their offending. Faraday and Plummer (1979, pp.776–7) also highlight this problem:

> Most social science in its quest for generalizability imposes order and rationality upon experiences and worlds that are more ambiguous, more problematic and more chaotic in reality. If we check our own experiences we know that our lives are flooded with moments of indecision, turning points, confusions, contradictions and ironies. Most social science glosses over this interstitial but central region of our lives. Questionnaires, experiments, attitudes scales, and even the perusal of existing social science literature and historical documents, give form and order to the world that it does not have. Researchers seek for consistency in subjects' responses when subjects' lives are often inconsistent.

It is commonplace within CBT for offenders to be asked to consider an offence using a 'before', 'during' and 'after' structure (Briggs *et al.* 1998, pp.43–51). This imposes a 'form and order to the world'. Although CBT does not directly ask the offender 'why' he or she committed an offence (Briggs *et al.* 1998, p.50), it asks him or her to explain 'how' he or she committed it; this requires him or her to select factors that are congruent with the story the worker wishes to hear and discount the many variables that are considered to be irrelevant from a cognitive standpoint. The role and task of the worker is to extract 'the truth' (about offending behaviour) from the offender. The part played by the worker in the interview or group process is rarely subject to scrutiny. However, from a constructionist perspective, consideration of the circumstances in which a story is told and the 'dialogical' nature of the 'therapeutic' process (individual/groupwork) is of key importance and it suggests that what emerges from such work is not objective 'truth' but rather the product of a 'joint action'.

A dialogical perspective

The dominant model of probation practice with sex offenders is located within a 'natural science' paradigm. The worker is considered to be the 'expert' who through the exercise of professional skills extracts from the offender information pertinent to formulating a treatment strategy. Franklin (1997, pp.100–1) has described this approach to interviewing as 'information extraction'. The interviewer is not personally involved in the interview/group processes. S/he remains detached and merely responds (within the prescribed cognitive paradigm) to what is said. In this model, the interviewer is a catalyst for the emergence of 'truth' from the person being interviewed. This approach to interviewing (and groupwork) is 'monological' in both its epistemological perspective and in its practical orientation (Shotter 1993, 1995). The offender and the worker do not engage in any form of reciprocal exchange, that is to say they do not engage in dialogue.

By recognizing two or more people are engaged in an interview or group process, dialogical approaches incorporate the necessity to theorize the role of the interviewer in the creation of knowledge (Gergen and Gergen 1986; Shotter 1993). The dominant psychological approach wherein the worker seeks to discover what is inside the head of the offender is rejected; the focus is instead on the process of creation that occurs within, for example, interviews or groupwork sessions (Harré 1995; Harré, Clarke and De Carlo 1985; Shotter 1993, 1995).

Central to this shift is the way in which language use is understood. In 'dialogical' approaches language is seen as constructive: the conversation of the parties *creates* what is being discussed. Shotter (1993, p.8) terms this understanding of language in action 'rhetorical-responsive'. Language no longer represents something outside of the speakers (for example the 'true story of what the offender "did"'); the dialogic exchange is creative rather than 'representational-referential'. And, of course, this process occurs within and as part of social and cultural influences. Here the later work of the philosopher Ludwig Wittgenstein is helpful in identifying and reflecting on the constructive processes that occur in work with sex offenders.

For Wittgenstein (1953), language is not a system of symbols representing an outer world; it is an active and changing system in use. Within dialogical interaction participants are inevitably engaged in a variety of 'language games', which emanate from a variety of 'forms of life'. Dialogue in all contexts follows a number of unexpressed but implicitly followed rules/conventions ('language games'). These conventions are specific to the context of the conversation. Gergen (2000, pp.34–5) describes a language game:

> To say 'good morning' gains its meaning from a game-like relationship called a greeting. There are implicit rules for carrying out greetings: each participant takes a turn, typically there is an exchange of mutual glances, and there are only a limited number of moves that one can legitimately

make after the other has said 'good morning.' You may respond identically, or ask 'how are you,' for example, but you would be considered 'out of the game,' if you responded by screaming or cuffing the other on the head. Further, the words 'good morning' are generally meaningless outside the game of greeting. If we are in the midst of a heated argument on unemployment, and I suddenly say, 'good morning,' you would be puzzled. Have I lost my mind? Wittgenstein termed the 'language and the actions into which it is woven, the "language game."' Or for Wittgenstein, 'the meaning of a word is in its use in the language.'

However, 'language games' are not free-floating 'rules for the conduct of conversation'. They are rooted in various contexts within cultures. Wittgenstein called these contexts 'forms of life'. Language games are embodiments of various 'forms of life'. McGinn (1997, p.51) clarifies this:

> ...our human life is fundamentally cultural (rather than biological) in nature. Coming to share, or understand the form of life of a group of human beings means mastering, or coming to understand, the intricate language games that are essential to its characteristic practices. It is this vital connection between language and the complex system of practices and activities binding a community together that Wittgenstein intends to emphasize in the concept 'form of life'.

Dialogical approaches highlight a 'constructive' approach to understanding what is happening in an interview; Wittgensteinian perspectives have narrowed the focus onto 'language games' and emphasized the cultural context of any interview by highlighting that all dialogue embodies various 'forms of life'. In work with male sex offenders, the two 'forms of life' that seem to be important are related to being a man and being a participant in a CBT programme.

Men, masculinity and masculinities

The vast majority of sex offenders are men and yet CB programmes appear to give little recognition to issues of gender and particularly the enactment of masculinities. In writing of men, masculinity and masculinities one could consider the study of the individual, a social grouping, or aspects of a particular culture. Defining terms and justifying usages has preoccupied many authors (Clatterbaugh 1998; Coleman 1990; Connell 1995; Hearn 1998). Early discussions about men focused on the notion of masculinity (Pleck 1976); however, this was challenged because it carried an assumption that there was only one form of masculinity and Carrigan, Connell and Lee (1985) suggest that 'masculinities' is a more appropriate term reflecting diversity amongst men. As a part of this notion there is recognition that not all masculinities are equally powerful. It is within this context that the concept of 'hegemonic masculinity' appeared. Connell (1995, p.77) describes hegemonic masculinity as: 'the configuration of gender practice which embodies the currently accepted answer to the problem of the legitimacy of patriarchy, which guarantees (or is taken to guarantee) the dominant position of men and the subordination of women'. Although this term has recently been criticized as vague (Hearn 2004), it is a useful concept in that it suggests there are dominant ways of *being* a man and these ways are linked to the subordination of women and some men.

However, the abstracting of masculinity and masculinities from men and what men do has caused problems for some commentators (Hearn 2004; Whitehead 2002). Clatterbaugh (1998, p.42) suggests that the terms have, at times, been used in an unclear and often tautological fashion: for instance, masculinity/ies is/are what men do and is recognizable because men do it/them. He suggests that, in the short term at least, the words 'masculinity' and 'masculinities' should be avoided and focus should be, more simply, on what men do (Clatterbaugh 1998, p.43).

Whilst focusing attention on the behaviour of men is a positive way forward, there are many ways in which that behaviour is interpreted (Connell 1995; Edley and Wetherell 1995). Perspectives range from essentialist approaches that assume there is something fixed (essential) that can be identified, defined and studied (see, for example, Thornhill and Palmer 2001), to social constructionist perspectives that focus on the fluid and varied identities that men enact (see, for example, Connell 2000). It is the social constructionist perspective(s) that I am concerned with in this chapter; particularly focusing on various 'forms of life' and 'language games' that pertain to being a man.

Mac an Ghaill (1994) suggests that masculinities are enacted in three discursive situations: fear of same sex attraction (homophobia), compulsory heterosexuality and fear or hatred of women (misogyny). Fielding (1994, p.47) has noted similar aspects in the way men behave in the police force. Scully (1990, pp.81–92) also identified the presence of these attitudes and ways of talking and behaving in her study of rapists and non-rapists in prison. Although prison culture is not homogeneous (Genders and Player 1995, p.154; Sim 1994, pp.110–12), it is this (hegemonic) masculinity that appears to dominate male prisons. However, Sim (1994) comments that this masculinity is not 'a pathological manifestation of abnormal otherness, but…part of the normal routine which is sustained and legitimated by the wider culture of masculinity…' (p.105). It is enacted as a form of (male) life both inside and outside prisons through the use of common language games.

The language games of CBT

> Roger: I couldn't hurt anybody now. I mean, you know, like, my step-daughters, all I wanted to do was apologize and to say…one day tell them why I did it, but I know that they wouldn't really want to hear that now. I just feel for them. What I did, what happened to me, gave me the biggest CD in my offending. Because I wasn't hurting them, I didn't think I was…because I wasn't hurting them physically, and they was getting this and getting that…erm, I mean they used to get this and that anyway, before I…before I'd abused. I was all…I never chastised them or anything. Even my little ones, I never hit them, you know.

> MC: When you said CD do you mean cognitive distortion?

> Roger: Yes. I mean, I've used…when I was abusing…it was love and affection, it was our love and affection, our special type of love, and I thought they was responding to it, but obviously they were as frightened and scared as what I was. I can see that now.

The other form of life and associated language games that require consideration are associated with CBT – whether delivered in individual work or in a groupwork programme. The dialogue that introduces this section is taken from recent research I undertook with male sex offenders in prison (Cowburn 2002). There are a number of language games Roger is inviting me to play – for example men as caring fathers who love too much – but the one of interest here is the CBT game. In introducing myself as researcher, I mentioned my past experience as a probation officer working with sex offenders. In this section Roger uses technical jargon to which I could respond in kind: 'CD'. This language game is characterized by clinical jargon regularly used in CBT[1] but that otherwise do not have common usage. Potentially, it (re)constructs the offender as someone who has changed through the course of therapy. However, participation by offenders in this game leads workers to become suspicious of offenders using such language – potentially this takes us back to the positivist paradox of how we distinguish between those offenders who 'talk the talk' and those who 'walk the walk'.

Power, forms of life and language games

The concepts of forms of life and language games focus on the constructive nature of human interaction but Wittgenstein's work does not in any depth consider issues of power within forms of life and language games (O'Connor 2002, pp.441–2). Much of the early part of CBT with sex offenders focuses on how they have used power to commit their offences. However, in this section I am more concerned to examine the presence of power within the CB programme.

Foucault (1976, p.63) notes that, in Western societies, discussion about sexual behaviour has generally taken the form of 'confession'. Initially this form of discourse was directed and controlled by the church but, from the mid-nineteenth century onward, it came to be dominated by 'scientific' investigators and particularly by the medical profession. The notion of confession has implicit within it the relationship of confessor and confessee: an unequal relationship in which the person confessing is judged within the terms of the value framework of the person receiving the confession. Speaking of medical science, Foucault (1976, p.54) describes how it provided an intellectual structure that justified the attitudes and values of the dominant class in a society. The 'scientific' method gave power to one group to categorize and 'treat' other groups within a society. The CBT discourse concerning the offender assumes prior knowledge of the individual (embodied in diagnostic manuals and classification systems). By claiming prior knowledge, this can lead to the construction of a therapeutic method that is potentially oppressive in its original conception and in the manner in which it is subsequently delivered.

As early as 1990, Sheath raised concerns about the methods employed by some cognitive programmes run by the Probation Service. He suggested sex offenders were verbally coerced into admitting to and agreeing with probation workers' version of how the offence occurred. Sheath's paper is a rare example of critiquing the operation of power within a therapeutic programme, and specifically within the dialogical context of direct work with offenders. Overall, however, the use of power in the process of CBT has not concerned theorists or programme developers. In three relatively recent publications (Briggs *et al.* 1998; Marshall *et al.* 1998; Morrison, Erooga and Beckett 1994), power is only considered in the context of the offender committing his offences. There is no consideration of how the power of the worker affects the process and outcome of the therapy.

The nature of the relationship between sex offender and probation worker is very different to that found in psychodynamic therapy (where the client voluntarily enters the relationship), and the presence and operation of power seem to be obvious. The person (offender) no longer has a choice to engage in therapy, he or she is mandated to do so (Salter 1988, pp.85–7). The right to consent to treatment (with the exceptions of medical treatment and Drug Treatment and Testing Orders) whilst on probation in England and Wales was withdrawn in the 1991 Criminal Justice Act. The worker no longer views her/his client with 'unconditional positive regard', as stipulated by Carl Rogers for example (Rogers 1959), but with suspicion and mistrust (Salter 1988, pp.84–95). Along with the assumption that the offender frequently lies is the suspicion that he may lie about how the programme has affected his attitudes and behaviours.

Workers have mandated power that can significantly alter the future lifestyle and life chances of offenders. How a man performs on a programme or in individual work may affect whether he is allowed to rejoin his family. Inevitably, with such serious consequences, men learn to 'talk the talk' – they learn the language game of the treatment programme. This inevitably leaves doubt, despite the most rigorous positivistic evaluation, as to whether anything other than a script in a specific setting has changed. A way forward from this position of sceptical pessimism is to identify the range of forms of life and the diversity of language games associated with being a man and then to critically examine whether workers participate in or seek to change language games that are supportive of male sexual coercion. Additionally, consciously addressing how masculinities are performed within and beyond programmes may strengthen parts of the established cognitive programme – particularly relapse prevention.

Towards constructive work with male sex offenders

This chapter began by problematizing the CB paradigm that underpins and dominates work with sex offenders in the penal system (Joint Prison/Probation Accreditation Panel 2000–2001 (2001)). However, it is not my intention to suggest that constructive work with sex offenders cannot occur within this framework. I suggest that a constructive approach to working with sex offenders can be developed alongside the dominant approach and I focus on three areas where this may be possible:

1. developing an explicit value-base

2. thinking about cognitive distortions

3. working with(in) male forms of life and language games.

Developing an explicit value-base

In many ways this is not a new area of development. In the past I have outlined the values underpinning my work with sex offenders (Cowburn 1990, 1993; Cowburn and Modi 1995; Cowburn, Wilson and Loewenstein 1992); however, this is essential for developing constructive work with sex offenders because it is a way of explicitly stating the standpoint from which practice is developed (for a fuller discussion of standpoint see Harding 1991). In making explicit the values that inform work with sex offenders, workers recognize that all work inevitably embodies values particularly in relation to masculinity/ies, sexualities, coercion and the operation of power. The commonplace encounters in work with sex offenders embody ways of performing, ways of doing masculinities. An explicit value-base may help workers to become more aware of the commonplace and reflect on how their work performs (or not) the tasks of hegemonic masculinity. I suggest an appropriate starting point for values in work with sex offenders is feminist and pro-feminist analysis of the operation of gendered power.

A pro-feminist standpoint is the male complement of a feminist standpoint. Key features of it are familiarity with feminist critiques of patriarchy and male power, reflexivity and a desire to change dominant forms of male behaviour. Both Hearn (1998) and Pease (2000) consider an essential element in a pro-feminist position being an awareness of and sympathy to feminist critique and theory.

Such value-bases do not construe male sexual coercion as a 'deviant' but rather as part of the continuum of male behaviour identified by Kelly (1988). Male power and the ways it is used to harm others is a key element. Further work could be done to identify aspects of hegemonic masculinity that underpin or support male sexual coercion (for example compulsory heterosexuality, homophobia and misogyny) and particularly in explicitly developing a critical standpoint to these so-called 'normal' male attitudes.

To develop this aspect of work with sex offenders is to move away from the 'scientific' standpoint that is implicit in the CB programmes. The 'scientific' standpoint aspires to objective practice; however, as Harding (1991) has clearly demonstrated, this objectivity is the objectivity of the white heterosexual able-bodied middle-class man. And, as Foucault (1977, 1984) suggests, the knowledge developed privileges this group by creating a 'deviant' group, thus maintaining the dominance of the hegemonic group (Connell 1995) and leaving the attitudes and practices of the majority of men unquestioned. This is brought sharply into focus when considering the key concept of current cognitive work with sex offenders – the 'cognitive distortion'.

Thinking about cognitive distortions

Murphy (1990) identifies three approaches to understanding and working with cognitive distortions; the cognitive-behavioural, the feminist and the criminological. From a CB perspective 'distortions refer to self-statements made by offenders that allow them to deny, minimize, justify and rationalize their behavior (Abel, Becker *et al.* 1984; Wolf 1984; Rouleau, Abel *et al.* 1986)' (Murphy 1990, p.332).

Understanding of cognitive distortions from a feminist perspective highlights attitudes supportive of rape, sex role stereotyping, adversarial sexual beliefs and acceptance of interpersonal violence against women (Burt 1980; Koss and Dinero 1987; Malamuth 1986; Murphy, Coleman and Haynes 1986; Rapaport and Burkhart 1984). This body of literature makes links with wider male attitudes and behaviours but still considers them to be distortions in need of individual remedy.

In what Murphy (1990, p.332) calls the 'criminological literature', cognitive distortions are construed as a wider feature of offenders' lives rather than being closely linked to their offending behaviour. They are, however, viewed as a pathological problem, which is the principal focus of treatment.

The types of thinking which are generally identified by all models as being 'distorted' relate to how women and children are construed by male sex offenders: for example, Briggs and his colleagues (1998, p.105) cite as distorted thinking when offenders construe women who wear short skirts as being sexually available to any man. Other examples relate to how offenders describe their responsibility for offending and for the harm that their offences have caused.

Although these models differ in their emphasis, they share the view that the types of thinking identified as 'distorted' are aberrant thought processes. By this it is meant that they are not typical of the usual thought processes of the non-convicted population (of men). However, an alternative and more productive way of construing some of the thinking identified as distorted is to see it as ordinary and typical of many men. For example, in some of the language games around misogyny and compulsory heterosexuality, women are commonly construed as both sexually provocative and 'asking for it'. To construe such thinking as aberrant or distorted is to miss the point completely. Within certain male forms of life and language games, this thinking is commonplace. Scully (1990) was unable to distinguish rapists from non(convicted)-rapists when she examined their attitudes to women and their views of responsibility and harm in relation to rape. A more productive way forward may be to identify the wider language game and begin to challenge the misogynistic attitudes more widely prevalent in society. Many years ago, colleagues and I discussed the difficulties in running cognitive programmes (for individual offenders or groups) in which men learned to 'talk the talk' and yet still bought newspapers that objectified women and portrayed them solely as sexual objects. Our discussions ended in pessimistic resignation; however, if consideration is given to engaging critically with hegemonic forms of male behaviour and associated language games perhaps there is a way of naming, challenging and changing some hegemonic practices.

Working with(in) male forms of life and language games

Forms of life are ways of being located in and part of various cultures and subcultures. The forms of life that I am interested in here relate to being a man. There are many ways to begin to identify the diversity of male forms of life. In this chapter I have already used Mac an Ghaill's (1994) three sites for the development of male identities. Additionally, Connell (1995) studied three diverse groups of men and identified three areas of male praxis: power relations within families, employment and intimate desire. These areas are also sites for diverse male forms of life, each with their own language games.

The challenge for workers is two-fold: to identify how they are participating in various language games (or not) and to consider how alternative language games may be developed. I address the latter area in the final section of this chapter.

Participation in language games is, typically, unreflexive and automatic. This was highlighted to me, when working with a man convicted of rape. I was co-working with a female colleague. At one point in the interview, when the man was discussing his personal relationships, he turned to me and said, 'You know what women are like…' The words were phrased not as a question, but as a statement. He did not require an answer; he assumed that we shared a common understanding – that we were playing the same language game. On that occasion, I was not required to respond to him; I very consciously did not nod my head in affirmation of his point but I did not disturb his subsequent misogynistic discourse. More recently in my research with male sex offenders (Cowburn 2002), I was aware that my physical presence (as a man) appeared to facilitate the men in expressing themselves in a wide range of ways including using some of the problematic language games identified above. However, when I was invited to participate in these language games I either remained silent or asked naïve questions about the taken-for-granted element of the language game (for example women or gay men). The challenge for workers varies according to their different identities; however, the initial problem is to recognize language games and how they are linked to certain ways of being a man.

Then, they need to reflect on how and if they are participating in language games. Finally consideration needs to be given as to whether language games can be changed.

Alternative language games, alternative forms of life: Towards a new relapse prevention?

Within CBT helping the offender avoid re-offending is crucial. This process is termed 'relapse prevention' (Laws, Hudson and Ward 2000). Patterns of offending are deconstructed and thinking errors are identified, the offender is helped to identify how his offences occurred and how to avoid such situations in the future. Generally the emphasis is negative in that the offender learns what he must not do. However, to differing degrees, some approaches do consider what supports the offender needs to avoid relapsing into offending (Hudson, Wales and Ward 1998). This section identifies the potential of constructive work to develop new forms of life and language games that may consolidate and strengthen the more conventional cognitive approaches.

O'Connor (2002) considers the creative potential for self-consciously developing new language games that then create new forms of life. She highlights that 'the language available to individuals limits the meanings they can make of their experiences, and thus limits their worlds' (p.432). However, she emphasizes that developing new language games is not an internalized process, but a dialogical one. This necessarily raises issues for workers as to how they initiate and support the acquisition of new language games.

In O'Connor's work, the people (who were helped to develop new forms of life and new language games) recognized the destructive power of previous forms of life and sought less toxic ways of being. The issues with men convicted of sexual offences is how to help them to identify what they would like to change about themselves and how they behave. Without dialogical engagement that recognizes power in the worker–offender relationship, it is likely that the relationship may slip back into a coercive therapeutic form of life where offenders merely 'talk the talk' in the individual sessions or the group programme sessions.

However, the following areas may produce new language games and ways of being a man: expressing feelings and expressing love. In developing ways of speaking and being in these areas, other negative language games (misogyny, compulsory heterosexuality and homophobia) may be challenged and replaced.

I have observed sessions in cognitive programmes for sex offenders where they were expected to identify and non-verbally demonstrate a range of emotions. Initially, the workers helped the men identify feelings such as 'sad', 'angry', 'happy', 'fed up' and 'bored'. These words were written on cards and then each man, in turn, drew a card and tried to mime the emotion. The main objective of the exercise was to help the men recognize and show feelings. The process was essentially monological – the workers were the catalysts for the session and when the session was over the next component of the programme was addressed. Quite appropriately, within the constraints of CBT, no further attempts were made to address or more specifically enact such issues. No language game was developed or rehearsed. To develop language games and new forms of life these (and other) feelings would need to be contextualized and repeatedly rehearsed and adapted, with workers taking an active part in the process, not merely being passive expert bystanders. The language game for anger would, for example, need to be developed in ways that did not easily fall back into using homophobic or sexist stereotypes, even if anger was felt towards a woman or a gay man or lesbian. This is all very complex and requires a lot more of workers than merely completing (successfully) a training course in CBT techniques. It requires much exploration and a commitment to change and to develop personally during the work with sex offenders. The expert role is rejected and replaced with one of co-participant in developing (new) language games and forms of life.

The focus of the above work is strongly linked with Connell's (1995) notion of *cathexis* in so far as emotional repertoires (or not) play a part in close relationships. More specifically, however, language games relating to love are problematic. In my study of 2002, men conflated love with sex and spoke of showing parental love sexually. They also described having childhoods devoid of parental love and yet insisted they had 'the best parents in the world'. It is a challenging area for academic research and probation/clinical practice to identify forms of life and associated language games in relation to love (parental, friendship and sexual) but it is an area that is overlooked by most relapse prevention programmes.

The nature of a dialogical approach in working with sex offenders brings into stark relief the problem of 'treatment integrity' (also called 'programme integrity'). The term is concerned with the application of treatment in rigorous and similar manner over many programmes. The role of the worker is to implement a prescribed programme in as replicable way as possible (Aubut *et al.* 1998, p.222; Gordon and Hover 1998, pp.11–12). This potentially reduces the worker to an automaton delivering similar, preferably identical, programme sessions to many and diverse sex offenders over a long period of time. The aspiration behind this notion is one of scientific objectivity. The worker is the catalyst unaffected by the programme. The programme is seen as a monological process and aspires to the standards of scientific practice and so it can be evaluated scientifically (see Smith 2004 for a systematic critique of this approach). Such a concept, as it is currently configured, is both unrealistic and irrelevant to a constructive approach.

Constructive work with sex offenders reveals the world to be more complex than is assumed by those working within a natural science paradigm. Working self-consciously from a constructive perspective recognizes that dialogical processes (interview/groupwork) cannot be delivered clinically in an identical way each time. They involve different workers who have different ages, ethnic identities, sexualities, physical and mental abilities and, of course, different genders. The challenge of constructive work is not to aspire to deliver increasingly sterile packages in an unchanging fashion, but rather to develop reflexive practice based on an awareness of values, difference and most particularly themselves. Delineating such training is beyond the scope of this chapter but it points (again) in the direction of anti-oppressive practice and an exploration of values in action, and this requires workers to develop a critical awareness of themselves and how they contribute to the construction of male forms of life and language games.

Note

1. Examples of such 'jargon' would be (the list is not exhaustive): CD, cognitive distortion, cognitive restructuring, cycle of behaviour, masturbation and fantasy cycle, motivation to offend, my victim(s), offending behaviour, relapse, relapse prevention, responsibility, victim, victim empathy.

References

Abel, G.G., Becker, J.V., Cunningham-Rathner, J., Rouleau, J.L., Kaplan, M. and Reich, J. (1984) *The Treatment of Child Molesters*. Available from G.G. Abel, Behavior Medicine Institute, 5791 Kingston Cross, Stone Mountain, GA 30087.

Aubut, J., Proulx, J., Lamoureux, B. and McKibben, A. (1998) 'Sexual Offenders' Treatment program of the Philippe Pinel Institute of Montréal.' In W.L. Marshall, Y.M. Fernandez, S.M. Hudson and T. Ward (eds) *Sourcebook of Treatment Programs for Sexual Offenders*. New York: Plenum Press.

Beech, A.R., Fisher, D. and Beckett, R. (1999) *Step 3: An Evaluation of the Prison Sex Offender Treatment Programme*. London: Home Office.

Briggs, D., Doyle, P., Gouch, T. and Kennington, R. (1998) *Assessing Men Who Sexually Abuse: A Practice Guide*. London: Jessica Kingsley Publishers.

Burt, M.R. (1980) 'Cultural myths and supports for rape.' *Journal of Personality and Social Psychology* 38, 217–30.

Carrigan, T., Connell, R.W. and Lee, J. (1985) 'Toward a new sociology of masculinity.' *Theory and Society* 14, 551–604.

Clatterbaugh, K. (1998) 'What is problematic about masculinities?' *Men and Masculinities* 1, 1, 24–45.

Coleman, W. (1990) 'Doing masculinity/doing theory.' In J. Hearn and D. Morgan (eds) *Men, Masculinities and Social Theory.* London: Unwin Hyman.

Connell, R.W. (1995) *Masculinities.* Cambridge: Polity Press.

Connell, R.W. (2000) *The Men and the Boys.* Cambridge: Polity Press.

Cowburn, M. (1990) 'Work with male sex offenders in groups.' *Groupwork* 3, 2, 157–71.

Cowburn, M. (1993) 'Groupwork programmes for male sex offenders: Establishing principles for practice.' In A. Brown and B. Caddick (eds) *Groupwork with Offenders.* London: Whiting & Birch.

Cowburn, M. (2002) 'Men and violence: Life hi/stories of male sex offenders.' PhD thesis. School of Health and Related Research. Sheffield, University of Sheffield.

Cowburn, M. and Modi, P. (1995) 'Justice in an unjust context: Implications for working with adult male sex offenders.' In D. Ward and M. Lacey (eds) *Probation Working for Justice.* London: Whiting & Birch.

Cowburn, M., Wilson, C. and Loewenstein, P. (eds) (1992) *Changing Men: A Practice Guide to Working with Adult Male Sex Offenders.* Nottingham: Nottinghamshire Probation Service.

Crowle, T. (1990) 'I don't know why I did it.' In R. Bhaskar (ed.) *Harré and his Critics: Essays in Honour of Rom Harré with his Commentary on Them.* Oxford: Basil Blackwell.

Edley, N. and Wetherell, M. (1995) *Men in Perspective: Practice, Power, and Identity.* Hemel Hempstead: Prentice Hall/Harvester Wheatsheaf.

Faraday, A. and Plummer, K. (1979) 'Doing life histories.' *Sociological Review* 27, 4, 773–98.

Fielding, N. (1994) 'Cop canteen culture.' In T. Newburn and E.A. Stanko (eds) *Just Boys Doing Business? Men, Masculinities and Crime.* London: Routledge.

Foucault, M. (1976) *The History of Sexuality: An Introduction.* London: Penguin.

Foucault, M. (1977) *Discipline and Punish: The Birth of the Prison.* London: Allen Lane.

Foucault, M. (1984) *The History of Sexuality: An Introduction.* London: Peregrine.

Franklin, M. (1997) 'Making sense: Interviewing and narrative representation.' In M.M. Gergen and S.N. Davis (eds) *Toward a New Psychology of Gender.* London: Routledge.

Genders, E. and Player, E. (1995) *Grendon: A Study of a Therapeutic Prison.* Oxford: Oxford University Press.

Gergen, K.J. (2000) *An Invitation to Social Construction.* London: Sage.

Gergen, K.J. and Gergen, M.M. (1986) 'Narrative from and the construction of psychological theory.' In T.S. Sarbin (ed.) *Narrative Psychology: The Storied Nature of Human Conduct.* New York: Praeger.

Gordon, A. and Hover, G. (1998) 'The twin rivers sex offender treatment program.' In W.L. Marshall, Y.M. Fernandez, S.M. Hudson and T. Ward (eds) *Sourcebook of Treatment Programs for Sexual Offenders.* New York: Plenum.

Harding, S. (1991) *Whose Science? Whose Knowledge? Thinking from Women's Lives.* Milton Keynes: Open University Press.

Harré, R. (1995) 'Agentive discourse.' In R. Harré and P. Stearns (eds) *Discursive Psychology in Practice.* London: Sage.

Harré, R., Clarke, C. and De Carlo, N. (1985) *Motives and Mechanisms: An Introduction to the Psychology of Action.* London: Methuen.

Hearn, J. (1998) 'Theorizing men and men's theorizing: Varieties of discursive practices in men's theorizing of men.' *Theory and Society* 27, 781–816.

Hearn, J. (2004) 'From hegemonic masculinity to the hegemony of men.' *Feminist Theory* 5, 1, 49–72.

Hudson, S.M., Wales, D.S. and Ward, T. (1998) 'Kia Marama: A treatment program for child molesters in New Zealand.' In W.L. Marshall, Y.M. Fernandez, S.M. Hudson and T. Ward (eds) *Sourcebook of Treatment Programs for Sexual Offenders*. New York: Plenum.

Joint Prison/Probation Accreditation Panel 2000–2001 (2001) *Second Report from the Joint Prison/Probation Accreditation Panel*. London: JPPAP.

Kelly, L. (1998) Surviving Sexual Violence. Oxford: Polity Press.

Kendall, K. (2004) 'Dangerous thinking: A critical history of correctional cognitive behaviouralism.' In G. Mair (ed.) *What Matters in Probation*. Cullompton, Devon: Willan Publishing.

Koss, M.P. and Dinero, D.E. (1987) *Predictors of Sexual Aggression among a National Sample of Male College Students*. New York: New York Academy of Sciences Conference on Human Sexual Aggression: Current Perspectives.

Laws, D.R., Hudson, S.M. and Ward, T. (eds) (2000) *Remaking Relapse Prevention with Sex Offenders: A Sourcebook*. Thousand Oaks, CA, and London: Sage.

Leberg, E. (1997) *Understanding Child Molesters*. London: Sage.

Mac an Ghaill, M. (1994) *The Making of Men: Masculinities, Sexualities, and Schooling*. Buckingham: Open University.

Malamuth, N.M. (1986) 'Predictors of naturalistic sexual aggression.' *Journal of Personality and Social Psychology* 45, 432–42.

Marshall, W.L., Fernandez, Y.M., Hudson, S.M. and Ward, T. (eds) (1998) *Sourcebook of Treatment Programs for Sexual Offenders*. New York and London: Plenum Press.

McGinn, M. (1997) *Wittgenstein and the Philosophical Investigations*. London: Routledge.

Morrison, T., Erooga, M. and Beckett, R. (eds) (1994) *Sexual Offending Against Children: Assessment and Treatment of Male Abusers*. London: Routledge.

Murphy, W.D. (1990) 'Assessment and modification of cognitive distortions.' In W.L. Marshall, D.R. Laws and H.E. Barbaree (eds) *Handbook of Sexual Assault: Issues, Theories and Treatment of the Offender*. New York and London: Plenum Press.

Murphy, W.D., Coleman, E.M. and Haynes, M.R. (1986) 'Factors related to coercive sexual behavior in a nonclinical sample of males.' *Violence and Victims* 1, 255–78.

O'Connor, P. (2002) 'Moving to new boroughs: Transforming the world by inventing language games.' In N. Scheman and P. O'Connor (eds) *Feminist Interpretations of Ludwig Wittgenstein*. Pennsylvania: The Pennsylvania State University Press.

Pease, B. (2000) *Recreating Men: Postmodern Masculinity Politics*. London: Sage.

Pleck, J.H. (1976) 'The male sex role: problems, definitions, and sources of change.' *Journal of Social Issues* 32, 155–64.

Rapaport, K. and Burkhart, B. (1984) 'Personality and attitudinal characteristics of sexually coercive college males.' *Journal of Abnormal Psychology* 93, 216–21.

Rogers, C.R. (1959) 'A theory of therapy, personality and interpersonal relationships as developed in the client-centered framework.' In S. Koch (ed.) *Psychology: A Study of a Science: Formations of the Person in the Social Context*. New York: McGraw-Hill.

Rouleau, J.L., Abel, G.G., Mittelman, M.S., Becker, J.V. and Cunningham-Rathner, J. (1986) *Effectiveness of Each Component of a Treatment Program for Non-incarcerated Pedophiles*. NIMH-sponsored Conference on Sex Offenders, Tampa, FL.

Salter, A.C. (1988) *Treating Child Sexual Offenders and Victims: A Practical Guide*. Newbury Park, London and New Delhi: Sage.

Scully, D. (1990) *Understanding Sexual Violence: A Study of Convicted Rapists*. Cambridge, MA, and London: Unwin Hyman.

Sheath, M. (1990) 'Confrontative work with sex offenders: Legitimised nonce-bashing?' *Probation Journal* 37, 4, 159–62.

Shotter, J. (1993) *Conversational Realities: Constructing Life through Language*. London: Sage.

Shotter, J. (1995) 'Dialogical psychology.' In J. Smith, R. Harré and L. Van Langenhove (eds) *Rethinking Psychology*. London: Sage.

Sim, J. (1994) 'Tougher than the rest? Men in prison.' In T. Newburn and E.A. Stanko (eds) *Just Boys Doing Business? Men, Masculinities and Crime.* London: Routledge.

Smith, D. (2004) 'The uses and abuses of positivism.' In G. Mair (ed.) *What Matters in Probation.* Cullompton, Devon: Willan Publishing.

Thornhill, R. and Palmer, C.T. (2001) *A Natural History of Rape: Biological Bases of Sexual Coercion.* Cambridge, MA, and London: MIT.

Whitehead, S.M. (2002) *Men and Masculinities: Key Themes and New Directions.* Cambridge: Polity Press.

Wittgenstein, L. (1953) *Philosophical Investigations.* Oxford: Blackwell.

Wolf, S.C. (1984) *A Multi-factor Model of Deviant Sexuality.* Third National Conference on Victimology, Lisbon, Portugal.

Chapter 10

Dispensing [with?] Justice
Young People's Views of the Criminal Justice System

Monica Barry

Introduction

The principles of justice have never been so challenged as they currently are
in relation to youth offending. A dictionary definition of 'justice' includes
words such as 'fairness', 'integrity', 'impartiality' and 'rightness', concepts
that are increasingly undermined by our present criminal and youth justice
systems. Young people have never been a political priority and yet they have
received an unprecedented amount of adverse political attention in recent
years, notably in respect of law and order. Whilst the majority of criminal
convictions apply to young people in the age range 16–21, only a small percentage of this age group becomes embroiled in the criminal justice system.
For example, in Scotland in 2001, only 4 per cent of all 16–21-year-olds
had a charge proved (Scottish Executive 2002). Thus, the problem of youth
offending – for the criminal justice system at least – is not as extensive as
politicians and the media would have us believe, and yet young people are
bearing the brunt of increased political and media hype about a widespread
and growing youth crime problem that can only seemingly be curtailed
through increased and more punitive political directives.

This chapter takes a critical look at the criminal justice system from the
perspective of young people aged approximately 16–25 who have been
involved in offending. It is argued that what young people want from
criminal justice professionals to help them stop offending and what the government wants to be seen to be doing with young people who offend are
diametrically opposed in both principle and practice. The chapter also questions whether current policy is not only 'dispensing justice' in a merely

administrative fashion but also perhaps more accurately 'dispensing *with* justice', in the pursuit of spiralling political one-upmanship.

Whilst criminal justice practitioners in England and Wales are part of the Probation Service and are referred to as 'probation officers', in Scotland they remain part of the remit of local authority social work departments and are thus referred to as 'criminal justice social workers'. However, throughout this chapter, they will be referred to as 'criminal justice practitioners', since it is argued that there is little to differentiate between them both north and south of the border.

Likewise, although the views of young offenders presented here come from one particular jurisdiction within the UK, namely Scotland, with its own system of criminal justice legislation and practice, the views of offenders in Scotland are nevertheless comparable with those of their counterparts in England and Wales in stressing the need for practical and emotional support irrespective of offending behaviour (Barry 2000, 2005). This strength and consistency of opinion is all the more remarkable given the different legislative and practice procedures in each jurisdiction.

Later sections of this chapter describe the context in which recent changes to the criminal justice system in the UK have taken place and highlight the differences between these views and those of the 'What Works' literature, for it is the latter which holds the key to understanding many of the changes in criminal justice policy and practice in recent years.

What works for young people

The following views of young offenders were elicited from two qualitative research studies undertaken in Scotland involving samples who had had experience of probation under the new 'regime' of a 'What Works' agenda. They are known here as the Probation Study (McIvor and Barry 1998) and the Desistance Study (Barry 2004). The Probation Study fieldwork was undertaken in 1995 and comprised both quantitative analysis of 155 probation orders and in-depth interviews with 65 probationers about their current probation orders. The respondents, the majority of whom were men, ranged in age from 16 to 50, with 54 per cent aged 25 or under. The aim of the research was to assess the impact of 100 per cent funding for community-based criminal justice social work services and the effectiveness of National Standards (both policies having been introduced in Scotland in 1991). The Desistance Study fieldwork was undertaken in 2000/1 and comprised qualitative interviews with 40 current and previous offenders (who had also been on probation in the past) about their experiences of starting and stopping offending. The age range was 18 to 33, with 29 respondents aged 25 or under, and there was an equal mix of men and women.

When exploring with young people their views about 'What Works' in criminal justice interventions, certain key themes emerge which are consistent across both time and jurisdiction. These themes are that practitioners should foster a friendly, caring and encouraging relationship with their clients; interventions should be premised on the importance of giving practical help and advice to clients, depending on their perceived needs; and practitioners should build on their clients' strengths rather than focus on their weaknesses. These themes are not peculiar to young offenders alone, nor only to offenders in Scotland. On the contrary, they have been cited by offenders of all ages throughout the UK (Barry 2000; Farrall 2002; Maruna 2001). These themes are categorized below and used in the sections that follow to highlight the views of young people to:

- build up a relationship with the client based on trust, listening and respect

- focus more on practical circumstances than on addressing offending behaviour per se

- offer encouragement for the future.

The relationship with the client

One of the key components of effective practice in the vast majority of professions, not just in criminal justice, is the relationship between worker and client, because only through that relationship can meaningful dialogue and action be sustained. Young people in particular need the 'sounding board' element that relationships can enable, so as to encourage appropriate development, positive learning experiences and meaningful interaction with others. In the later stages of the transition to adulthood, relationships with 'adults' tend to have an increased significance to many young people, whilst relationships with peers may become less essential to the building of one's own identity (Barry 2001; Shover 1996). Whilst for the women in the Desistance Study having one's own child or partner were also strong influencing factors in their decision to stop offending, invariably the people most likely to influence young people in their decision to desist from crime were parents (usually a renewed relationship in early adulthood following a breakdown in communication during adolescence) and professional workers (e.g. social workers, probation workers, teachers and youth workers):

> I don't think I'd have known what to do without [probation worker] half the time. It was him I first told about my drugs problem, the very first person I told. (17-year-old man, Probation Study)

> I connected with the people [in an intensive probation project]... I liked [the project worker] although he was English!...but he seemed a nice enough person, so I let him basically get inside my brain. If you felt you wanted to ask something, he said 'ask away, I'll answer as truthfully as I can'. And the older I'm getting, the more I'm feeling...[he] is an exceptional man. I could really connect with him. (24-year-old man, Desistance Study)

The importance of relationships to these young people was the fact that they generally brought mutual respect and trust, and it was the resultant feeling of self-worth that gave the young people the support they needed to change their behaviour:

> You get respect... I feel proud because you're not committing offences. You're not letting people down. (18-year-old man, Desistance Study)

> People don't look down their noses at you any more 'cos they don't see you as a hooligan. It sort of gives you a bit, sort of, respect. (24-year-old man, Desistance Study)

When the respondents in both studies put themselves in the role of criminal justice practitioners, the majority took an holistic view of the client and his/her needs, stressing the importance of getting to know the person, their lifestyle, their family background, their current problems and their future aspirations. They did not see this as an intrusion into somebody's privacy if it was clear to the probationer that sharing information that the individual *wanted* to share might help to resolve their current problems:

> Let [the client] talk about what he wants to talk about, and not what you want to know. (17-year-old man, Probation Study)

There was also a stress on the need for the practitioner to have a genuine rather than tokenistic interest in the client:

> It's not just ten to fifteen minutes in the office once a month. [The probation worker] has got to be someone who wants to help. (19-year-old man, Probation Study)

> I know they're busy people, but they should be there for you when you need to see them. (22-year-old man, Probation Study)

Finally, the art of listening was crucial for criminal justice social work intervention to be effective:

> It was great to know there was someone there to listen to me and to understand where I was coming from. (22-year-old woman, Probation Study)

Practical help versus addressing offending

Offending is often seen by young people as a manifestation of more deep-rooted problems in their lives, whether past or present: a symptom rather than a cause of current circumstances. There is thus a need to address the circumstances rather than the offending behaviour per se. Most thought that there was little else a criminal justice practitioner could do, other than offer practical and emotional support. They felt on the whole that criminal justice practitioners could do little to reduce offending, whereas they could do a lot to alleviate other problems in their lives. Reducing offending was very much seen as something that had to come from the individual, as the following quotes illustrate:

> [Y]ou can only change yourself. Nobody else can change you. (17-year-old man, Probation Study)

> I don't think I would have changed at 17. I don't think I was ready to talk about anything that had happened to me or anything…until the person's ready to talk about it and settle down…they have to be ready for it. They have to be ready within themselves…ready to see the light. (23-year-old female, Desistance Study)

Whilst approximately a third of probationers in the Probation Study thought that tackling offending should be a key aim of probation, not least because further offending would result in breaching the order, they also recognized the greater importance of tackling other problems in their lives, since offending was invariably seen as a by-product of other issues such as poverty, boredom, peer group pressure or unfair discrimination by the police, for example. One young woman in the Desistance Study wanted a greater emphasis to be placed on drug use rather than on offending per se:

> …sit and listen to what they're doing, what their day-to-day routine [is], what their background is, why they're doing it, how are they doing it, do they want to come off it. If they don't want to come off it, there's no point in trying to help them… If you're offending, you're offending for a reason. (21-year-old woman, Desistance Study)

Equally, a 'one-size-fits-all' approach (Pitts 2001, p.11) to probation supervision is not what young people want, as one 27-year-old woman in the Desistance Study explained:

> Give them support that suits that individual because everybody – there's that many different people out there that need that many different types of support. But people assume, like, because like you've been sexually abused, they think you just need counselling for abuse, but there's a lot more to it.

The factors aiding desistance which were cited by the majority of these respondents included motivation (having something to lose by renewed offending), having support to stabilize or reduce substance misuse, having responsibilities (through employment, child-rearing or having one's own tenancy) and having access to constructive activities and relevant advice. These factors were unlikely to be offered through, for example, cognitive-behavioural programmes looking at the consequences of offending or victim awareness. Whilst important in their own right, cognitive-behavioural programmes need to operate alongside one-to-one support of a more practical rather than supervisory nature. Many young people seek help from criminal justice practitioners to access education or employment opportunities, to find their own tenancy or to negotiate state benefits, and many suggest that once they have got their own house in order, they are more likely to be amenable to more cognitive-behavioural approaches.

Encouragement for the future

According to many offenders, irrespective of age, supervision should not focus on the past but on the future, since it is positive opportunities in the future that are likely to reduce the need or desire to re-offend. This is where taking an holistic approach to the practical and emotional needs of offenders is crucial in helping to motivate them to change their lifestyles and behaviour. Farrall (2002) suggests that offender motivation is more likely to aid desistance than probation supervision per se, but that the supervisory relationship may be crucial in helping to build that motivation. Encouragement and praise, both of which can boost self-confidence, were always noted when present in the supervisory relationship, as the following two quotes suggest:

> [I gained] a wee bit of confidence in myself. Just with [my probation worker]…saying that I was good staying out of trouble for this amount of time. I felt a lot more confident than what I was. I thought I was a loser, the

only thing I could do was steal things, but he made me feel a bit more confident in myself. (22-year-old male, Probation Study)

I was still dealing when I went to probation and I really did get a lot of help there and that was when I stopped the dealing and I was trying to come off all the time and they really did, you know, [tell me] 'keep going, you're doing well'. They were brilliant, absolutely brilliant. (23-year-old woman, Desistance Study)

A major factor which restricts young people's ability to focus on the future is their reputation as an offender. Much of one's reputation springs from one's own actions and Emler (1990) suggests that for young people with no other status or power, a bad reputation is often preferable to no reputation at all, since it at least attracts attention and recognition from one's peers. Law-abiding behaviour only offers one a reputation by default, whereas deviance has a more profound and immediate effect on one's reputation amongst one's peers (Emler 1990). However, whilst wanting to maintain the attention and kudos amongst their peers through their former reputation as an offender, young people, when they decide to stop offending, often find that their previously 'bad' reputation within the community goes before them. One 27-year-old woman in the Desistance Study, who had stopped offending completely two years prior to interview, suggested that the local community still labelled her as an offender:

Everyone would look down on me, they still actually do...and names stick.

Many young people felt that the police were not encouraging:

I'm too well known by the police – they stop and question me for no reason, and people judge me. (23-year-old man, Desistance Study)

Having a criminal record was also seen by many young offenders as exacerbating their chances of 'turning over a new leaf', as one 18-year-old man in the Desistance Study explained in relation to employment opportunities:

Nobody's gonna accept me...because of my criminal record.

The Desistance Study found that having positive opportunities which would replace the need to offend, and having something or someone to be responsible for, were factors which had a major influence on young people's propensity to stop or reduce offending:

Well now I've got a job...I've got something to look forward to...when I get up in the morning. (22-year-old man, Desistance Study)

I've got something better, that I thought I never could have – a good man, a lovely house, a nice life. (25-year-old female, Desistance Study)

Nobody wants to go on like that for the rest of their life… [I stopped] for my family, for the people I care about, the people that matter. (22-year-old female, Desistance Study)

However, it is difficult within the criminal justice system as it presently stands (partly because of the long time scale between offence and disposal and partly because of the restrictions placed on offenders as a result of certain disposals) for young people to be offered the opportunity for a 'clean slate', wherein they have the space, the resources and the support to reorder their lives. In that respect, many young people talk of a 'vicious circle' of offending–sentencing–stigmatization–marginalization–deprivation– offending, and so on. That vicious circle is likely to be exacerbated by changes in criminal justice policy that focus even more narrowly on the individual at the expense of his/her wider circumstances. Yet, this is exactly what is envisaged by the wholesale adoption of 'What Works' principles in criminal justice policy, as the following section demonstrates.

What works for policy-makers

The criminal justice 'What Works' agenda had its origins in the 1980s when it developed in response to the criticism that 'nothing works' from a rehabilitative perspective in reducing offending (McGuire and Priestley 1995) and that a greater focus should be placed on a more centralized, administrative approach to law and order (Harris 1996). Large-scale quantitative studies, notably from North America, have since the 1980s increasingly influenced policy-makers in the UK to focus on cognitive-behavioural approaches to offending, almost totally to the exclusion of the wider social environment within which such behaviour takes place. A set of common needs and risk factors were identified by academics as a result of meta-analyses of these quantitative studies which seemingly enabled offending behaviour to be predicted, contained and modified. It was concluded from this 'What Works' research that effective practice can only be achieved through interventions that are closely monitored and evaluated, and consistently replicated throughout the criminal justice system.

Thus 'hard evidence' replaced 'gut feelings' as the driving force for criminal justice practitioners (HM Inspectorate of Probation 1998, p.viii). Evidence-based practice is practice which is based primarily on external research findings rather than on practitioner expertise, and some would argue that this has resulted in increased managerialism and accountability at the expense of a concern for individual need and welfare (Smith 2004). Trotter (1999) suggests that evidence-based practice can only in effect work with the presenting problem (offending) rather than wider socio-economic concerns because the presenting problem is more amenable to measurement and evaluation. It is also politically more expedient to blame and change individuals rather than to blame and change social structures. Thus, since the 1980s, there has been an increasing focus on the offender's behaviour rather than his/her circumstances that has allowed psychology (which focuses on the individual) rather than sociology (which focuses on wider socio-economic factors) to become the theoretical mainstay of criminal justice policy (Kendall 2004). And yet, as the young people in these studies often suggested, offending behaviour can be a manifestation of troubles external to and beyond the control of the individual.

To ensure that criminal justice practitioners were made accountable for and could demonstrate effectiveness in their interventions with offenders, National Standards were published in the early 1990s, setting out procedures and guidelines for various criminal justice services. Whilst it is acknowledged as important to have standards against which practice can be measured, these should complement rather than replace professional discretion and well-established methods of effective practice with offenders. However, National Standards focus on addressing offending behaviour by prescribing assessment procedures, requiring standardized groupwork programmes and specifying targets and outcomes, often to the exclusion of the wider circumstances for individual offenders. Assessments focus almost entirely on risk of re-offending, groupwork programmes by definition cannot be tailor-made to individual needs, targets encourage 'number crunching' and the primary outcome of interventions remains one of changing behaviour – reducing the frequency or seriousness of offending – in order to protect the public rather than to rehabilitate the offender (Robinson and McNeill 2004).

Groupwork programmes became standard practice within probation in the early 1990s throughout the UK, with the expectation that standardized programmes would bring national consistency and value for money and allow greater measurement of effectiveness. Irrespective of them often being inappropriate to young people's intellectual and maturational capacities, such group-oriented programmes by definition also restrict the adoption of an holistic and tailor-made approach to young people's problems (Barry 2005). 'What Works' principles rest on cognitive-behavioural approaches not only because they are easier to measure than less structured approaches, but also because they tend to lessen the need to emphasize the wider social and economic context, a facet of the 'What

Works' literature that has received much recent academic criticism (Kendall 2004; McIvor 2004; Rogowski 2003/4; Smith 1998).

> While offenders may benefit to varying degrees from structured interventions aimed at changing their attitudes and behaviour, such benefits are likely to be limited and short-lived if attention is not similarly paid to their wider social and personal needs. Greater emphasis correspondingly needs to be placed upon social inclusion and upon putting 'people' back into the equation by recognizing the importance of the supervisory relationship in enhancing offenders' motivation not to re-offend. (McIvor 2004, p.305)

It could be argued that groupwork programmes focus on commonalities within behaviours at the expense of the wider difficulties young people face as individuals in society. Equally, groupwork programmes operate in a socio-economic vacuum and cannot differentiate between individuals, in terms of level of risk, needs and circumstances. Thus such programmes discourage workers from addressing individual problems. There are also high drop-out rates from accredited programmes (Spencer and Deakin 2004), which has resulted in the government halving the numbers required to undertake accredited programmes since they were first introduced (see Chapter 1, this volume).

Andrews (1995) identifies several factors which he considers are 'promising targets' based on 'What Works' research:

- changing anti-social thinking

- improving cognitive-behavioural skills

- reducing substance misuse

- changing other attributes which are linked to criminal conduct.

These factors require change only to the individual: they do not look at the context in which behaviour and personality development take place, they do not address extraneous factors, they focus on negative rather than positive factors and they do not require a genuine one-to-one relationship between worker and client. They are also relatively conducive to quantitative measurement. However, Andrews also identifies less promising targets for change – which are less measurable and, by inference, should receive less attention. These are:

- increasing self-esteem (without simultaneously addressing anti-social attitudes and behaviour)

- focusing on 'vague emotional/personal complaints' that have not been linked to criminal conduct

- improving living conditions (without simultaneously addressing anti-social attitudes and behaviour)

- increasing conventional ambition in school and work (without offering concrete support to realize those ambitions).

Although these subsidiary factors acknowledge the need to address more practical issues for offenders, the first three have the proviso that there should also be an emphasis on changing individual behaviour rather than the wider society. None of these factors was drawn up in consultation with young offenders. On the contrary, they seem totally at odds with the views of young people in the criminal justice system, as evidenced by the research cited in the previous section.

Whilst National Standards focus predominantly on the presenting problem, in Scotland they do leave some discretion with the practitioner to address other client needs, such as personal or social problems (McIvor 2004), but only where these directly contribute to offending or affect community integration (so-called 'criminogenic needs'). Scotland has not become as centralized or specific in its programming of offender work as have England and Wales and it has been suggested (McIvor 2004; Robinson and McNeill 2004) that this is because criminal justice social work in Scotland is still tied into generic social work departments wherein social justice is a founding principle. However, the preferred agenda for policy-makers in Scotland, following devolution, is now the management of risk and reducing the likelihood of further offending (Robinson and McNeill 2004) – irrespective of the cause of that behaviour and, more important perhaps, irrespective of the views and concerns of the clients themselves. Certainly, from the preceding qualitative data from young people 'at the coal face', it would seem that such a criminal justice policy is at best misguided and at worst counterproductive.

Many academics argue for criminal justice policies to be placed within the context of wider social policies. Drakeford and Vanstone (2000), for example, suggest that:

> The myth that criminal justice services, by themselves, can tackle crime and protect the public is one which has both made the realisation of those essential goals less attainable and caused substantial harm to those services themselves, subverting traditional aims and purposes and substituting ambitions which are unrealisable at both individual and corporate levels...
> Rather than pursue criminal justice outcomes through social policy measures, the government is in danger of reaching always for criminal justice solutions to problems which more appropriately lie in the civic

space in which the benefits of an education, an income and a place to live are distributed. (p.378)

Constructive work with young offenders

It would seem that the official view of 'What Works' differs dramatically from young people's assessment of 'What Works'. The official view of 'What Works' is that one needs to address anti-social thinking, increase cognitive-behavioural skills and contain or change individual behaviour – all preferably within a groupwork setting. The official view, in effect, sees young offenders as problematic and 'set apart' from the mainstream. Mair (2004, p.2) suggests that the 'What Works' 'juggernaut' implies a medical or deficit model of deviance that can only be ameliorated through educating offenders using cognitive-behavioural methods. The young offender's view of 'What Works', on the other hand, is that the professional relationship should be genuine and based on listening and respect; that young people need more proactive, practical advice and greater opportunities for employment, education and leisure; and that young people want a greater stake in society and integration within the mainstream.

According to Parton and O'Byrne (2000, p.1), social work 'has become very defensive, overly proceduralised and narrowly concerned with assessing, managing and insuring against risk'. This results in the depersonalization of the intervention and a focus on the presenting behaviour of the client. Thompson (2000, p.4) argues that although social work has a dual function of care and control, if control becomes dominant at the expense of care, then practice can become oppressive and counterproductive: 'a failure to address the client's needs is likely to make for a more stressful situation, and therefore to make the need for policing even greater'. Equally, Thompson (2000) identifies five types of what he describes as 'dangerous' practice in social work: routinized, defensive, defeatist, oppressive and chaotic. It could be argued that the current emphasis within criminal justice on a narrow 'What Works' agenda could meet at least four of these five criteria for bad practice. Whilst arguably not chaotic in their arrangements – although recent government u-turns on achievable targets might suggest otherwise – such interventions could arguably be described as routinized, defensive, defeatist and oppressive. Routinized practice fails to respond in a 'tailor-made' fashion to particular problems for individual offenders; defensive practice may result in workers not addressing clients' perceived needs but focusing disproportionately on risk factors; defeatist practice can result when workers are not encouraged to use their professional discretion; and oppressive practice means focusing solely on the offender's behaviour at the expense of addressing wider social problems which may exacerbate that behaviour.

The focus of this book as a whole has been on a constructive approach to work with people involved in the criminal justice system. The views of young people in this chapter about 'What Works' – the relationship with the criminal justice practitioner and the need for practical support and encouragement for the future – are also views which are highly compatible with the theory and practice of social constructionism. Listening, talking and collaboration between worker and client are crucial components of constructive practice, and this relationship is inextricably linked to the success or otherwise of professional supervision. Constructive practice also encourages clients to seek solutions for positive futures rather than to dwell on the problems of their negative pasts. However, one limitation of the present approach to constructive work with young offenders is that such work does not overtly confront the fact that there are socio-economic and political restrictions placed on young people's ability to mobilize their own resources. An over-emphasis on changing behaviour and ignoring structural inequalities may result in young people yet again blaming themselves, or being blamed by others, for their inability to improve their circumstances. Much of the desistance literature would concur that behaviour cannot be changed in a vacuum; changed behaviour requires a simultaneous change of circumstances – and a change of policy direction – if that modified behaviour is to be sustained (Barry forthcoming).

Constructive work with offenders requires the building of positive solutions between worker and client based on a negotiated understanding of the client's social world. However, such a negotiated understanding needs to be a collaborative effort between more than just the worker and the client; policy-makers and other key stakeholders with the power to influence the criminal justice system also need to be involved in a wider debate with both practitioners and clients. In recent years, this consensus building between interested parties has not been in evidence and the views of young offenders about 'What Works' are not shared by those with the power to manage or reform the criminal justice system.

A commitment to social justice should be a key component of work with offenders, allowing practitioners to challenge oppression and discrimination. Thompson (2000, p.118) suggests that: 'To work alongside social injustice without seeking to address it as a serious social problem can clearly be seen as an unethical form of practice, in so far as it involves leaving oppressive structures and established practices intact.' Current criminal justice policy which isolates the offending behaviour from the external circumstances in which that behaviour is manifested is not only 'dispensing justice' in a cold and calculated vacuum, but is also 'dispensing *with* justice' because of its oppressive and discriminatory focus.

New Labour is more willing than the previous Conservative government to listen to the findings of research into effectiveness, but there are still several problems in relation to criminal justice that New Labour has failed to address. First, the government still sees punishment through criminal justice policy, as opposed to rehabilitation through social policy, as being the appropriate response to offending behaviour. Second, 'What Works' research focuses too narrowly on measurable outcomes relating only to offending behaviour. Finally, the 'What Works' literature ignores the views of the clients themselves, possibly because their views highlight the unpalatable truth that offending behaviour is closely correlated with and influenced by structural inequalities.

Conclusion

This chapter has described the views of young people about criminal justice social work and contrasted these with the recent shift in policy towards the management and containment of offenders. Young people consistently want one approach whilst the 'What Works' literature consistently recommends another. It would seem that young people define effective practice in terms of traditional social work values of justice, respect, empathy, rehabilitation and integration. They see offending more as a symptom of other problems in their lives rather than the cause of those other problems. They want emotional and practical support to gain opportunities to lead law-abiding lives. Current policy and practice, however, is tending to erode traditional social work values and is becoming oppressive, discriminatory and reactive, based more on political expediency than on any commitment to addressing root causes of offending. Cognitive-behavioural programmes have their place, but only, it is argued here, in conjunction with – not instead of – proactive professional support.

Young people need incentives (carrots, not sticks) to change their lifestyles, but the 'What Works' agenda offers little in the way of such incentives. Young people have become pawns in a struggle between political parties to be seen to be 'tough' on crime and populist approaches to politics flourish on superficial reviews and the constant tinkering of policies aimed at the presenting problems of a minority group. Regrettably, young people are just such a minority group and criminal justice policies are always ripe for new political initiatives which catch the headlines but fail to truly address the problems. As the title of this chapter suggests, a narrow focus on past behaviour at the expense of encouraging future opportunities is a mechanistic way of dispensing justice, and could arguably be better described as dispensing *with* justice.

References

Andrews, D. (1995) 'The psychology of criminal conduct and effective treatment.' In J. McGuire (ed.) *What Works: Reducing Offending.* Chichester: Wiley.

Barry, M. (2000) 'The mentor/monitor debate in criminal justice: "What Works" for offenders.' *British Journal of Social Work* 30, 575–95.

Barry, M. (2001) *Challenging Transitions: Young People's Views and Experiences of Growing Up.* London: Save the Children/Joseph Rowntree Foundation.

Barry, M. (2004) 'Understanding youth offending: In search of social recognition.' Unpublished PhD thesis, Stirling, University of Stirling.

Barry, M. (2005) 'A curriculum by any other name... The parallels between youth work and criminal justice.' *Youth and Policy* 86, 19–32.

Barry, M. (forthcoming) Youth Offending and Youth Transitions: In search of social recognition. Abingdon: Routledge.

Drakeford, M. and Vanstone, M. (2000) 'Social exclusion and the politics of criminal justice: A tale of two administrations.' *The Howard Journal* 39, 4, November.

Emler, N. (1990) 'Social reciprocity.' In W. Stroebe and M. Hewstone (eds) *European Review of Social Psychology, Vol. 1.* Chichester: John Wiley and Sons.

Farrall, S. (2002) *Rethinking What Works with Offenders.* Cullompton: Willan.

Harris, R. (1996) 'Telling tales: Probation in the contemporary social formation.' In N. Parton (ed.) *Social Theory, Social Change and Social Work.* London: Routledge.

HM Inspectorate of Probation (1998) *Evidence Based Practice: A Guide to Effective Practice.* London: Home Office.

Kendall, K. (2004) 'Dangerous thinking: A critical history of correctional cognitive behaviouralism.' In G. Mair (ed.) *What Matters in Probation.* Cullompton: Willan.

Mair, G. (2004) 'Introduction: What works and what matters.' In G. Mair (ed.) *What Matters in Probation.* Cullompton: Willan.

Maruna, S. (2001) *Making Good: How Ex-convicts Reform and Rebuild their Lives.* Washington DC: American Psychological Association.

McGuire, J. and Priestley, P. (1995) 'Reviewing "What Works": Past, present and future.' In J. McGuire (ed.) *What Works: Reducing Offending.* Chichester: John Wiley.

McIvor, G. (2004) 'Getting personal: Developments in policy and practice in Scotland.' In G. Mair (ed.) *What Matters in Probation.* Cullompton: Willan.

McIvor, G. and Barry, M. (1998) *Social Work and Criminal Justice: Volume 6 – Probation.* Edinburgh: The Stationery Office.

Parton, N. and O'Byrne, P. (2000) *Constructive Social Work: Towards a New Practice.* Basingstoke: Macmillan.

Pitts, J. (2001) 'Korrectional karaoke: New Labour and the zombification of youth justice.' *Youth Justice* 1, 2, 3–15.

Robinson, G. and McNeill, F. (2004) 'Purposes matter: Examining the "ends" of probation.' In G. Mair (ed.) *What Matters in Probation.* Cullompton: Willan.

Rogowski, S. (2003/4) 'Young offenders: Towards a radical/critical social work practice.' *Youth and Policy* 82, 60–74.

Scottish Executive (2002) *Criminal Proceedings in Scottish Courts, 2001.* Statistical Bulletin, Criminal Justice Series. Edinburgh: Scottish Executive.

Shover, N. (1996) *Great Pretenders: Pursuits and Careers of Persistent Thieves.* Boulder, CO: Westview Press.

Smith, D. (1998) 'Social work with offenders: The practice of exclusion and the potential for inclusion.' In M. Barry and C. Hallett (eds) *Social Exclusion and Social Work: Issues of Theory, Policy and Practice.* Lyme Regis: Russell House.

Smith, D. (2004) 'Introduction.' In D. Smith (ed.) *Social Work and Evidence-Based Practice.* London: Jessica Kingsley Pubishers.

Spencer, J. and Deakin, J. (2004) 'Community reintegration: For whom?' In G. Mair (ed.) *What Matters in Probation.* Cullompton: Willan.

Thompson, N. (2000) *Understanding Social Work: Preparing for Practice.* Basingstoke: Macmillan.

Trotter, C. (1999) *Working with Involuntary Clients: A Guide to Practice.* St. Leonards, Australia: Allen & Unwin.

Chapter 11

Offenders 'r' Us
The Story of This Book

Marilyn Gregory with Kevin Gorman,
Michelle Hayles and Nigel Parton

What is our story?

The seed for this book was sown when two of the editors, Kevin Gorman
and Marilyn Gregory, were invited, together with one of the contributors,
Monica Barry, to address a conference of probation practitioners in Oxford
in the summer of 2002. The title of the conference was 'Used and Abused:
The Politics of Probation', and it developed some of the themes explored at
a similar conference in 2001 entitled 'What Really Works? Robots or Relationships?'. Kevin had also addressed this earlier conference, at which
Monica Barry had shared her research findings about consumers' views on
social work as expressed by young offenders in Scotland. Kevin, who in
2001 had expanded on his published concerns about the 'What Works'
evidence and orthodoxy (Gorman 2001), now suggested alternatives to the
dominant narrative of constructive social work practice, drawing on the
ideas put forward by Parton and O'Byrne (2000).

Everyone present in 2001 and 2002 was only too aware of the punitive
and managerialist direction of criminal justice at the time. Practitioners
(probation officers and Probation Service officers) at both conferences were
nevertheless keen to develop ways of working that prioritized their relationships with service users and respected people's abilities to understand
their difficulties and work out their own solutions. There was a strong
feeling among the 50 or so people present on each occasion that though the
circumstances of practice were difficult there was still value in creating
positive working relationships with 'clients'. Discussion at the second

conference led to the idea of a book, by and for practitioners within criminal justice settings, to contribute to practice debates and demonstrate that constructive practice is still possible. Approaches were subsequently made to the eventual contributors, who were targeted because of their known commitment to practice and, above all, their combined decades of direct experience as practitioners in the criminal justice field.

In early discussions about the book's title, 'Constructive Probation Practice' was mooted, but from the outset we had wanted to address a wider audience than the statutory sector of criminal justice practice (which in any event may not be called 'probation' by the time this is published). Whilst expressing our own discomfort with the term, we had to acknowledge that 'offender' is the common policy/practice terminology used by students, academics and practitioners to whom we hope the book will be of interest.

In the time that has elapsed between the sowing of the original seed and the present, the political climate has become, if anything, less propitious for constructive practice (see Chapter 2, this volume). As the full implementation of the National Offender Management Service looms, we appear to be poised on the brink of the demise of the kind of Probation Service England and Wales has known for just short of 100 years, signalling the complete embracing of a US-style correctional system (Chapter 1). Media coverage of contemporary political debates on criminal justice indicates only too clearly that the pre-1979 party political consensus on crime is well and truly dead (Chapter 3). Key contributors to the debate on UK criminal justice policy paint a uniformly gloomy picture (see Garland 2001; Tonry 2004), summed up by Nellis:

> So the future is indeed as bleak as Garland envisages it at the end of *The Culture of Control* – humanistic values, the only standpoint from which one might resist the onslaughts of managerialism, and the debasements which follow, are ceasing to have credibility in criminal justice. Quite apart from the fact that a justice system which disregards such values may not be all that effective in reducing crime, the costs in terms of civilisation and decency are likely to be very high. (Nellis 2004, p.131)

Putting the book together, the editors gathered to discuss for the second or third time how we wanted to draw together the book's ideas in this final chapter. We acknowledged the difficult moment in criminal justice, but asked ourselves some basic questions: What is our story? Who is the book for? What is our message? A subject that we had revisited a number of times was again discussed. Why call the book 'Constructive Work with Offenders', when we take issue with a dominant narrative which regards people who have committed offences as fundamentally different and separate from the rest of society?

The key components of the official narrative with its focus on offenders are addressed particularly in Chapters 1, 2 and 3. It is founded upon an understanding of penality that is concerned with the 'responsibilization' of the good citizen and the 'othering' of the less good (Chapter 3). It is less interested in the causes of crime and more in its management and control. It places value on evidence that relates to outcome-based, statistically demonstrable results such as meta-analyses of reconviction scores, demonstrating 'effectiveness' across categories of 'offender' rather than in individual 'offenders'. Risk is this *new penology*'s key focus (Feeley and Simon 1992), with the emphasis increasingly on the avoidance of risky behaviour altogether by the exclusion and incapacitation of risky populations (Chapter 4).

We reflected that between the four of us we had recently acquired two speeding offences and six penalty points which though not standard list[1] offences are part of a process which enables the government to claim an increase in 'clear up rates' as do other fixed penalties which now of course include the more controversial Penalty Notices for Disorder, introduced by the Criminal Justice and Police Act 2001. We do not usually think of ourselves as offenders nor, we would suggest, are we the kinds of people being discussed in the increasingly shrill tones that permeate discussions in the media at the time of writing. Quite right too, our readers may think, as they share the irritation expressed by a High Court judge on Radio 4's *Today* programme recently when asked to comment upon the value of fixed penalties: 'Excellent idea, except when imposed upon people like me for doing 31 miles an hour in a 30 mile an hour speed limit!' The dominant view is clear here: offenders *are not us*.

Our own culpability, our different careers involving working with 'offenders' as well as teaching and research about social work and its diverse client group, our collective life experiences, these all lead us to oppose this position. The title of this chapter, 'Offenders 'r' us', is the slightly tongue-in-cheek signal of a more serious point. For offenders *are us*; they *are* our neighbours, they *are* corporate executives, they *are* parents, they are, in short, our fellow citizens.

Certainty versus uncertainty

A key feature of the dominant narrative is the tendency to deny uncertainty, to talk in absolutes about what the government can produce or achieve in relation to crime; in order to do so they focus on readily identifiable 'yobs' or 'bogus asylum seekers' whilst attempting to develop a sense of responsibility among 'respectable' citizens. A paradox of this tendency to eliminate uncertainty is that it heightens anxiety and fear of crime among the very population the government is seeking to reassure (Chapter 3). Drawing broadly on sociological, psychological and neuro- scientific literature, this certainty–uncertainty paradox has been framed by McCann (2003, 2005a) as a paradox generated by claustrophilia, love of enclosure, and claustrophobia, fear of enclosure. McCann argues that the tendency to think that uncertainty can be or should be eliminated tends to be inversely proportional to a person's experience of uncertainty (2005a). Garland (2001) has also suggested this as helping to understand why criminal justice professionals have, to some extent, capitulated to the more punitive ways of working they are now expected to adopt (Chapter 3).

What we hope is clear from the preceding chapters is that constructive practice actively resists the tendency to eliminate uncertainty. Working constructively involves embracing uncertainty and engaging with the day-to-day, mundane, messy reality of people's lives – indeed, the kind of evidence generated by data collection methods whose aim is to 'prove' the efficacy of predetermined policy objectives may prove little of real value (see Chapter 1).

Inclusion versus exclusion

The other contradiction of criminal justice policy, highlighted in Chapters 2 and 3 in this volume, is that, while social exclusion and its effects are key concerns, there is a bifurcation in policy rhetoric when it comes to people who have committed offences. Garland explains this bifurcation by suggesting that governments use the twin strategies of 'punitive segregation' and 'preventive partnership' (see Chapter 3 of this book). The contradiction is evident in the contrasting narratives of the new National Offender Management Service (NOMS) and the Social Exclusion Unit. Taking an example from NOMS, the Offender Management Model is claimed to have a 'human service approach' and citizenship does get a mention, albeit in the context of preserving it in the process of imposing punishment (NOMS Offender Management Workstream Team 2005). In all other respects the model depersonalizes the individual who is at the centre of the process, referring to him or her as 'the offender', 'the case', and even 'the project'. The work of 'offender managers' and 'offender supervisors' is discussed in terms such as 'tasks' and 'functions', with a core assumption of 'the offender' as inherently uncooperative:

> Supervision is the term used by the model to describe the sequence of day-to-day, face-to-face tasks and activities which will be required in most

cases to secure compliance, generate the motivation to co-operate, and achieve cohesion of the plan. Most offenders will not co-operate actively with their Sentence Plan simply because one exists. This is true whether the offender is in custody or in the community. (NOMS Offender Management Workstream Team 2005, p.8)

There is a very careful avoidance of words such as 'relationship', 'person' or 'negotiation' which would identify the 'offender' and the worker as thinking, feeling human beings and the work between them an exchange of ideas, values, or expertise. Our prologue, written by Jeremy Cameron without sight of the Offender Management Model, is obviously a spoof, but eerily prescient of the document's contents. The view of human nature implied here is a neo-liberal one, characteristic of the kind of retributivist penal policy we now see in many Western democracies, for the reasons discussed in chapter three. The individual is seen as self-serving and rational; to avoid being punished, he or she can simply opt not to commit a crime (Hudson 2003). In this formulation, the social context of the person's offending is hardly relevant. Whilst the expressed intention of policy here is not exclusionary, we would suggest that its effects are.

In contrast, the website of the Social Exclusion Unit (www.social exclusion.gov.uk) provides a social context for offending. Here the 'offender' can be seen as part of a community or neighbourhood, as a young person, as elderly, as vulnerable, and as socially excluded. Whilst the message is clear that it is the socially responsible citizen who *deserves* protection from crime within their neighbourhoods, the problems of offenders are acknowledged:

> The Social Exclusion Unit has a range of work looking at the causes of crime and interrelated problems, such as unemployment, education and training, substance misuse, housing, mental and physical health, attitudes and self-control, institutionalisation, debt and family breakdown. (Social Exclusion Unit 2005)

The neo-liberal view of human nature remains present, with, as Jordan notes, an emphasis on the toughness, rather than the love, in the soundbite 'tough love' (Chapter 2 of this volume). There is in addition a weakness in the understanding of social inclusion, which plays down poverty and inequality and emphasizes instead the individual contributions of each citizen (Jordan with Jordan 2000). There is an assumption of fear of crime, coupled with hopelessness and despair among decent citizens in high-crime neighbourhoods. However, this is not, according to some recent evidence, always present. Foster (1995) found the law-abiding residents of the area in which she conducted her research did not feel hopeless; indeed they felt there was something they could do to tackle some of the often-cited difficulties on their estate. More recently, it has been demonstrated from ongoing longitudinal work in both Glasgow and Trinidad that high crime rates do not necessarily lead to high fear of crime, even in those areas assessed as vulnerable to crime because of low levels of situational security (Ditton and Chadee, 2005). The issue has also been raised that high crime communities may be well integrated and therefore have good access to social capital, but it is a social capital particular to an oppressed, rundown area with few opportunities for legitimate work, and is therefore tolerant of offending (Spencer and Deakin 2004). This is not a new idea. The 'taking care of business' analysis of drug users of the 1960s and 1970s takes a very similar approach (Preble and Casey 1969). The former mining communities in South Yorkshire where I, Marilyn Gregory, began my probation career had a history of oppression by the police during the miners' strike of 1984 which has left indelible scars. This means that 'decent' citizens are far more likely to be afraid of the police than they are of local youths who are hooked on heroin. Pearson's analysis in *The New Heroin Users* (Pearson 1987) supports this understanding. Furthermore, I have written Pre-Sentence Reports upon middle-aged parents with no previous convictions who came before the courts for such offences as defrauding the DSS, in sheer desperation to pay off their son's or daughter's drug dealer. I am sure that every practitioner reading this can think of many clients like this who do not fit the dominant vision of an offender.

There are other stories

A mother with a school-aged child and family dog is walking through her local park. She looks up from talking to her child to observe that, jogging quite quickly toward her, is a young black man with shoulder-length dreadlocks. As he approaches, he slows his pace and they come face to face. Placing a hand on each of her shoulders, he breaks into a beaming smile and plants a kiss on her cheek. Then she remembers. This is Michael, someone she met three years ago when she was working as a probation officer in a category 'c' prison. They catch up. Michael has been away from trouble now for two years. He is working, and is living with his girlfriend. 'You helped me, Miss,' he says, embarrassing her with both the sentiment and the title prisoners apply to every woman staff member they encounter. 'I was only doing my job,' she says, 'and I'm so thrilled to see you looking so well and happy.' 'Yeah, well, some of 'em never bothered,' he says, and he's off, with a wave and another big smile.

When we posed ourselves the question 'What is our message?' Michelle Hayles made the remark 'There *are* other stories.' Working on the draft of this final chapter, I was reminded of my own story, my own motivations for becoming a probation officer, and of some of the many stories I encountered during that part of my working life. I was the probation officer referred to in the vignette above – I can already hear the cries of 'sentimentality', 'harking back to outdated models' and 'inappropriate role boundaries' that are likely to ensue when I say that it is stories like this that encouraged and supported my work as a probation officer. However, in considering the question 'What is our message?' my co-editors and I were clear that people's stories are fundamental to the constructive way of working, which considers that the person's story, their narrative, contains the seeds of the solution to whatever problem it is that they need to solve.

'There but for the grace of God go I'

Another key element of the message we hope this book gives is that our view of human nature is not the neo-liberal one we have suggested is part of the dominant criminal justice narrative. Constructive practice assumes service users are fellow citizens with all the respect and dignity rightly accorded to that status. It assumes that they know more about themselves than we do; they, not us, are the experts. It regards their views on practice interventions as important evidence in policy development. It incorporates realism about the efficacy of professional interventions. After all, practitioners are only ever a very small part of another person's life. To be able to make a difference we need to form a meaningful relationship with the person, in which we support them *as they solve their own problems*, and in so doing are able to move away from offending.

When we as practitioners find we have been able to make a difference in someone's life, we can achieve real job satisfaction, which is infinitely more valuable than meeting a key performance indicator. In this sense the work of helper and helped is a real exchange. Of course, it is more difficult when the person being helped is difficult or dangerous, but we have suggested that the same basic principles still apply; in fact this is at the heart of constructive professional practice (see Chapters 4, 5, 6, 8 and 9 of this book).

It also means recognizing that the way constructions operate can have a series of very negative consequences if not dealt with in a constructive way (see Chapter 7). A sense of humility is a quality that the constructive practitioner would bring to the work. After all, how many distressed parents of teenage offenders have we spoken to, with whom we can completely empathize? How hypocritical have we felt conducting a Pre-Sentence Report interview for motoring offences with that speeding ticket tucked into our briefcase? How many clients can we remember over the years, who have taught us important things about supporting others in a crisis, or dignity, or surviving adversity?

Reparation and restoration not punishment

Finally, although constructive practice can be carried out in prisons, as we can see from Sue Carless's account of work with women prisoners, the philosophy of constructive practice means that it fits far more comfortably with the principles of restorative justice than with the retributivist practices of late modern criminal justice (see Chapter 8; also Chapter 3). It is an approach which favours community penalties as the way of dealing with all but the most dangerous offenders.

Most of those working within the field, whether practitioners, academics or Home Office civil servants, acknowledge that the criminal justice system deals with only about 2 per cent of the offences the British Crime Survey estimates are carried out in the UK each year (Garside 2004). As such there is an important question about the honesty of government pronouncements on the effectiveness of *any* of the different elements of the system in reducing crime. This unequivocally includes imprisonment, and there is thus a very strong argument for working with offenders constructively in their communities, because it is more humane and it is more cost effective. It is clearly unnecessary to imprison such huge numbers of people. We have suggested in the preceding chapters that there is a growing body of evidence demonstrating the value of constructive practice focusing on *desistance* from offending as opposed to reconviction rates (Chapters 3 and 4). The more punitive, enforcement driven practice currently in place and strongly advocated in the NOMS Offender Management Model is leading to a substantial increase in the numbers of people in prison for community penalty breaches, as a similar approach has done in the US (Clear 2005; Solomon 2005).

The art of the possible

Throughout human history there are examples of people individually and collectively finding solutions to their problems even in the most extreme of adverse conditions. Constructive practice draws on this ability, and what we have put forward in this volume are different *sites of engagement* for such practice. It may be that, for many practitioners within the National Probation Service (now NOMS), the possibilities for constructive practice seem extremely limited. We have put forward ways of seizing the opportunity within various areas of probation practice: risk assessment (Chapter 4), courts (Chapter 5), Pre-Sentence Reports (Chapter 6), work with women (Chapter 8) and work with sexual offenders (Chapter 9). What we also believe is that probation practitioners will recognize the kinds of dialogue identified by Jordan, in Chapter 2, which demonstrates how contemporary policy rhetoric is reclaimed by service users and can be used to justify developing practice in ways which enable them to move from illegitimate to legitimate ways of sustaining themselves.

In Chapter 3, it is suggested that an alternative way of focusing the practice of probation work would be away from individual wrong-doers and toward the communities in which they live. At the time of drafting this chapter, I felt that such a radical transformation in probation practice might be seen as 'pie in the sky', but on reading the May 2005 issue of the *Howard Journal* I find something very similar is being put forward for American probation practice (Clear 2005). Clear makes a strong argument that the US Probation Service, which the government here seeks to emulate in the development of NOMS, is actually contributing to the decline of deprived communities because the more efficient the 'casework model'[2] of probation is, the more likely it is that they will enforce court orders, resulting in people being sent to prison (Clear 2005).

Neither the US nor the UK Probation Service is likely to be changed in the ways we suggest in the very near future. It is therefore important to recognize the other *sites of engagement* that make constructive practice possible. These of course lie in any of the many statutory and voluntary sector agencies throughout the country which provide human services, because, as we have argued, the person who comes through the door is not an offender first and foremost, he or she is a fellow citizen. The constructive ways of working put forward here can be used by practitioners in any number of agencies and indeed, under New Labour, the number of roles for 'human services practitioners' has been expanded, although there is clearly a reluctance to call them social workers (Jordan with Jordan 2000).

In a broader sense, the *site of engagement* for constructive practice is the social capital which every citizen needs if they are to enjoy the full status of citizen in a developed economy like ours. We have suggested that there is a growing body of evidence that developing access to social capital is more effective in encouraging *desistance* from offending than more punitive measures (Chapters 2, 3 and 4). We believe that the government's civil renewal agenda requires it to take seriously the possible contribution people who have committed offences can make to their communities. Faulkner and Flaxington (2005) put forward a number of ideas from a seminar sponsored by the Active Citizenship Centre about how to conduct research into civil renewal's contribution to crime reduction and victim support. These include looking at citizens' motivation for working with offenders, what difference that work makes, whether statutory agencies can provide both their 'mainstream' functions in ways which contribute to civil renewal, and how local citizens can be engaged in a dialogue about criminal justice issues. We have argued that in keeping with other social policy areas, service users' views on what criminal justice services should provide must also be sought (Chapter 10). Constructive practice goes beyond an interest in what contribution *citizens* can make in working with *offenders* and regards offenders fundamentally as citizens themselves.

Constructive practice as sustainable practice

The concept of sustainability is one that is familiar to us in debate and policy relating to global and local ecology and, more recently, urban regeneration. In what has become the norm in the funding of urban regeneration, complex and time-consuming bids to a variety of UK or EU funds are made by local councils, 'partnership' organizations, or community groups. A crucial requirement that applicants have to demonstrate is: 'How will the project/development/scheme be sustained for the future?' It is a perfectly reasonable question. There is no point in making improvements to your local park if there are no funds available for regular maintenance and upkeep, or if it will not be used because local people feel unsafe since there are no staff present in the park (DLTR 2002).

Sustainability is, we suggest, a concept that can be applied to work with vulnerable groups of people, helping them to reconstruct their lives and move forward in a positive way. Including 'offenders' in this process is in our view far more likely to result in their achieving sustainable change to their lives but, just as important, their contributing to sustainable change within their communities. Social capital is the ideal *site of engagement* for this work because both sectors of the community, poorer and better off, express themselves as fearful of crime, although not in the ratios we usually expect, even in communities in which rich and poor are closely juxtaposed (Ditton and Chadee 2005).

In order to engage successfully in sustainable work with offenders at the moment, practitioners may well have to find one of the many other *sites of engagement* that are available in the voluntary sector, as well as some specialist sites within the statutory sector, such as the Youth Conferencing Service in Northern Ireland (NIO 2005). This is a working example of restorative justice in practice and demonstrates that, if it so chooses, the government can decide to take a less punitive approach to justice for young offenders.

Hope, gentleness and sustainable change

McCann puts forward interrelated notions of *hope* and *gentleness* as concepts which can be deployed in the achievement of change in positive ways. In his formulation, *hope* can be helpfully understood as:

1. an acknowledgement that nothing is fixed (though much is experienced as stable), nothing is necessary, nothing has to be the way it is

2. an acknowledgement that we are active participants in our experience of meaning, power and social interaction.

In and through that participation we are always/already making a difference (McCann 2005b).

Gentleness is both a possible and powerful politics (McCann 2005a). McCann suggests that we eschew dominant narratives with their tendency to allure us into thinking that uncertainty can be or should be eliminated. We should instead recognize 'the importance of embracing rather than denying our experience of uncertainty in order to also embrace and affirm our experience and exercise of power' (McCann 2003, 2005a).

McCann is addressing social life in its broadest sense, but we suggest that constructive practice with 'offenders' can deploy hope and gentleness in achieving the sort of sustainable change we have suggested is a more realistic policy goal for an honest criminal justice. CPLC is a project in the US that we suggest is an example of people using social capital as *site of engagement*.

> The origins of Los Chicanos por la Causa (CPLC) are in the 1960s when students from Arizona State University began a campaign to improve the rights of Mexican-Americans in terms of their involvement in local services. Beginning with a campaign to get the local school system to employ more Latino teachers and to allow Mexican parents a say in their children's schooling, the project has developed considerably since then. It is now a fully established development corporation, one of the largest in the US. It provides services to the Latino community in Arizona within three broad sectors: Housing, Economic Development and Social Services. It also has some subsidiary companies including a mortgage company, a women's care centre, a construction company and a house purchase/real estate company. Its social services sector addresses issues such as drug abuse, domestic violence, HIV/Aids, services for elderly people, counselling support for a variety of groups and two after-school programmes working with first-time young offenders (Los Chicanos por la Causa 2005).

CPLC is a clear example of an organization developed by and for an oppressed minority group to provide services to community members deemed by the dominant narrative as 'the Other'. Starting with a specific issue, it has grown into a comprehensive provider of social and economic services to the Chicano community in ways that are respectful and inclusive. It is proof that people can resist the labels placed upon them and work toward their own positive solutions, in a climate where the dominant message is very much against them. Whilst the 'othering' of offenders remains the dominant narrative in the UK at the time of writing, with a recent suggestion from a newly appointed Home Office Minister that people on community service are issued with uniforms so that they can be easily identified, there are also more optimistic developments. Parents and Addicts against Narcotics in the Community (PANIC), founded by the mother of a heroin addict, is a voluntary, community-led support service for drug users and their families, providing a free helpline, counselling, advocacy and peer support (PANIC 2005).

Projects like these demonstrate the *hope* that people sustain even in the most difficult circumstances and, we would suggest, the fact that an approach embodying *gentleness* can lead to the development of accessible, respectful service provision for those of our fellow citizens who are some-times 'offenders'. A constructive approach to practice with offenders would eschew the soundbite politics so easily generated by punitive strategies addressing the 2 per cent of offences dealt with by the criminal justice system. In its place we advocate an honest social policy that sees the whole picture: offending is just one aspect of people's complex lives. Small projects like PANIC should be nurtured to enable them to develop into the kind of sustainable provision demonstrated by Los Chicanos por la Causa. Only when people are treated like fellow citizens are they likely to behave accordingly.

Notes

1. 'Standard list offences' are offences for which the name of the offender and details of each sentence have been collected by the Home Office since 1963. These are linked by the person's name and Police National Computer number to enable research into criminal histories. The offences include all indictable offences; triable either way offences and *some* summary offences – exceptions which may seem sur-prising include speeding and kerb crawling (Garside 2004).

2. This is not the social work understanding of casework, but describes the strongly correctionalist practice in the US in which probation officers hold high caseloads of offenders, but the focus is on enforcement and control.

References

Clear, T.R. (2005) 'Places not cases? Re-thinking the probation focus.' *The Howard Journal of Criminal Justice* 44, 2, 172–84.

Ditton, J. and Chadee, D. (2005) 'People's perceptions of their likely future risk of criminal victimisation.' *British Journal of Criminology* Advance Access article, 17 October, doi:10.1093/bjc/azi092.

DLTR (2002) 'Green spaces, better places.' *Final Report of the Urban Green Spaces Taskforce.* London: Department of Transport, Local Government and the Regions.

Faulkner, D. and Flaxington, F. (2005) 'NOMS and civil renewal.' *VISTA* 9, 2, 90–9.

Feeley, S. and Simon, J. (1992) 'The new penology: Notes on the emerging new criminal law.' In D. Nelken (ed.) *The Futures of Criminology.* London: Sage.

Foster, J. (1995) 'Informal social control and community crime prevention.' *British Journal of Criminology* 35, 4, 563–83.

Garland, D. (2000) 'The culture of high crime societies.' *British Journal of Criminology* 40, 347–75.

Garland, D. (2001) *The Culture of Control: Crime and Social Order in Contemporary Society.* Oxford: Oxford University Press.

Garside, R. (2004) 'Crime, persistent offenders and the justice gap.' *Discussion Paper No 1.* London: Crime and Society Foundation.

Gorman, K. (2001) 'Cognitive behaviourism and the Holy Grail: The quest for a universal means of managing offender risk.' *Probation Journal* 48, 1, 3–9.

Hudson, B. (2003) *Understanding Justice* (2nd edition). Buckingham: Open University Press.

Jordan, B. with Jordan, C. (2000) *Social Work and the Third Way: Tough Love as Social Policy.* London: Sage.

Los Chicanos por la Causa (2005) www.cplc.org/About_Us/index.html (accessed 27 May 2005).

McCann, A. (2003) *Beyond the Commons: The Expansion of the Irish Music Rights Organisation, the Elimination of Uncertainty, and the Politics of Enclosure.* Warrenpoint: Anthony McCann.

McCann, A. (2005a) Personal communication.

McCann, A. (2005b) www.beyondthecommons.com/hopearchive.html (accessed 27 May 2005).

Nellis, R.M. (2004) '"Into the Field of Corrections": The end of English probation in the early twenty-first century?' *Cambrian Law Review* 35, 115–34.

NIO (2005) *Interim Evaluation of the Northern Ireland Youth Conferencing Scheme.* Belfast: Northern Ireland Office.

NOMS Offender Management Workstream Team (2005) *The NOMS Offender Management Model.* London: National Offender Management Service.

PANIC (2005) www.stockton.gov.uk/citizenservices/33404/82711/87921/ (accessed 27 May 2005).

Parton, N. and O'Byrne, P. (2000) *Constructive Social Work.* London: Macmillan.

Pearson, G. (1987) *The New Heroin Users.* Oxford: Basil Blackwell.

Preble, E. and Casey jr, J.J. (1969) 'Taking care of business – the heroin user's life on the street.' *Internal Journal of the Addictions* 4, 1, 1–24, March, quoted in *Drugs Crime and Criminal Justice* Vol II.

Social Exclusion Unit (2005) www.socialexclusion.gov.uk (accessed 5 June 2005).

Solomon, E. (2005) *Recycling Offenders Through Prison.* London: Prison Reform Trust.

Spencer, J. and Deakin, J. (2004) 'Community reintegration, for whom?' In G. Mair (ed.) *What Matters in Probation.* London: Willan.

Tonry, M. (2004) *Punishment and Politics.* London: Willan.

Epilogue

Jeremy Cameron

'All right, mate?'
'All right, mate?'
'You all right, Wayne?'
'You all right, John?'
'How's your mum?'
'How's *your* mum?'
'Got the tests back.'
'Yeah?'
'All clear.'
'Glad to hear that.'
'Your mum?'
'Got the tests back.'
'Yeah?'
'Given her six months.'
'Oh no.'
'Yeah.'
'Oh Wayne, I'm sorry.'
'Bummer innit.'
'Bummer.'
'Best I don't go away.'
'You mean…'
'That report of yours.'
'You need to talk to your solicitor, Wayne.'
'You go to the game last night?'
'Crap, eh?'
'Bollocks. Total bollocks. They got to buy a goal scorer.'
'And a goalkeeper.'

'And a midfield.'
'And a central defender.'
'You go to the game?'
'Nah. You?'
'Nah.'
'What did you do last night?'
'Spot of thieving...'
'...'
'Got you there, eh?'
'Wayne, you winding me up?'
'I got this hot piece.'
'A gun?!'
'Woman.'
'Hot...?'
'Tell me about it.'
'What?'
'She was boiling.'
'Er, yes. Did you go to the cinema?'
'How's your missus?'
'She's just fine thank you. How's your missus?'
'Only six weeks to go now.'
'You must be looking forward to that.'
'Yeah.'
'Have you booked the day off?'
'Nah. See her when she gets home.'
'She prefer it on her own?'
'Yeah. Me, I'm the same.'
'You reckon it's the same for men and women?'
'I reckon.'
'You think women feel the same?'
'Nah. Never no sympathy. They reckon men can handle prison but women it's different. Even release.'
'Still, she's only got six weeks to go.'
'Yeah, be gone in no time. How's the kids?'
'Not bad. James, he's in the under-twelves. How's your James?'
'He's in the under-twelves. And special counselling.'
'Yeah? He scoring?'
'Now and then. Getting some goals too.'
'What?'
'Only joking. Bit young. Mind you, his counsellor... Your James scoring?'

'He got one on Saturday. Left foot. On the volley.'

'Jeez. Thought he was right-footed.'

'I always thought he was. Now I'm afraid we've been oppressing him. Suppressing his left foot.'

'Jeez that's terrible, John. He repressed? Stays in his room?'

'Sometimes. Your James?'

'Nah. We encourage freedom of expression. He's integrated.'

'Maybe we ought to rethink.'

'Mind you, it was that freedom of expression got his mum locked up.'

'Maybe. And you last time.'

'Me?'

'You remember what you said to that police officer?'

'Only freedom of expression John.'

'And to the horse. And that's not what the judge called it. He had to send for a dictionary.'

'Hah!'

'Then he was sick over his clerk.'

'I experienced remorse for that clerk, John. And that empathy you taught me. Public servant. Only doing his job.'

'Exactly.'

'You made me think there.'

'Fancy a cup of tea?'

'You got any of them organic biscuits made by them peasants?'

'Now you mention it.'

'I bought that honey from that socialist bees' cooperative to go with them.'

'Socialist bees?'

'They done away with the queen they reckon. Manage on their own.'

'Wow.'

'And that wholefood compost you gave me from the allotment, it's going down a treat on my muesli.'

'Oh I'm very glad.'

'Stopped me offending, course.'

'Yes?'

'All I needed was a regular lifestyle, John.'

'Wow.'

'Get the kids' tea. Keep the appointments with you. Visit my mum. Visit the missis. Eat my muesli and stay regular. All I think about.'

'Wayne, you've done really well.'

'You changed my life, John. I ain't committed no offences since I been seeing you.'

'Is that the truth, Wayne?'

'Course.'

'It's remarkable the changes a person can make in a fortnight.'

'Changed my life. Made me feel worthwhile. Gave me confidence.'

'Changed my life too. Made me feel worthwhile. Gave me confidence.'

'You bring the kids round one night?'

'Yeah, I think I will. How about Sunday?'

'You're putting one over on me, John, innit?'

'How's that?'

'You know how I always committed them offences on Sunday nights. After evensong.'

'Oh yes. Your problem…'

'You know how you told me to look at my problem? My problem was evensong. Them bells drive me mad. Just when I was having my Sunday kip.'

'Now you have your kip after lunch.'

'I looked at the problem.'

'Found a solution.'

'Crafty, eh? Yeah, come round Sunday, John. Bring the missus.'

'If she's free from her patchwork homework.'

'And your mum.'

'Your mum be there?'

'If she's out. They can talk operations.'

'Mutual support.'

'Good, this probation, John. I never felt so respected before. Member of society.'

'I'm very glad to hear it.'

'My firm, they're putting me up for the Rotary now.'

'Your firm?'

'Not that firm, John. Not them robbers. My bosses.'

'Yeah?'

'Pillar, they reckon. That's me. Pillar.'

'We can go together maybe.'

'Yeah. You got any more of that tea John?'

Contributors

Monica Barry has worked as a research fellow at the University of Stirling since 1994, focusing on research into youth offending, youth transitions, desistance and criminal justice social work. She formerly worked in the offender field as a practitioner, first in the voluntary sector as a project worker and then as a social worker in intensive probation. She is the criminal justice research advisor to the Association of Directors of Social Work and the editor of a recent volume entitled *Youth Policy and Social Inclusion: Critical Debates with Young People.*

Jeremy Cameron worked in social work for 30 years, including 8 years' residential work and 20 years as a probation officer. He finally left the Probation Service in despair at government policy, in particular the change of the service from welfare to punishment and the reduction of individual contact between worker and client. Jeremy has written extensively in social work and probation publications. He has also had five novels published, including *Vinnie Got Blown Away*, *It Was An Accident* (filmed with Chiwetel Ejiofor and Thandie Newton) and, most recently, *Wider Than Walthamstow*. He continues to work regularly for the probation trade union NAPO.

Sue Carless has worked for 23 years in the Probation Service in a variety of grades and roles. She has pursued an active involvement in working with women, including ten years as voluntary treasurer of a women's hostel which she helped to found. She developed good practice as a trainer in public protection and in multi-agency domestic violence training. She was also a practice teacher for seven years. Sue has managed numerous contracts and partnerships including those with mental health organizations, substance misuse agencies and delivery of sex offender and domestic violence programmes. Since 2001 she has been the manager of a probation team in a women's prison, where her responsibilities include public and child protection.

Malcolm Cowburn has worked at the University of Sheffield since 1994. His research interests are focused on sexual violence and masculinities. They originate from his work as a probation officer where he was involved in developing cognitive-behavioural programmes for adult male sex offenders. He has extensive experience both as a trainer and a consultant in issues related to sex offending. His research incorporates psychological and sociological understandings of sexual violence, and he is interested in finding ways to incorporate both of these approaches to sexual violence into different ways of thinking about men, male behaviours, male sex offenders and community safety.

Lena Dominelli is Director of the Centre for International Social and Community Development at the University of Southampton, Past President of the International Association of Schools of Social Work (IASSW) and the United Nations Liaison Officer for IASSW. She has worked in social work settings, including community work, social services and probation. She has been a researcher, educator and author for many years. Her most influential single-authored books include: *Anti-Racist Social Work; Women and Community Action; Women Across Continents: Feminist Comparative Social Policy; Feminist Social Work Theory and Practice; Anti-Oppressive Social Work Theory and Practice; Social Work: Theory and Practice for a Changing Profession*. Her current research interests cover the changing nature of welfare under globalization and shifting relationships in families. Her latest research project is called 'Fathering Within Child Welfare'.

Kevin Gorman is a Senior Lecturer at the University of Huddersfield, where he contributes to degree courses in applied criminology, social work and police studies. Between 1977 and 2004 he was employed as a probation officer, a role in which his supervisory and report-writing responsibilities covered virtually the whole spectrum of offending behaviour. He was also heavily involved in practice development and practice teaching, including the training of probation officers. A critical friend of both cognitive behaviourism and groupwork, his article 'Cognitive behaviourism and the Holy Grail: The quest for a universal means of managing offender risk' (2001, *Probation Journal*, 48(1)) earned him brief notoriety but no retirement yacht.

Marilyn Gregory spent 16 years in the Probation Service, working as a main grade officer in a former mining community, as a prison-based officer, court welfare officer and, finally, specialist practice teacher, teaching students initially on the diploma in social work and latterly the diploma in probation studies. For the past four years she has taught social work at the University of Sheffield, maintaining her interest in the Probation Service by teaching in the area of crime, abuse and public protection, and by conducting research about the work of probation officers. She is also interested in the continuing professional development of professionals within the social work/social care field. Recent publications include: with Margaret Holloway (2005) 'Language and the construction of social work' (*British Journal of Social Work* 35, 1, 37–53).

Michelle Hayles spent 12 years as a probation officer in a range of community contexts and in a women's prison. From 1991 to 1994 she managed a Home Office student training unit and continued to maintain links with practice in her subsequent role as a manager responsible for staff development and for qualifying training. She moved into a full-time academic post in 1999 to manage the university's involvement in the new probation officer training. She is currently a Principal Lecturer in community justice at the University of Huddersfield where she has leadership responsibilities for the BSc (Hons) in applied criminology and for an innovative foundation degree in police studies.

Bill Jordan is Professor of Social Policy at Plymouth and Huddersfield Universities, and Reader in Social Policy at London Metropolitan University. He was a probation officer 1965–75, and a social worker for the following ten years. He has held visiting chairs in several European countries, and has written more than 20 books, including *Sex, Money and Power: The Transformation of Collective Life*, published by Polity in 2004.

Geoff Kenure is a self-employed coach and teacher specializing in court practice. During 37 years in the Probation Service he worked in staff development for seven years and from 1990 to 2001 managed a combined Crown and Magistrates Courts team. For his last two years until 2003 he worked as a court officer with a special interest in enforcement proceedings. Since 1990 he has been a member of the Advisory Committee to the Leeds Centre for Criminal Justice. He also works as an occasional lecturer in criminology and as a part-time hospital manager hearing mental health appeals.

Patrick O'Byrne has worked as a probation officer in West Yorkshire and then as probation tutor at the University of Huddersfield. His special interests include work with offenders' families and using constructive interventions (based on solution-focused and narrative methods) with young offenders and drug users. He lectures and provides training in solution-focused practice for a range of agencies and is co-author with Nigel Parton of *Constructive Social Work: Towards a New Practice* (Palgrave/Macmillan 2000).

Nigel Parton is Professor in Child Care and Director of the Centre of Applied Childhood Studies in the School of Human and Health Sciences at the University of Huddersfield. He has a particular interest in the area of child protection and is the author of *Safeguarding Childhood: Early Intervention and Surveillance in a Late Modern Society* (Palgrave/Macmillan 2006) and was author, with Patrick O'Byrne, of *Constructive Social Work: Towards a New Practice* (Palgrave/Macmillan 2000). From 1995 to 2005 he was co-editor of the journal *Children and Society* (published by John Wiley in association with the National Children's Bureau).

Subject Index

Author Index